CHARLES F. HEMPHILL, JR., Doctor of Jurisprudence,
is a member of the Texas Bar. He has written
or coauthored nine prior books on legal or business subjects,
including *Basic Criminal Law* and *Criminal Procedure:
The Administration of Justice.*

PHYLLIS D. HEMPHILL, is professor of communications
at Rio Hondo College, Whittier, California. She is the author
of *Business Communications with Writing Improvement Exercises*
and *Career English.*

THE
DICTIONARY
OF
PRACTICAL
LAW

CHARLES F. HEMPHILL, JR.
PHYLLIS D. HEMPHILL

A SPECTRUM BOOK

PRENTICE-HALL, INC., Englewood Cliffs, N.J. 07632

340
HEM

Library of Congress Cataloging in Publication Data

Hemphill, Charles F.
    The dictionary of practical law.

    (A Spectrum Book)
    1. Law—United States—Terms and phrases.
I. Hemphill, Phyllis D., joint author.
II. Title.
KF156.H45   340'.03   79-14697
ISBN 0-13-210567-5
ISBN 0-13-210559-4 pbk.

©1979 by Prentice-Hall, Inc.
Englewood Cliffs, New Jersey 07632

A SPECTRUM BOOK

10   9   8   7   6   5   4   3   2   1

Printed in the United States of America

Editorial / production supervision
and interior design by Norma Miller Karlin
Manufacturing buyer: Cathie Lenard

PRENTICE-HALL INTERNATIONAL, INC., *London*
PRENTICE-HALL OF AUSTRALIA PTY. LIMITED, *Sydney*
PRENTICE-HALL OF CANADA, LTD., *Toronto*
PRENTICE-HALL OF INDIA PRIVATE LIMITED, *New Delhi*
PRENTICE-HALL OF JAPAN, INC., *Tokyo*
PRENTICE-HALL OF SOUTHEAST ASIA PTE. LTD., *Singapore*
WHITEHALL BOOKS LIMITED, *WELLINGTON, New Zealand*

To
Gregory, Brian, and Christopher

INTRODUCTION

Every profession or field of endeavor has its distinctive vocabulary. This is a specialized dictionary, written to help in the understanding and use of legal terms.

This dictionary was prepared for the needs of law students, paralegal courses, legal secretaries, and students in the administration of justice, corrections, and rehabilitation. It was also written for the needs of working police officers, and for those who simply want a definition of legal terms in everyday language.

This volume was designed as a manageable, practical alternative to the bulky, comprehensive law dictionaries that remain on reference shelves or in law libraries. Some of the old historical terms found in bulky dictionaries have been left out, since many of these terms have almost no modern usage. Some new terms, used today by attorneys and the courts, have been included.

Many English words, common in standard usage, mean something quite different when spoken or written in a legal sense. Some other words are shaded away from usually understood meanings. Then too, legal phrases of only a few words in length may be used to express complex legal ideas. Some of these phrases do not have the directness of basic English but have persisted for hundreds of years because of the clarity and pithiness with which they depict fundamental legal concepts and principles.

Introduction

It is also pointed out that some words in legal usage are not spelled to conform to their sounds.

Latin terms, still in legal usage in the United States, had their origin in the legal language of Britain's Roman conquerors, nearly 2000 years ago. French terms were introduced into English law by the Norman invaders of A.D. 1066. Some foreign legal words and phrases have become so common that they are now considered a part of everyday English.

Guides in pronouncing some Latin terms have been included. Anglicized versions of these terms have become rather common in legal circles, and variations between both the Latin and English are also heard.

This dictionary sometimes includes at least two wordings for the meaning of one legal term. Differently worded but related definitions of this kind are separated by a semicolon.

Legal terms may be used with more than one meaning, depending on the area or branch of the law in which they are used. When two distinct definitions are given for one term, the different meanings are given separate numbers. (See *abandonment*.)

There are always changes in language. New meanings arise through interpretations of the courts and through common understanding of the general public. Yet there seems to be unvarying continuity in the meaning of many legal terms. This is sometimes due to the law's basic philosophy of providing stability for the activities of individuals and of business.

We want to thank Ross H. Hemphill of the Texas Bar and Carol A. Chase of the California Bar for their assistance and interpretations. Mrs. Margaret A. Morse and Anita M. Hemphill were also very helpful in manuscript preparation.

It is hoped that we have made these definitions practical, with the semantic color, clarity, and spirit that they deserve.

CHARLES F. HEMPHILL, JR.
PHYLLIS D. HEMPHILL

A

A.B.A. Abbreviation for American Bar Association.

a·*ban*·don·ment. (1) The relinquishment, disclaimer, or surrender of property rights; giving up of a thing absolutely, such as vacating property with no intention of return. (2) Desertion of a spouse or child. See *desertion*.

ab an·te. (Latin–ab *an*·tee) *Before.* In advance. For example, it is understood that a legislature cannot agree *ab ante* to approve an amendment to legislation that may be passed later.

a·*bate*. (1) To quash; to put an end to. For example, the public health officer may *abate* a nuisance by putting an end to the unsanitary or dangerous condition that constituted the nuisance. (2) To reduce in value or amount.

ab·di·*ca*·tion. The act of giving up an office, power, or authority. The term generally refers to a sovereign who renounces a throne, but it may refer to anyone leaving a position of trust or authority.

ab·*duc*·tion. Originally, the term meant the unlawful taking away of a woman for marriage, concubinage, intercourse, or prostitution, either by enticement or by open violence. *Abduction* is currently a crime in most jurisdictions, and by statute in some jurisdictions it includes enticing a husband away and causing him to abandon his wife. In some states it includes the taking of a female ward. There is great variation in abduction laws from state to state. In one form or an-

1

other, most prohibit: **(a)** Enticing or taking away a female to introduce her into a house of prostitution; **(b)** taking, detaining, or alluring away a female under a specified age, without the consent of her parent or guardian; **(c)** taking or detaining a female against her will, with intent to engage in sexual relations or to be married. In a number of jurisdictions, violations of abduction statutes may also be violations of kidnapping laws.

a·*bet.* To induce or encourage another to commit a crime.

a·*bet*·tor. One who encourages, incites, procures, commands, or counsels another to commit a crime. One who promotes or sets on another to commit a crime. It is usually used synonymously with the term, *one who aids and abets.* The courts usually say that an *abettor* must be present or in the neighborhood, and must have encouraged or agitated the actual perpetrator, before a conviction will be sustained.

a·*bey*·ance. **(1)** In suspension; temporary inactivity. **(2)** In the law of estates or succession, a time when there is no living person in whom the title (freehold) is vested. This may occur when there is a tenant and the remainder has not yet vested. See FREEHOLD ESTATE; VESTED INTEREST; LIFE ESTATE. **(3)** The rights of property of a bankrupt, pending adjudication, may be said to be *in abeyance.*

a·*bid*·ing con·*vic*·tion. A term sometimes used by a criminal court judge to mean that the judge has a positive conviction of guilt, based on a thorough examination of the entire case.

ab in·i·ti·o. (Latin–ab in·*ish*·ee·oh) *From the beginning;* from the very outset.

ab·*jure.* **(1)** To abstain from. **(2)** To renounce under oath; to foreswear; to recant or retract; to withdraw a vow or oath. For example, upon being sworn as a U.S. citizen on naturalization, the new citizen must *abjure* all allegiance to any other government or ruler.

ab·ro·gate. To repeal or annul a law or legal duty through the operation of a legal process. For example, an existing law (statute) can be *abrogated* by the enactment of a new statute. Or, the common law is *abrogated* or abolished by the passage of a statute.

ab·*scond.* To depart suddenly and secretly, especially to avoid arrest or prosecution. To flee outside the jurisdiction of law enforcement officers or a court. *The cashier absconded with the company cash.*

ab·so·lute es·*tate.* An estate that is free from all manner of incumbrance or condition; an ESTATE IN FEE SIMPLE. See ESTATE.

2

ab·*sten*·tion (doctrine). The legal principle that a Federal court may decline to render a decision in a case in which the Federal court has jurisdiction, since the matter is also within the jurisdiction of a state court and is being handled under state laws.

ab·stract of *ti*·tle. A condensed summary, or history, of the TITLE to real estate. The *abstract* begins with a legal description of the land covered, and then shows the original government grant and all subsequent deeds, mortgages, releases, wills, judgments, mechanic's liens, foreclosure proceedings, tax sales, or any other document that has been recorded about this property. By examining the *abstract,* it can then be quickly determined what encumbrances exist against the property, in the event the title is not clear. *Abstracts of title* are regularly kept current in those states where this system is used. Without the *abstract,* it might be necessary to search through voluminous county records to glean the information on the *abstract.*

a·*buse*. (1) Any action which is contrary to right or proper usage or accepted order. (2) To make improper or excessive use of a thing, or to use it in a manner contrary to natural or legal rules for its use. (3) The crime of sexually molesting a child. (4) The destruction of the substance of a thing in using it.

a·*buse* of dis·*cre*·tion. The failure to exercise reasonable, sound judgment, especially by a judge in the handling of a legal matter. A discretion exercised by a judge to an end or purpose not justified by and clearly against evidence and reason.

a·*buse* of *pro*·cess. The perversion or improper use of a legal process in a way in which it was never intended to be used. For example, a male police officer arresting a female on a warrant and keeping the female in the police car for several hours without taking the prisoner to jail.

a·*but*·ting *own*·er. (1) One whose land touches or joins that of another. (2) Sometimes used as the owner whose land touches a highway or other public place.

ac·cel·er·*a*·tion clause. A statement, or clause, in a contract evidencing debt (such as an installment contract or a mortgage), providing that if the payment or interest is not paid when due, the entire debt becomes payable immediately. Unless an acceleration clause is incorporated into the wording of the instrument, it would be necessary for the lender to sue for the amount of each payment as it falls due.

3

ac·*cep*·tance. (1) In contract law, agreeing to an offer and thereby being bound under the terms of a contract. (2) In sales law, receiving goods that had been purchased, with the intention of keeping those goods. (3) In real property law, the act of receiving the deed to property purchased, with the intention of VESTING title or ownership in the buyer. (4) Taking something offered by another individual with the intent of keeping it. (5) The act of honoring, or paying off a negotiable instrument, such as a promissory note, bank check, etc.

ac·*ces*·sion. Any acquisition of property by its union, addition, or incorporation to other property.

ac·*ces*·so·ry. (1) In criminal law, one who is not the chief actor in a crime, but who contributes or aids in the commission of the offense, although not present when the crime actually takes place. See ACCESSORY BEFORE THE FACT; ACCESSORY AFTER THE FACT. Some courts have held that in certain crimes there can be no *accessories;* all who participate are PRINCIPALS, as in the crime of TREASON. Most courts also agree that there are only PRINCIPALS in all violations below the degree of FELONY (MISDEMEANORS and LESSER OFFENSES). (2) Anything which is joined to property or another thing. For example, growing timber is considered an *accessory* to a parcel of land; a rear view mirror is considered an *accessory* to an automobile.

ac·*ces*·so·ry *af*·ter the fact. An individual who has knowledge that a crime was committed, conceals it from the authorities, and harbors, assists, or protects the person charged with or convicted of the crime. The aid rendered may consist of any aid to avoid or escape from arrest, trial, conviction, or punishment.

ac·*ces*·so·ry be·*fore* the fact. One who incites, procures, urges, commands, or aids another to commit a crime, yet who is not present when the crime is actually committed. This crime is usually a FELONY, if the violation perpetrated by the principal is a FELONY.

ac·*ces*·so·ry *con*·tract. A contract which is incidental to a principal contract. For example, the contract to engage a SURETY to stand good for the default of another contract.

ac·*ci*·dent. An unforeseen event, misfortune, or an event that happens without human will. The word has a great variety of meanings in different legal situations. For example, the negligent driver of an automobile may be legally responsible for damages caused by an *accident.* On the other hand, an *accident of navigation,* under maritime or marine law is a mishap caused by the elements, which could not be avoided by the exercise of proper prudence, foresight, and skill.

ac·com·mo·*da***·tion** *pa***·per.** A PROMISSORY NOTE, BILL, or DRAFT, signed or endorsed by one individual as an *accommodation* or favor to help the ACCOMMODATED PARTY obtain a loan. This practice is used in instances in which the accommodated party does not have sufficient credit to obtain a loan.

ac·com·mo·*da***·tion** *par***·ty.** An individual who, for the purpose of assisting another individual to obtain credit, signs a note without receiving value.

ac·com·mo·*da***·tion per·son·***nel.*** Individuals who serve as incorporators of a joint stock company (CORPORATION), merely to provide the required number of individuals needed to comply with incorporation requirements.

ac·*com***·plice.** An individual who knowingly, and with criminal intent, helps another in the perpetration of a crime. Most courts say that an ACCESSORY BEFORE THE FACT and an ACCESSORY AFTER THE FACT are both *accomplices.* There are, however, decisions holding that an *accessory after the fact* is not an *accomplice.* See ACCESSORY AFTER THE FACT; ACCESSORY BEFORE THE FACT.

ac·*cord*** and sat·is·***fac***·tion.** An agreement between two parties, one having a legal right of ACTION against the other, that the latter should accept something in discharge of the right of action that is different from (usually something less than) that which might be legally enforced. For example, Smith may owe Brown $1,000 on a promissory note signed by Smith that has not been paid. Smith is unable to pay. Brown may take an oil painting in *accord and satisfaction* of the debt, although the painting might bring only about $800 on a forced sale. Brown may feel that he does not want to expend time or money in court when Smith has little in the way of assets.

ac·*count*** stat·ed.** An account submitted by a creditor, that has been examined and admitted to be correct by the person owing the debt. The correctness of the account may be admitted expressly, or by implication of law when the debtor has had an opportunity to object and has failed to do so.

ac·*counts*** pay·able.** Contract obligations owed by individuals or corporations on an open account.

5

ac·*counts* re·*ceiv*·able. A balance due from a debtor on a current account.

ac·*cred*·it. (1) To give official authorization or approval. (2) In international law, to send a diplomatic representative with credentials, such as an ambassador, to another nation. (3) To accept or acknowledge the credentials of a diplomatic representative sent out by another nation.

ac·*cre*·tion. Increase of the size of land by natural causes. This buildup in size could be by the gradual buildup of soil by river action or by accumulation from a windstorm.

ac·cu·mu·*la*·tion trust. A TRUST in which income is allowed to build up during the trust period, rather than being paid out on a regular basis to a beneficiary.

ac·cu·*sa*·tion. The bringing of a criminal charge before a magistrate or court having jurisdiction to inquire into criminal offenses.

ac·*cused*. One charged with committing a criminal offense. See PARTIES.

ac·*knowl*·edg·ment. A declaration by a person before a NOTARY PUBLIC or other official that he executed (signed) a legal document in the required manner. A formal INSTRUMENT drawn by a qualified officer, stating that the execution of an accompanying legal paper was proper —this is to ensure legal validity. To confirm as binding or of legal force. *He made an acknowledgment of his guilt.*

ac·qui·*es*·cence. The giving of implied consent to an act performed, or to the accrual of a right, by mere silence or failure to protest and without express approval.

ac·qui·*si*·tion charge. See PREPAYMENT PENALTY.

ac·*quit*·tal. A VERDICT of not guilty, setting free someone formally charged with the commission of a crime.

act of God. A loss or catastrophe caused solely by the forces of nature, for which a lawsuit for damages cannot be sustained. The courts say that an *act of God* is a misfortune or accident which human prudence could not foresee or prevent. In TORT law, a salesman would not be liable for fire loss of a manufacturer's goods carried in his car while the car was stored in a public garage struck by lightning, unless negligence was involved. If the salesman carelessly and negligently parked the car overnight in a dry creek bed, and a flood destroyed the car and contents, many courts would say that the salesman would be liable in damages, even though the loss was an *act of God.* If the salesman was under a contract obligation to use only a fireproof garage, and if the garage was negligent in providing fire protection required by law, there would be additional grounds for recovery, either against the salesman or the garage.

ac·tion. (1) A proceeding in a court, instituted by one party against another. A suit in court for the enforcement of a legal right. A judicial process. Also called a LAWSUIT or legal action. (2) Behavior; conduct; something done.

ac·tion·able. That which provides the legal basis to sustain a LAWSUIT (legal action) in the courts.

ac·tu·al *no*·tice. See NOTICE.

ad cu·riam. (Latin–add kew·reiam) *To court,* or *at a court.*

ad *dam*·num. (Latin) *To the damage.* That clause of a declaration or writ which sets forth the plaintiff's claim regarding money damages or loss.

ad·dit·ur. The right of a trial judge to increase the amount of the jury award, with the consent of the DEFENDANT, and as a condition for denying a new trial. *Additur* is usually handled in the judge's chambers in conferences between the judge and the lawyers for both sides, although it can be done without the consent of the PLAINTIFF. This procedure is used in cases when the jury obviously makes an inadequate money award to the plaintiff, and the plaintiff has made a motion for a new trial. It is an effective method for giving a just award of damages, without the trouble and expense of a new trial. See REMITTITUR.

add-ons. New purchases made by an INSTALLMENT buyer before the previously purchased merchandise is completely paid for. This usually requires the drafting of a new installment purchase contract.

a·demp·tion. The failure of a specific legacy in a will, because the property or item in question no longer belonged to the TESTATOR'S ESTATE at the time of death. For example, Smith wrote a will in 1970, leaving an antique to his son John. In 1975, forgetting the provision in the will (which does not take effect until death), Smith gave the antique to his granddaughter Marie. John cannot obtain the antique upon the death of Smith, since Marie has owned it since 1975.

ad hoc. (Latin–ad hock) *For this special purpose, or duty.* For example, a guardian *ad hoc* is one appointed to represent an infant or incompetent in a particular legal action in which the appointment was made.

ad hom·in·em. (Latin–add *hom*·un·nem) *To the person.* An argument that appeals to emotions, personal interests, or prejudice, rather than to reason or logic.

ad i·dem. (Latin–add *eye·*dem) *To the same effect.* An argument that goes to prove the same proposition or point of law.

ad in·fi·ni·tum. (Latin–add in·fuh·*ny·*tum) *Without end or limit;* indefinitely.

ad in·ter·im. (Latin–add *in·*tuh·rim) *In the meanwhile.* For example, an appointment *ad interim* is one made to fill a temporary vacancy.

*ad·*jec·**tive law.** That body of the law which provides procedures and methods for enforcing legal rights. *Adjective law* is synonymous with PROCEDURAL LAW. It is that part of the law concerned with methods for enforcing or maintaining rights. Adjective (procedural) law is distinguished from SUBSTANTIVE LAW—that body of law which the courts are established to administer.

ad·*journ·***ment.** The act of a judge, court, legislature, or other official body in dissolving a meeting or postponing business. An *adjournment* may be temporary or may be a final act.

ad·*judge.* To pass on, or decide judicially.

ad·ju·di·*ca·*tion. The pronouncing or giving of a judgment or decree in a case under trial or under legal consideration.

ad·ju·*ra·*tion. A swearing or *binding* to tell the truth under oath.

ad·*just·***ment.** In insurance law, the settlement of a loss claim between the insurance company and the insured. If more than one insurance UNDERWRITER is involved, the *adjustment* may set the percentage of loss that will be paid by each of the companies.

ad·*just·***ment se·*cu·***ri·ties.** Stocks or securities that are issued as a part of a corporate reorganization. *Adjustment stocks* may have less PAR VALUE than the shares that they replace, and consequently may have less market value.

ad *lit·*em. (Latin) *For the suit.* Pending this lawsuit, or for purposes of this lawsuit. A *guardian ad litem* might be appointed by a court to protect the legal interests of an individual in a lawsuit being brought for damages sustained in an automobile accident. This would be an appointment for purposes of this lawsuit only.

ad·min·is·*tra·*tion. (1) The handling of the settlement of an ESTATE of a deceased individual. (2) The officials in charge of the EXECUTIVE branch of the government. (3) The practical management and direction of a business or industry, society, organization, or branch of government.

ad·*min·*is·tra·tive law. (1) That body of law which concerns the organization, operation, responsibilities, and functions of administrative

8

agencies of the government. (2) Those rules, having the force of law, that are prescribed and administered by administrative bodies of the government. Typical of these rules would be those set up by the U.S. Department of Internal Revenue in collecting income taxes.

ad·*min*·is·tra·tive *rem*·e·dy. A procedure for establishing and enforcing legal rights by going to an administrative agency of the government, rather than filing a lawsuit in the courts. A lawsuit may be filed eventually, but the courts say that an administrative matter must first be pursued with the governmental commission, board, or agency handling the matter. Judicial consideration is given only after *administrative remedies* have been exhausted or found inadequate. For example, an individual seeking a license as an airplane pilot would be obliged first to seek issuance of the license from the administrative agency giving examinations of pilots, with recourse to the courts if the agency did not act when requirements had been met.

ad·mi·ral·ty court. A court having jurisdiction over all maritime contracts, injuries and damage suits (torts) and over criminal offenses on the high seas.

ad·*mis*·si·ble. (1) That which is legally proper in reaching a decision. (2) When applied to evidence, that which is *admissible* is of such a character that the judge is obligated to allow it to be presented in the course of the trial.

ad·*mis*·si·ble ev·i·dence. That evidence which was properly obtained, and which the judge will therefore allow the jury to consider, if it is pertinent to the issues of the trial. See *admissible.*

a·*dopt*. (1) To accept as one's own; to appropriate. (2) To put into operation, or make legally effective, such as the adoption of a constitution, resolution, ordinance, bylaws, etc. (3) To take into one's family the child of another, giving that individual the legal privileges, rights, and duties of a natural child and heir. (Under statutes in some states, the person *adopted* may be a fully grown adult.)

a·*dop*·tion. (1) Legally making one who is no prior relation a child of the family, with all rights, duties, and privileges of any child. *Adoption* is regulated by statute. In some jurisdictions an adult may be *adopted* in order to make that individual an heir. (2) The passage of a statute, ordinance or law, putting it into effect. (3) To legally accept, appropriate, or choose to make that one's own which was not so originally.

ad pros·e·*quen*·dam. (Latin) *To prosecute.*

9

a·*dul*·tery. Voluntary sexual intercourse of a married man with someone other than his wife, or between a married woman and someone other than her husband. Under the definition followed by most states, this activity on the part of any married party is *adultery,* while the same conduct by an unmarried person is fornication. See *fornication.*

ad va·*lo*·rem. (Latin) *According to value.* A tax or duty set by the value of item being taxed. An *ad valorem tax* is distinguished from a *specific duty* or tax, which is imposed on each article, regardless of value.

ad·*vance.* See *motion to advance.*

ad·*vance*·ment. Money or property given to an heir that is intended to be deducted from the heir's share of an inheritance. This is usually a payment by a living person who does not intend to leave a will. If a will is subsequently written, the maker may refer to *advancements* made during the maker's lifetime, with instructions that the *advancement* be deducted from the donee's legacy under the will.

***ad*·ver·sary pro·*ceed*·ing.** See explanation under ADVERSARY SYSTEM.

***ad*·ver·sary *sys*·tem.** The system followed by courts in trying cases in the United States and England. In this procedure there are two clearly drawn sides, with the judge as an impartial arbitrator. Each side presents the facts known to it. The theory is that each side is in the best position to present the evidence favorable to their claim. Thereafter, the truth is more likely to be found when the searchers are closing in on each side. If presentations are clearly made, the truth should be self-evident to a fair-minded jury. This is distinguished from the so-called INQUISITORIAL SYSTEM for conducting a trial, which is commonly used in most other trial systems in continental Europe, South America, etc. Under the latter system, the judge is not an impartial party, but conducts investigation and inquiries, representing the state's interests, especially in a criminal prosecution.

***ad*·verse pos·*ses*·sion.** A means of acquiring TITLE to REAL PROPERTY after a lapse of time, based on continued possession. Under the decisions and statutes in most states, there are five essentials before title can be acquired by *adverse possession:* **(a)** possession of the property must be by actual occupation and must be open and notorious, **(b)** possession must be hostile to the true owner's title, **(c)** possession must be under some adverse claim of right, such as a defective deed, **(d)** possession must be continuous and uninterrupted, **(e)** the claimant must have paid all taxes levied during the statutory period. Statutory periods in some states may vary from 5 years to 20 years, with some other variations in statutes from state to state. Generally, public lands cannot be acquired by *adverse possession*. In most jurisdictions a mere SQUATTER cannot get title by *adverse possession*, since the SQUATTER has no adverse claim of right.

ad·verse *wit·*ness. A witness whose attitude and answers indicate a hostile bias toward the party questioning the witness.

ad·*vise·*ment. Legal deliberation or study. The study and deliberation of a court after arguments have been presented by both sides and before an opinion is delivered.

ad·*vi·*so·ry *ju·*ry. A jury that may be called by the trial judge in a Federal case to decide questions of fact, even though it is a case in which the judge has the right to function as both judge and jury.

ad·*vi·*so·ry o·*pin·*ion. An opinion rendered by a judge or an appellate court on a legal matter presented by an executive official of the government, or by the legislature. It does not involve an actual court suit between interested parties. In effect, an *advisory opinion* merely furnishes guidance, but is not binding on anyone and does not really settle any legal dispute. It is an *extra-judicial opinion.* Court opinions are never binding in hypothetical situations or in any matter which is not squarely before a court in an adversary lawsuit. A *trumped up lawsuit,* merely to get an opinion from a court, would not be considered as binding by future judges faced with the same legal question.

ad·vo·cate. One who pleads the cause of another, aids, defends, or assists. A legal *advocate* is, of course, an attorney.

af·*fi·*ant. An individual who makes and signs an AFFIDAVIT under oath. The term *affiant* is sometimes used interchangeably with DEPONENT. See AFFIDAVIT.

af·fi·*da·*vit. A written or printed statement of facts given voluntarily and under oath before magistrates or other officials designated by law to take such statements. The purpose of the *affidavit* is to set down facts that may later be in dispute. The *affidavit* may be used as evidence or as an essential part of a subsequent court case or action. It is not necessary to notify the adverse party to a legal dispute when an *affidavit* is taken. If a potential witness gives an *affidavit* to certain facts, then the AFFIANT (person making the statement) cannot later testify to opposite facts without the likelihood of being prosecuted for the crime of PERJURY.

af·fi·*da·*vit of *ti·*tle. An AFFIDAVIT given by the seller of real estate to assure the buyer that there are no defects in the seller's TITLE to the property. This affidavit supplements the title examination and includes matters which may not be disclosed by a title search. In a sense, an *affidavit of title* provides additional protection to the purchaser since the delivery of an *affidavit of title* containing false information is a criminal offense in some states.

af·fil·i·a·tion pro·ceed·ings. Has same meaning as PATERNITY SUIT.

af·*fin*·i·ty. A relationship by marriage, rather than by blood; relationship which one spouse because of marriage has to blood relatives of the other.

af·fir·*ma*·tion. A solemn declaration made under penalty of PERJURY by an individual whose religious persuasions forbid the taking of an OATH. An *affirmation* is considered to be of the same legal effect as an oath. Quakers and some other religious groups have religious beliefs against swearing under oath, even in the courts.

af·*fir*·ma·tive de·*fense*. That part of a defendant's pleadings (answer) that are in addition to answering or denying the plaintiff's charge, furnishing additional facts and arguments that might lead to a judgment for the defense, even if the claims (pleadings) of the plaintiff turn out to be true.

a for·ti·o·ri. (Latin-ay for·*she*·or·ee) *With stronger reason.* A term used in legal logic to draw a conclusion that is inferred to be even more certain that one conceded to be true. For example, a man who lost two legs in a car accident is, *a fortiori,* disabled if the state disability commission has set loss of one leg as constituting disability.

af·ter-ac·*quired ti*·tle. A principle in property law, that if an individual attempted to convey ownership in real estate, but did not actually have good TITLE yet subsequently got good title, the ownership would automatically pass to the individual to whom the real estate was originally conveyed (transferred).

a·gen·cy. The legal relationship by which one individual represents or acts for another in the latter's business, with authority of the latter. The relationship may be legally created by specific agreement, or by an implied contract.

a·gen·cy by ne·*ces*·si·ty. An AGENCY relationship recognized by the courts which enables a wife to obtain whatever is reasonably necessary for her maintenance and support on her husband's credit. The courts that follow this reasoning state that this is an IMPLIED AGENCY. See AGENCY; IMPLIED AGENCY.

a•**gent.** One authorized to carry on business for another, or for a firm. The general rule of law is that the agent must have authority from the PRINCIPAL before the principal is bound by the agent's acts or contracts. However, this right may be lost by the principal who intentionally, or by carelessness, leads a third party to believe the *agent* has authority.

ag•**gra**•**va**•**ted as**•*sault.* A type of special assault, usually defined by statute, with the definition varying from state to state. Assault and BATTERY were only MISDEMEANORS at common law. Some crimes classified in these categories by state law are, however, far more serious, and have special penalties. Assaults in which it appears the attacker may intend to kill, rob, rape, or do great bodily harm are usually designated as assaults in a distinct, technical aggravated assault violation, punishable as a felony. Examples would be ASSAULT WITH INTENT TO KILL, ASSAULT WITH INTENT TO RAPE, etc. Some states classify all such assaults as *aggravated assault,* or *assault with a deadly weapon,* etc.

ag•*grieved par*•**ty.** One who has been injured, or who has suffered from a denial or infringement of that individual's legal rights.

aid and a•**bet.** To assist another in the accomplishment of a common design or purpose. An example is one who may *aid and abet* in the commission of a crime. Most courts say that one who *aids and abets* is guilty as a *principal,* but the individual who does so must have a criminal intent. See ACCESSORY BEFORE THE FACT; ACCESSORY AFTER THE FACT; ACCOMPLICE.

a•**le**•**a**•**to**•**ry** *con*•**tract.** A contract that turns on a contingency, or uncertain event. For example, the amount of compensation payable to an executive may depend on the amount of profit or loss made by the business.

a•**li**•**as.** An assumed name. Using an *alias* has, of course, long been a technique used by criminals to evade apprehension.

a•**li**•**as** *sum*•**mons.** A replacement SUMMONS issued when the original has been ineffective because of defective form or improper manner of service. It is a duplicate of the original, except the word *alias* precedes *summons.* If it should be necessary to prepare a third summons, the third is called a PLURIES SUMMONS.

al•**i**•**bi.** A form of defense to a criminal charge, whereby the accused individual attempts to prove that he was elsewhere when the crime in question was committed. *His alibi was that he was in a bar in Houston when the bank was robbed in Boston.*

a·li·en. An individual who is not a citizen of the United States.

a·li·en·a·ble. That which is subject to transfer or CONVEYANCE. The term is usually used to denote a transfer of title or conveyance of real estate, but it may be used to mean any transfer.

al·ien·*a*·tion of af·*fec*·tions. The winning away of the affection, love, and companionship of one of the spouses in a marriage that formerly served as the basis for a lawsuit. At one time *alienation of affection* suits for damages were rather common, but most states have enacted statutes doing away with this as the basis for a civil suit.

al·i·mo·ny. Court-ordered payments by a husband to his wife for maintenance while they are separated or after they are divorced. If the wife is the major breadwinner, the court may order the wife to pay *alimony* for the husband's support.

al·i·mo·ny pen·dente lite. ALIMONY, or support money, paid to one spouse in a divorce action, pending court settlement of the divorce action; temporary alimony.

al·i·quot. (1) Any definite legal interest, although only a fractional part. (2) A proportionate or fractional part of anything.

al·le·*ga*·tion. (1) The claim or assertion made in the pleadings of one side in a lawsuit, outlining what is expected to be proved. (2) A charge of criminal wrongdoing.

al·lo·*cu*·tion. The procedure in which a trial judge asks a convicted prisoner, before sentence, whether the prisoner has legal cause to show why judgment should not be pronounced against the prisoner on the verdict of conviction. The judge is allowed to handle this within his or her own discretion, but normally will permit any reasonable statement by the prisoner explaining why the crime was committed, mitigating circumstances, family or personal condition, or anything else that would reasonably bear on the sentence. The judge would not allow this speech by the prisoner to continue indefinitely, but would almost invariably accept any reasonable statements made.

al·lo·graph. A writing or signature, done by one individual for another, who may be physically unable to write.

al·*longe*. (French) A blank piece of paper affixed to a negotiable INSTRUMENT (bill of exchange, promissory note, etc.) to provide additional space for endorsements when there is no more room on the instrument itself.

A.L.R. Abbreviation for American Law Reports, in the library or lawyer's office.

al.*ter*.na.tive re.*lief*. The second of two kinds of relief asked of the judge in pleadings in a lawsuit. For example, in a lawsuit for breach of contract, the pleadings would ask for specific enforcement of the contract, or, in the alternative, for monetary damages to the extent which the plaintiff has been injured.

a.mal.ga.*ma*.tion. An act of consolidation, or merging. The blending of two or more into one, such as the merger of two corporations.

am.bu.lance chas.er. A lawyer, or someone working with a lawyer, who obtains clients by persuading victims of accidents to file damage suits.

am.bu.la.to.ry. (Latin) *To walk about.* Legally, the term may have two or more meanings: **(1)** That which is movable. For example, an *ambulatory court* is one that holds trials in various locations. **(2)** That which is subject to change, or is alterable. For example, a will is *ambulatory,* in that it may be altered by the person making the will up to the time of death.

a.*mend*. To modify or alter a writing or document; to correct. For example, defective pleadings submitted by one side in a lawsuit may be *amended.*

a.*mend*.ment. **(1)** Any alteration or writing proposed as an improvement or addition to some principal writing. **(2)** A provision of the U.S. or a state Constitution, ratified since the original constitution was adopted. **(3)** A change made to a bill or proposal of Congress or a legislature. **(4)** In legal practice, it is the correction of an error in any pleading or process, done either by consent of the parties to the lawsuit or procedure, or upon motion of the court where the matter is pending.

a.mi.cus cu.ri.ae. (Latin–uh.*mee*.kus *kure*.ee.eye) *Friend of the court.* A third party (other than the plaintiff and defendant) who is allowed to appear in a lawsuit, with the consent of the trial judge. Sometimes this third party is allowed to present evidence and take an active part, but is generally restricted to filing a legal BRIEF. This procedure is permitted when the judge feels there may be broad community interests that should be represented, and that these basic interests go far beyond differences between the plaintiff and the defendant. This procedure may also be allowed when the trial involves matters that may be beyond the knowledge of the judge. This is usually in a technical or scientific dispute.

am·nes·ty. A general pardon or proclamation of forgiveness by the government for past criminal offenses. It has the effect of erasing the offense of a whole class of persons who may have committed a particular violation. The pardoning official may grant *amnesty* either before or after conviction and sentence.

a·mor·tiz·*a*·tion. The process of paying off a debt by regular payments. It may also apply to paying off bonds, stocks, or other legal indebtedness.

an·ar·chy. A state of lawless or political disorder, where there is no governmental power; a society where there is absolutely no control or restraint on anyone.

an·cient lights (doctrine of). An old legal principle followed in some jurisdictions, to the effect that windows in the wall of a building along the property line cannot be obstructed by new construction on the adjoining property line, if the windows have been in use for 20 years or more.

an·cient *writ*·ings. In evidence law, documents that are 30 years of age or more, giving every evidence of authenticity, and being introduced from regular custody, are admitted as genuine without any further proof of origin.

an·cil·lar·y. Auxiliary; attendant upon; helping. The term *ancillary* is used to mean court proceedings that are auxiliary to the main action. A motion to suppress evidence, for example, would be *ancillary* to a criminal prosecution.

an·cil·lar·y ad·min·is·*tra*·tion. A proceeding in a state where a deceased owned property, but which is a different state from the one is which the deceased lived and where the main part of the estate is being settled.

an·i·mo. (Latin–*ahn*·ee·mo) *With intent.* A Latin term generally coupled with another word, as *animo revocandi* (with intent to revoke), *animo testandi* (with intention to make a will), or *animo furandi* (with intent to steal, or having the necessary criminal intent [MENS REA] to steal).

an·no·tat·ed *stat*·ute. See CODE ANNOTATED.

an·no·*ta*·tion. An explanatory comment or explanation. Legal *annotations* for a legislative enactment, for example, may state when the statute was first passed into law, whether there were amendments, or whether it was repealed and passed a second time, and so forth. In addition to the history, the *annotation* may list the decided court cases that have interpreted the statute, with the caption, legal citation, and a brief description of the holding in each.

an·*nul*. To nullify or make void, as a law or a marriage. To make invalid. To deprive of operation.

***an*·swer.** The DEFENDANT'S formal statement of defense against the PLAINTIFF'S claims in a lawsuit.

ap·*peal*. The procedure by which the decision of a lower court is brought to a higher court for review. The procedure for taking a case to a higher court is set by the rules of the highest state court, or by rules of the United States Supreme Court in Federal *appeals*.

ap·*peals* court. The court (higher ranking court) to which a matter may be appealed, when a prejudicial error was committed in the trial court.

ap·*pear*·ance. (1) In legal terminology, the required coming into court of a party to a lawsuit, either as PLAINTIFF or DEFENDANT. In many instances the appearance may be by attorney, or by filing an ANSWER in the court pleadings. The *appearance* is obligatory in the sense that a DEFAULT JUDGMENT may be entered against the party that fails to appear. (2) In a criminal case, the failure of the accused to make an *appearance* can be expected to result in a bench warrant for the arrest of the accused.

ap·*pel*·lant. A party to a legal action who makes an APPEAL to a higher court.

ap·*pel*·late court. See APPEALS COURT.

ap·*pel*·late ju·ris·*dic*·tion. The authority and power of a review court (higher court) to take over the adjudication and review of a matter that has been tried in a court of original jurisdiction (trial court, lower court, inferior court, or whatever it may be called). *Appellate jurisdiction* includes the power to correct errors in judgment of the matters under review, and may require the case to be sent back to the lower court for additional clarification of the issues.

ap·pel·*lee*. One against whom an appeal is taken. See PARTIES.

17

ap·*pose*. To examine a custodian of records about the preparation, maintenance and use of those records.

ap·*pur*·te·nance. (1) An incidental property right, such as a right of way, attached to a principal property right, and passing with the principal right when transferred in ownership. (2) Annexed to, or attached to something else. For example, a built-in dish cabinet, permanently affixed to a structure is an *appurtenance*. It could also be described as a *fixture*.

a pri·o·ri. (Latin–ay pry·*or*·eye or ay pree·*or*·ee) *From the cause to the effect*. A term used in legal logic, which takes a known truth or principle, and proceeds to deduce from it the effects which must necessarily follow. When it rains, *a priori* the earth will be wet.

ar·bi·trage. Transactions by stock traders in which securities are bought in one market, and sold almost simultaneously in another market where the price is higher. For example, a trader might buy U.S. Steel stock on the American Stock Exchange at 63½ and sell it on the New York Stock Exchange, where it is quoted at 64¼ per share.

ar·bi·*tra*·tion. The submission of a disputed matter to a disinterested individual or body for settlement. The persons judging the dispute are called *arbitrators*. *Binding arbitration* is that in which both sides agree in advance to be bound by the decision of the *arbitrator* or *arbitrators*.

ar·*raign*·ment. The formal bringing of one charged with crime to the bar of the court to answer this charge.

ar·*ray*. The whole group, or listing of jurors called in for duty for a particular term of court.

ar·*rest*. To restrain or take into custody by legal authority. It is for the purpose of detaining to answer a criminal charge or a civil demand of a court. The courts usually say that mere words alone will not constitute arrest. There are two requirements: **(a)** the individual must be deprived of liberty of movement (not merely restricted by keeping out of an area), and **(b)** the restraint must be done under real or assumed authority. Physical force is not a requirement, if the individual detained submits peacefully.

ar·*rest* of *judg*·ment. The act of suspending or staying a JUDGMENT, since it is apparent to the trial judge that there is some defect in the proceedings or on the face of the record which would make a JUDGMENT erroneous or reversible.

ar·ro·*ga*·tion. To seize or claim something without a legal right. To appropriate property of another, or to assert a claim without any real basis.

ar·son. The malicious burning of the house or building of another. In most jurisdictions, common law *arson* has been extended to any kind of building, although at one time, only the home and outbuildings were covered. Modern statutes also frequently prohibit the malicious burning of boats, automobiles, or any kind of structure, to the injury of another, or in defrauding an insurance company.

ar·ti·cles. (1) A connected set of propositions, or a system of rules. (2) The separate parts of a document, constitution, or statutory enactment. (3) A contractural document, such as ARTICLES OF CONTRACT.

ar·ti·cles of in·cor·po·*ra*·tion. The instrument or charter by which a private CORPORATION is formed and organized.

ar·ti·*fi*·cial *per*·son. A creation of the law; a CORPORATION.

as·por·*ta*·tion. The illegal carrying away of goods, money, or other objects that is one of the requirements of the crime of LARCENY. It is the physical act of taking away whatever is being stolen.

as·*sault*. An unlawful offer of bodily injury to another by force, or by force unlawfully directed toward the person of another, under such circumstances as to create a well-founded fear of immediate peril. Words alone are not sufficient to constitute an *assault,* but will be enough if coupled with some menacing act or threatening gesture. Put in other words, the placing in fear of an immediate battery is an *assault.* If the assailant goes ahead and uses force, the crime is a BATTERY. Therefore, an *assault* is a battery in the making. In actual usage, *assault and battery* is used as one term, since an assault frequently results in a battery.

as·*sess*. (1) To ascertain worth, or fix the value of something. (2) To determine a taxing base for property. (3) To evaluate or determine size, importance, or relationship. (4) To apportion costs for accounting purposes.

as·sets. (1) From a legal meaning, the term generally denotes money, property, and other valuables which comes to the representative of a deceased person, to pay off debts or that belong to the estate. (2) From an accounting meaning, all money, property, or valuables that are owned by an individual or organization. Assets may be used in whole or in part to pay off liabilities (debts).

as·*sign*. **(1)** To turn over or assign property or a property interest to another. An example would be to *assign* assets for the benefit of creditors. **(2)** To particularize, point out, or specify, as to *assign* errors in a writ of error (appeal). This would be to point out errors to an appellate court as the basis for an appeal.

as·*signed* risk. In insurance law, those questionable or unwanted risks that are *assigned* to insurance companies because of a legal obligation by the insurance company to cover all risks, regardless of desirability.

as·sign·*ee*. An individual or firm to whom an ASSIGNMENT is made.

as·*sign*·or. The individual who makes an ASSIGNMENT.

as·*sign*·ment. The transfer or signing over of any property or legal right to another. *Assignments* may be made of personal or real property, whether in possession on in litigation, or in any kind of an estate. Normally, an *assignment* is limited to CHOSES IN ACTION, and the rights in or connected with property, as distinguished from the property itself. Generally, real or personal property is transferred by deed or bill of sale, with assignments made of choses in action.

as·*signs*. A phrase that may be used in deeds to designate those to whom property is being transferred.

as·sump·sit. (Latin) *He promised.* **(1)** An undertaking or promise by which one party undertakes to do some act or pay something to another. Technically, it is one side of a contract, and it may be either oral or in writing. **(2)** *Assumpsit* was also the old English name for a type of lawsuit or legal action brought for non-performance of a contract.

as·*sump*·tion of *mort*·gage. Taking over the mortgage when buying real estate.

as·*sump*·tion of risk. The legal doctrine in which one exposed to injury or damage has consented to relieve others of obligation to remove the harm, either by **(a)** express agreement, or **(b)** implication from the conduct of the parties. As to an express agreement, a highwire trapeze artist could sign a contract with a circus, agreeing to hold the circus harmless in the event the trapeze performer fell during either practice or performance. Courts sometimes hold contracts of this type invalid as a matter of public policy, especially if it appears to be an effort to completely circumvent workmen's compensation laws. As an example of the second situation, **(b)**, a spectator at a baseball game is usually legally regarded as consenting that the players may go about the game without taking unusual precautions to protect the spectator from being hit by a ball.

at·*tach*·ment. The method by which a debtor's property, real or personal, is taken by legal means and held as security pending the outcome of a lawsuit by a creditor. Pending decision in the case, the debtor cannot sell or transfer the property, or place it beyond the reach of the creditor. In most states the attaching creditor must put up a bond with the court. In turn, the debtor can then release the property by putting up a counterbond. An *attachment* is normally used when the debtor is evading the creditor or is in hiding, when the debtor is apparently going to conceal, remove, or transfer title to the property.

at·*tain*·der. The loss of civil rights and privileges that takes place when an individual is sentenced to death on conviction for treason or felony.

at·*tempt*. In criminal law, an endeavor to commit a crime, carrying beyond mere preparation, but falling short of execution of the ultimate criminal design. *Attempts* are punished as separate crimes, with separate penalties from the offense attempted, for example *attempt to commit murder* is a separate offense from *murder,* with a lesser penalty in practically all jurisdictions. The prosecutive problem here is that it is often difficult to say when mere planning ends, and an *attempt* begins.

at·*test*. **(1)** To affirm to be true or genuine. **(2)** To authenticate by signing as a witness.

at·tes·*ta*·tion. The procedure for witnessing a legal document or instrument at the request of the party making the document, and subscribing to it as a witness.

at·*tor*·ney (or at·*tor*·ney at law). A lawyer, counsel, advocate, or officer employed to furnish legal advice or to prepare and try a cause (case) in the courts.

at·*tor*·ney in fact. An individual authorized to act for another, either for some specific purpose, or to transact business of a general nature. Authority to act in this manner is conferred by a written instrument called a *power of attorney* or a *letter of attorney.* An *attorney in fact* is actually a kind of agent who handles either a specific transaction or general business for the principal. Any mentally competent adult may serve as an *attorney in fact,* and the term does not refer to an ATTORNEY or LAWYER in the usually understood meaning of the term. An individual going on a trip around the world by ship could leave a *power of attorney* letter with a trusted acquaintance, instructing the acquaintance to sell some property. Acting under this written *power of attorney,* the acquaintance could sell the property and sign the necessary papers to make the transfer legal.

at·*tor*·ney of *re*·cord. The attorney whose name is entered on records as the lawyer representing the client, although a number of lawyers may be working on the case. The *attorney of record* is the individual the client has designated as his agent upon whom service of legal papers may be made. The *attorney of record* is distinguished from an *attorney of counsel,* who is a lawyer hired by the *attorney of record* to assist in the case.

at·*tor*·ney's lien. The right of a lawyer (attorney) to hold money or property of a client coming into the attorney's possession until charges for legal services have been paid.

at·*trac*·tive *nui*·sance *doc*·trine. The principle in tort law that one maintaining a dangerous machine, instrumentality, or condition on the premises to which young children may be attracted because of their inability to appreciate the peril, owes a legal responsibility to exercise reasonable care to protect children against the dangers of such attraction. The care that must be taken is that which a reasonably prudent man would take to prevent injury. Some courts say that the attraction must be visible from a public place or from a place where the children have a right to be. The person maintaining the attractive nuisance is held liable, regardless of the fact that the child may be a trespasser.

au·then·ti·*ca*·tion. A formal certification that a document is a legal instrument or record, or a certified copy thereof, so it may be entered in evidence. It is done with a view to having the document in due form of law, by an officer charged with responsibility to make an *authentication.* The procedure is set by law, and is quite formal.

***au*·top·sy.** The post mortem examination of a body to determine the cause of death. This is done by dissection. Usually, an autopsy is conducted by the coroner, if the coroner is a medical examiner.

a·*ver*. To allege or assert in legal pleadings.

a·*ver*·ment. (1) An allegation or statement in legal pleadings. **(2)** To declare positively that something is true.

a·*void*·ance. (1) A statement in pleadings in a lawsuit, admitting the truth of pleadings by the other party, but explaining why these facts should not be permitted to prevail in the legal dispute. **(2)** To make of no effect; to cancel or annul. **(3)** In parliamentary language, to evade or escape a decision on a pending question.

a·vul·sion. **(1)** A sudden cutting away of land by flood, current, or change in the course of a river or body of water, resulting in the loss of real property. **(2)** Any forcible detachment or separation.

a·ward. **(1)** The grant of monetary damages to the winning side in a lawsuit. **(2)** The decision of a referee, commissioner, or arbitration official in a dispute submitted for settlement. **(3)** To grant or give in a formal procedure or bid process, as to *award* a contract.

B

bad faith. Fraud, either actual or constructive, or an intent to mislead or deceive another.

badge of fraud. In the law of conveyances, a circumstance which points to an inference or possibility of fraud. A false statement about the consideration paid for a real estate transfer, transfer of all of a debtor's property at one time, or a fictitious consideration, are recognized in the law as examples of a *badge of fraud.*

bail. **(1)** Security given for a prisoner to obtain release from custody until the time of trial or disposition of a legal charge. **(2)** The money or property put up with the clerk of a criminal court to insure the appearance of a person released on a BAIL BOND.

bail bond. A bond executed by an individual who has been arrested, together with other individuals as sureties (sometimes a professional bail bondsman), promising that the accused will appear when wanted for trial. It is a contract which usually requires SURETIES. A professional bondsman usually charges a fee, such as 10% of the face of the bond in cash, frequently requiring the accused or some relative to sign over a home, property, etc., if the accused jumps BAIL.

bail·ee. The individual to whom property is bailed. See BAILMENT.

bai·liff. **(1)** An officer of a trial court who is assigned to maintain order, to keep custody of prisoners in the courtroom, to be responsible for the jury's security, and to take charge of the jury while it is deliberating.

23

On the judge's instructions, the *bailiff* may segregate the jury during the period of deliberations. Some courts call the *bailiff* a marshal. In some jurisdictions a *bailiff* may make arrests and serve legal papers or subpoenas, writs, and warrants. In other jurisdictions, the *bailiff* may be a court usher and message carrier for the judge. **(2)** A legal overseer of the property of another.

bail•**ment.** The delivery of goods or personal property, to be held in trust. It is a delivery for temporary holding, and ownership of the property does not change hands. But the transaction is a sale (rather than a *bailment*), and ownership of the property does change hands, if return of the same property is not contemplated. If the goods delivered, however, are FUNGIBLE GOODS, identical quantities or units of the goods may be returned, since individual units of fungible goods are indistinguishable. (See FUNGIBLE GOODS.) Money carried by an armored car service is a *bailment,* provided the money is delivered to an owner of the money. A pair of shoes, left with a repairman, is also a *bailment.* The individual handing over the property is the BAILOR, and the individual receiving it is the BAILEE. If the agreement is that the bailee is obligated to pay over a sum of money at the option of the bailor, the transaction is a sales contract and not a *bailment.* However, if some of the goods are sold by a bailee who is a traveling salesman, the transaction is a *bailment* with respect to the unsold items.

bail•**or.** One who delivers goods or money to another in trust. See BAILMENT.

bait and switch. A type of deceptive advertising in which a store will *bait* a customer into coming into the store to get an advertised bargain, and will then try to *switch* the customer to a more expensive item on the claim that the advertised item has been sold out. In some jurisdictions this is a criminal violation if the original item was never really available for purchase at the advertised price, or was different from the item advertised.

bal•*loon pay*•**ment.** A final payment on an installment loan or contract, when regular payments are relatively small and a large payment falls due as the final installment. If the final installment is unusually large, it may be necessary for the *balloon payment* to require refinancing. Federal Truth-In-Lending statutes require a disclosure of all *balloon payments,* and some state laws forbid installment payment contracts of this kind.

bank·**er's lien.** A charge or lien by which a bank can appropriate a customer's money or property in the custody of the bank to pay off a matured debt to the bank. This customer money cannot be taken if it is a TRUST FUND, of which the bank has notice.

bank·**rupt**·**cy.** (1) A procedure under Federal law, for filing for relief of debts. The procedure is initiated either by an individual's or corporation's voluntary petition to a court, or is invoked by a party's creditors. *Bankruptcy* is different from INSOLVENCY, which is an inability to meet obligations as they fall due. An insolvent could still have enough assets to pay off all debts, but may not be able to liquidate assets when they fall due. (2) Sometimes loosely used to mean INSOLVENCY.

bar. (1) The whole body of lawyers who are members of the legal profession. (2) The rail that separates the general public from judges, attorneys, jurors, and others concerned in a trial in a courtroom. This is the meaning in which we use the expression *prisoner at the bar.* (3) In contract law, an impediment or obstacle. (4) That which annuls, cancels out or defeats. For example, we may say that a lawsuit was a *bar* to development of the freeway.

bar as·**so**·**ci**·*a*·**tion.** A voluntary association of members of the bar, in a state or local area. This group is distinguished from the INTEGRATED BAR. See INTEGRATED BAR.

bar·**gain and sale deed.** A variation of a *quitclaim deed* which transfers whatever interest the grantor (sellor) has in the property at the time of its execution. See deed: QUITCLAIM DEED.

bar·**ra**·**try.** (1) The offense of stirring up lawsuits or any kind of groundless legal proceeding. AMBULANCE CHASING is a form of *barratry* of this kind. (2) Any act by the master (captain) or sailors on a vessel that defrauds the owner of the vessel. Selling off part of the cargo at an intermediate port and pocketing the money would constitute *barratry* by the master or sailors responsible.

bar·**ris**·**ter.** An attorney in England who pleads at the bar and tries cases in English superior courts. In the English court system, a *barrister* is a higher ranking attorney than a SOLICITOR.

base and me·*rid*·**i**·**an.** Imaginary lines used by surveyors to find and note the location of public and private lands.

bas·**tard.** A child born out of wedlock. Most states have statutes relating to the criminal liability of the father, as well as to the care and support of the infant, although these statutes are frequently not enforced.

Most jurisdictions regard the child as LEGITIMATE if the parents subsequently marry. Legitimization may be important for a number of legal reasons. For example, a will made by the father leaving property to his children will not include a *bastard* child under the law in most jurisdictions.

bas·**tardy** *ac*·**tion.** The method provided by statute for proving an individual is the father of a BASTARD child, and to force the father to provide proper maintenance for this offspring. This legal action is sometimes called a *bastardy process* or PATERNITY SUIT.

bas·**tardy** *pro*·**cess.** See BASTARDY ACTION.

bat·**tery.** Any wilful beating, striking, or use of force on another in an unlawful way. It is the slightest touching of another, or of the clothes or anything else attached to his or her person, if done in a rude, insolent, or angry manner. The actual threat or offer to use force to the injury of another is an ASSAULT; the use of it is a *battery,* and always includes an ASSAULT. As a result, the two terms are commonly joined in the phrase *assault and battery.*

bear·**er.** (1) Someone who carries, holds, or transports a thing. (2) In the law of negotiable instruments, the individual in possession of a check, bill, or note that is made payable to *bearer.* A check endorsed in blank, or that is made out *payable to bearer* is a *bearer instrument.*

be·*lief.* A conviction of the truth of a statement or proposition. A state of mind in which confidence is placed in alleged facts, or the reality of some being or phenomenon, especially when gained from evidence and from other persons. Legally, *belief* is stronger than mere suspicion.

bench. (1) The place of judgment of a court; the court itself, or the group of judges that make up a court. The old-English term *King's bench* was the name for the King's court, or the King's judges. (2) The seat itself, occupied by a judge in a court.

bench **leg**·**is**·*la*·**tion.** A term for JUDGE-MADE LAW.

bench marks. Descriptive locations for property boundaries placed on permanent markers by land surveyors.

bench *war*·**rant.** An arrest WARRANT issued from the court itself (from the judge) rather than from a magistrate. Normally, a criminal arrest warrant originates with a magistrate, who issues the warrant after receiving a complaint from an investigating officer or a victim of a crime. The magistrate's warrant brings the offender into the custody of the judicial system through an arrest. Thereafter, the accused may be released on bond and subsequently tried. A *bench warrant* is issued by the judge if the accused jumps bail or fails to report for trial, or if a witness ignores a subpoena in the trial process. Also, the judge will bring the accused into court on a *bench warrant* after an indictment has been returned (voted) by a grand jury.

ben·e·*fi*·cial *in*·ter·est. The financial advantage, profit, or benefit that results from a contract, an estate, or property, as distinguished from absolute legal ownership itself.

ben·e·*fi*·ci·ar·y. A person or organization benefitting under a will, trust, insurance policy, or agreement.

***ben*·e·fit.** That which is financially useful, profitable, or advantageous.

be·*nev*·o·lent cor·po·*ra*·tion. A CORPORATION formed for the improvement of social, spiritual, mental, or physical well-being of the general public, rather than for profit. Under the law in most jurisdictions, an association or corporation of this type may be exempt from the payment of some taxes, or receive tax advantages.

be·*queath*. (1) The giving of personal property in a will. This is distinguished from the giving of real property, which is by DEVISE. (2) In recent years the term has been used more to mean the giving of any kind of property by will.

be·*quest*. A disposition, bestowal, or gift made in a will. Property or money left to another in a will.

best *ev*·i·dence rule. The rule followed in all court trials requiring that only the original of written or printed documents be used, unless it can be shown that the original cannot be obtained and the copy is an exact one. The object of the rule is to eliminate the possibility of errors in copying, or to prevent using a document as evidence that could have been subject to tampering or change. The courts sometimes state the rule as: "A written instrument or document is regarded as the best possible evidence of its existence and contents."

bes·ti·*al*·i·ty. Sexual relations between a human and any kind of animal. By statute, this is a criminal violation in most jurisdictions.

***bet*·ter·ment.** In real estate law, an improvement upon property which increases value and is considered a capital asset as distinguished from repairs or replacements, where the original cost or character is unchanged.

be·*yond* a *rea*·son·a·ble doubt. The kind of evidence or proof that convinces to a moral certainty, or that fully satisfies. This is the degree of proof that is needed for conviction in a criminal trial. While nothing is ever completely certain, it is the kind of conviction which leaves little room for doubt.

bi•**as.** A set, preconceived opinion on a cause or issue which does not leave the mind completely receptive to evidence, either for or against. That which sways judgment and renders an individual or a judge unable to be impartial.

bi•*cam*•**er**•**al.** A division of a legislative body into two chambers, such as the United States Congress divided into the Senate and House of Representatives. The state of Nebraska uses a *unicameral,* or one-body legislative system, with other states using a *bicameral* system.

big•**a**•**my.** The act of entering into a marriage while still married to another.

bi•*lat*•**er**•**al** *con*•**tract.** A contract in which both the contracting parties are obligated under the terms of the agreement to fulfill obligations toward each other, reciprocally. It is a contract that is executory on both sides, where mutual promises are made and accepted. For example, one farmer may promise to cut the wheat crop of a second party, who promises to deliver three dressed sides of beef to the first.

bill. (1) Originally, a formal statement of particulars, a complaint, or a declaration. Today, the word has a number of applications, including: **(a)** a formal statement of complaint to a court of justice, **(b)** a type of writ, **(c)** a formal written petition, **(d)** a written statement of the terms of a contract, **(e)** promissory obligations in the law of negotiable instruments, **(f)** the terms of contracts in maritime law, **(g)** a statement of particulars in criminal law, and other applications. For example, a *bill of particulars* in criminal law is a statement of the specific charges that must be answered by the accused. **(2)** A proposed or projected law, presented for consideration to a legislature, but not yet enacted into law. **(3)** A type of negotiable instrument, such as a *bill of exchange.* **(4)** A statement of debt.

bill of at•*tain*•**der.** Any law passed by a state legislature or the Congress of the U.S. that inflicts punishment on anyone without the benefit of a judicial (court) trial. An IMPEACHMENT proceeding is the only exception allowed by the U.S. Constitution. The prohibition against a *bill of attainder* serves to guarantee a review of all the accused's rights in open court, with the right of judicial appeal in the event an error is made by the trial court. This system prevents Congress or the state legislature from taking over the functions of the court.

bill of ex•*change.* A written order from one person to another to pay a specified sum of money therein named at a given time. A draft is a *bill of exchange.* A check is a *bill of exchange* drawn on a bank, payable on demand.

bill of in·*dict*·ment. A written presentation to a grand jury, accusing a named person or persons of having committed a crime, and requesting the return of an INDICTMENT (a true BILL) by the grand jury.

bill of in·ter·*plead*·er. See INTERPLEADER.

bill of *lad*·ing. A document that gives written evidence of a contract between a shipper and carrier for the transportation and safe delivery of goods. A *bill of lading* has three legal functions: **(a)** it is a contract that sets out the terms under which the carrier agrees to carry the merchandise, **(b)** it serves as a receipt for the merchandise, and **(c)** it is the TITLE document. A *non-negotiable bill of lading,* or *straight bill of lading* requires delivery to the particular individual named as consignee. A *negotiable,* or *order bill of lading,* permits delivery at the order of the consignee. Firms often negotiate or transfer bills of lading to individuals buying goods, and the purchaser can claim the merchandise from the carrier by presenting the *bill of lading* obtained.

bill of par·*tic*·u·lars. A written statement of the details or particulars on which a plaintiff brings a lawsuit, or by which the defendant claims a COUNTERCLAIM or SET-OFF against such demand.

bill of re·*view*. A request brought before a court to have the court correct, review, or reverse a prior decree of the court that rendered it. It is in the nature of a WRIT OF ERROR. For example, it could involve an error appearing on the face of the court record.

bill of rights. Those individual rights and privileges, set out in constitutional declarations and legislative enactments, that must be accorded to every purpose. Sometimes the first ten amendments to the United States Constitution are spoken of as the *Bill of Rights,* but there are a number of other rights guaranteed by enactments of Congress and by U.S. Supreme Court interpretations. State constitutions and legislative enactments also set forth a number of rights of individuals that are deemed essential and fundamental. Some of these duplicate the rights guaranteed to everyone under federal law. The rights in the first ten amendments include the right to: freedom of speech, freedom of religion, freedom of the press, and freedom of assembly and petition for redress of grievances. These first ten amendments also include: the right to bear and maintain arms, freedom from being forced to maintain accommodations for soldiers in private homes, and protection from unreasonable searches and seizures. Also included are: the right to an indictment prior to a FELONY trial, a prohibition against

DOUBLE JEOPARDY, the right not to be forced to testify against one-self, the right not to be deprived of property without due process of law, the right to a speedy criminal trial, the right to an impartial jury and a jury trial, the right to confront witnesses and to call witnesses in one's own behalf, the right to a lawyer, the right to reasonable BAIL, and the right that punishment shall neither be cruel nor unusual. Some rights that have been legally established, such as the right of *habeas corpus,* are not included in the first ten amendments.

bill of sale. A document issued by a seller to a buyer evidencing the transfer of ownership of personal property that is listed or described in the document. Under state laws, the sale of some items cannot be made without the preparation of a formal *bill of sale.* An example would be the sale of an automobile, where a written document is needed for state registration procedures.

bind. To place under a legal duty, or obligation. We say that the terms of a contract, for example, *bind* the parties to the agreement. In similar manner, the agreement is *binding,* and each party is *bound.*

bind·**er.** **(1)** A written memorandum of agreement to show insurance coverage until a formal insurance policy can be issued. A fire insurance agent, for example, can give a home owner a handwritten *binder* consisting of only a few lines, that will give the home owner protection until a fire insurance policy is issued by the home office of the insurance company. Obviously, the *binder* cannot include all the provisions of the fine print of the policy, but gives coverage under the company's standard policy provisions. **(2)** Earnest money deposited for the purchase of real estate is sometimes called a binder. See EARNEST MONEY.

black·**mail.** Extorting money by threats to publicly expose weaknesses, bad business practices, sexual misconduct, crimes, or other activities that would damage the reputation or social standing of the victim. Generally, the term is used synonymously with EXTORTION. *Blackmail* is a statutory crime in some states, and is limited to specific types of extortion.

blank en·*dorse*·ment (or blank in·*dorse*·ment). An endorsement of a check, promissory note, bill of exchange, or any NEGOTIABLE INSTRUMENT by merely signing the name of the *endorser.* This has the effect of leaving the instrument negotiable.

blan·**ket *mort*·gage.** A kind of mortgage that covers two or more parcels of real estate. The mortgage may call for the release of individual parcels as certain payments are made in reduction of the loan. Unless there is a provision of this kind in the mortgage, however, the holder may retain the security of all the properties until the mortgage is satisfied.

blue laws Any set of rigid laws that regulates conduct on Sunday. Historically, the meaning comes from the so-called "Sunday laws" or "Blue laws" by authorities who settled the Connecticut colony in colonial America, with strict application of Mosaic principles. For example, a prohibition against a professional baseball game on Sunday is referred to as a "blue law."

blue sky laws. A popular name given to laws that regulate the sale of stocks, bonds, or share units to protect the public at large from fraudulent security sales.

board of di•rec•tors. The ruling body of a private CORPORATION, or other legally constituted organization.

body cor•por•ate. A private or public stock company or corporation.

bo•na fide. (Latin–*boh•*nuh fide, *boh•*nuh fide•ee). *In good faith.* In some civil lawsuits the courts look to the *bona fides* or good faith of the parties involved. Under some circumstances the courts will not allow one party to prevail in a lawsuit if that party entered into the original transaction in bad faith. According to the old legal maxim, "He who comes into equity (court) must come with clean hands."

bond. (1) A certificate or evidence of debt. (2) An obligation made binding by a money forfeit. (3) Property or money pledged as a bail or surety for an individual released from jail to answer criminal charges. (4) An interest bearing certificate of private or governmental indebtedness.

bot•tom•ry. A contract by which a ship owner obtains money for operating costs or repairs in return for a pledge of the ship. In maritime parlance it is pledge of the *bottom and keel* as security.

bound. See BIND.

boy•cott. A concerted refusal to have dealings with, or to do business with, a specific firm, individual, or group. A conspiracy to prevent the carrying on of business by another.

breach of peace. Any disruption of the public order, or tranquility. The criminal violation of breaking or disturbing the public peace by any forcible, riotous or unlawful activity or assembly. Going about in public with dangerous or unusual weapons, threatening another with violence and physical injury, and making extremely loud noises during the nighttime hours, are examples of activity usually recognized by the courts as a *breach of peace.*

breach of *pris•*on. The criminal offense of forcibly breaking out of a prison or jail. It is a statutory offense in many states.

breach of *prom•*ise. Violation of a promise, usually used in connection with a promise to marry. Formerly used as the basis of a suit for damages, legal action based on such a breach is seen with less frequency in modern times. In some jurisdictions it is prohibited by statute.

*break•***ing and** *en•*ter•ing. Another name for the crime of BURGLARY. State laws vary as to whether the breaking must be at night, and whether the building involved must be a dwellinghouse or outbuilding. See BURGLARY.

*bri•*ber•y. The offer of money, an advantage, or a favor, given or promised, to an individual in a position of trust to influence the latter's judgment. Offering something of value to influence action or a refusal to act in discharge of a legal or public duty. The gist of the offense is the attempt to pervert justice. It applies to both the actor and the receiver, and is a crime in all jurisdictions. To offer a city building inspector $100 to overlook a requirement in the city building code would be a violation.

brief. (1) A condensed or abbreviated statement of the pleadings, proofs, and affidavits in any legal proceeding. (2) A brief is a written or printed statement prepared by attorneys to serve as the basis for arguments to an appellate court. It includes case citations and points of law which the lawyer seeks to establish, along with any legal authorities cited. It is the vehicle by which the lawyer seeks to convey to the appellate court the essential facts of his client's case.

bring suit. To *bring suit* or *bring an action* has a settled, customary meaning at law. This refers to the commencement of court action or legal proceedings in a lawsuit.

*bug•*ger•y. (The definition varies from jurisdiction to jurisdiction). Generally three types of unnatural sexual relations are regarded as *buggery:* (a) a man or woman and a brute (any animal); (b) a man and a man; and (c) a man unnaturally with a woman. Some definitions include sexual relations between a woman and a woman. Most or all of these relationships are forbidden by statutes, but there is considerable variance between the states.

bulk sales acts. Statutes that forbid the sale in bulk of all or substantially all of a merchant's stock of goods to defraud the creditors of the merchant.

bulk sales law. A statute designed to protect creditors of a merchant who sells all or a considerable part of stock to a single buyer, leaving the creditors with no assets that can be attached or reached. Statutes of this kind vary from state to state. In general they provide that a buyer for a major portion of a merchant's stock, other than in the regular course of business, must obtain, under oath, a list of the seller's creditors. The buyer is then required to give notice to each creditor, usually about 10 days, to allow the creditors to press their claims before the merchant's stock and other assets are beyond their reach.

bulk *trans*·fer laws. Same as BULK SALES ACTS.

***bur*·den of *go*·ing *for*·ward.** Same as BURDEN OF PROCEEDING.

***bur*·den of pro·*ceed*·ing.** The affirmative duty to come forward with evidence on a particular issue in a lawsuit, rather than to wait for the other side to prove that the matter is not true.

***bur*·den of proof.** (1) In evidence law, the obligation or necessity to prove those facts in dispute in the trial of a lawsuit. Most courts say that the *burden of proof* involves two obligations: (a) the duty of producing evidence as the trial progresses, and (b) establishing the truth of the claim by a preponderance of the evidence. (2) In a criminal prosecution, the *burden of proof* is on the prosecutor (on the government) to prove all material issues that may be in doubt. This is an affirmative duty. At the outset of the trial, the defendant has no duty to prove innocence.

***bur*·*glar*·y.** At common law, breaking and entering the dwelling place of another, with intent to commit a FELONY therein, whether the felony was committed or not. The common law definition has been modified in most states to include *entering in the daytime,* and to prohibit the entry into any type of structure or building. The breaking and entering into a building merely to get out of a snowstorm would not be a burglary. But a breaking to determine whether there was property inside that could be stolen would be sufficient to constitute the crime, even though nothing was found and the building was then used to provide shelter. The FELONY intended on the inside of the building could be any felony—murder, rape, larceny, etc.

busi·ness *judg*·ment **rule.** The legal principal that a court will not interfere in the operation of a CORPORATION, so long as corporate officials and executives are acting within the scope of their powers and in the honest exercise of judgment. Mere stupidity or bad judgment is not sufficient to sustain a stockholder suit to turn the management over to a receiver or other stockholders.

busi·ness **trust.** A business set up in the form of a TRUST, and distinguished from a joint stock company. In a *business trust,* the property belonging to the business is placed in the hands of trustees, who manage and deal with it for the use and benefit of beneficiaries who hold certificates like corporate stock certificates. The trustees have permanent management responsibilities, unlike the directors of a corporation who change from year to year. Sometimes called a *Massachusetts Trust.*

by·laws. The rules adopted by a CORPORATION or other organization for its own operations and government. Normally, a corporation may change its *bylaws* at any time, so long as the *bylaw* is **(a)** not in opposition to an existing law, **(b)** consistent with the objectives for which the corporation was formed, and **(c)** not in violation of the rights of a company's stockholders. All states have laws that regulate incorporation and set up rules for government of the corporation by passage and implementation of *bylaws.*

C

cal·en·dar **(or court** *cal*·en·dar**).** The list of lawsuits (causes) ready for argument or trial.

cal·en·dar **call.** A roll call made by the clerk of a court to determine the presence of attorneys or others called in, in order to begin hearing of pending cases.

can·cel·*la*·**tion.** **(1)** An act which demonstrates an intent to annul a legal INSTRUMENT, putting the instrument in a condition where its invalidity is obvious on its face. **(2)** A means of bringing a contract to an end because the other party to the contract has already broken the agreement.

can·**on.** A guiding legal principle or legal rule. A basis for judgment, standard, or criterion.

can·**ons of con**·*struc*·**tion.** Those basic rules and maxims which are recognized in the law as controlling or governing the construction or interpretation to be given to legal INSTRUMENTS.

ca·*pac*·**i**·**ty.** (1) Legal qualification or authority. For example, the right to make an arrest. (2) Qualifications as to space, size, strength, power, or force. (3) The legal right to take certain actions, such as the *capacity to sue.* (4) Good perception and understanding, such as an understanding of the disposition made of property.

ca·*pi*·**as.** (Latin–*ka* pee us) *That you take.* The name for a writ that orders the sheriff or other peace officer to take the body of the defendant into custody. It is a writ of attachment or arrest.

cap·**i**·**tal** *as*·**sets.** Assets of a permanent nature used in the production of income, such as land, buildings, equipment and machinery. *Capital assets* are distinguishable from *inventory* for income tax law purposes, as *inventory* is property held for sale to customers in the ordinary course of business.

cap·**i**·**tal crime.** See CAPITAL OFFENSE.

cap·**i**·**tal gains tax.** A tax on the increase in worth of CAPITAL ASSETS upon sale. For example, a tax levied on the increase of value on common stocks, purchased at 27½ per share and sold at 38½.

cap·**i**·**tal** *lev*·**y.** A tax on real property or capital assets.

cap·**i**·**tal** *of*·*fense.* A crime for which the death penalty may, but need not necessarily, be imposed.

cap·**i**·**tal** *pun*·**ish**·**ment.** The infliction of the death penalty for commission of certain crimes.

cap·**i**·**tal stock.** (1) The amount of stock to be subscribed and paid in, as fixed by the corporate charter. (2) The term may also refer to the amount or limit of stock that a corporation may issue, according to the charter of the stock company.

cap·**i**·**tal**·**i**·*za*·**tion** *meth*·**od.** A method for determining the value of real estate by considering net income and percentage of reasonable return on the investment.

cap·**i**·**tal**·**i**·*za*·**tion rate.** The rate of interest which is considered a reasonable rate of return on the investment, and is used in the process of determining value based on net income.

cap·**i**·*ta*·**tion tax.** A tax fixed at an equal sum per person; a POLL tax, or tax per head.

care. (1) Attentiveness to detail, heed, discretion, or concern. Ordinary *care* is that degree of care which persons of ordinary prudence and discretion are accustomed to use under the same or similar circumstances. (2) Within custody or safekeeping.

car·nal *knowl·edge.* The act whereby a man and a woman have a sexual connection; sexual intercourse; copulation; coitus.

car·ri·er. A firm, organization, or individual doing business in the transportation of passengers or property for hire. A *carrier* may be either a *private carrier* or a *common carrier,* with the latter accommodating any member of the general public.

car·ri·er's lien. The right of a freight line or other carrier to retain the consignee's cargo until transportation charges have been paid.

car·tel. An association or combination of independent businesses in one or more countries, formed for the purpose of controlling production, sale and price, to obtain a monopoly in any particular industry or commodity. The objectives and activities of a *cartel* may be in violation of antitrust or monopoly laws.

case at bar. A case that is currently before a court, and under consideration.

case law. Reported decisions handed down by the courts. Prior decisions that are ordinarily binding on judges deciding a case.

case *meth·od.* A system of instruction used in most law schools requiring students to read and report on selected cases. These cases usually illustrate outstanding legal decisions and general legal principles. Cases that support basic principles as well as divergent viewpoints are studied and analyzed. This system forces the fledgling lawyer to dig out all the POINTS OF LAW, and to evaluate basic legal problems. It is also excellent for research training. The case method differs from the HORNBOOK or textbook method, in which legal principles are set out in a text, appropriately footnoted with case decisions. The *case method* evolved from trial and error, and is preferred by most legal teachers and scholars.

cash *ba·sis.* A bookkeeping system that reflects a profit or loss as money is received or paid out.

cas·u·al *e·ject·or.* See EJECTMENT.

cas·u·al·ty. An unfortunate mishap or accident; a contingency that comes about without design or without being foreseen. It usually involves loss from fire, lightning, shipwreck, property damage, or the unanticipated loss of life.

cau·sa mor·tis. (Latin–*kos*·uh *mor*·tis) *In contemplation of approaching death.* Usually used to refer to the giving of money or property immediately before death, in order to avoid INHERITANCE TAXES. Some states have statutes providing that gifts of this kind are taxable, if given in a specified time limitation before death occurs.

cau·sa prox·i·ma. (Latin–*kos*·uh *prox*·i·muh) See PROXIMATE CAUSE.

cause of ac·tion. The subject matter of a lawsuit; a redressable wrong; the right to recover something from another. The *cause of action* may exist, but this does not mean there will always be a practical remedy.

ca·ve·at emp·tor. (Latin–*kay*·vee·at *emp*·tor) *Let the buyer beware.* The ancient rule of commercial law, tracing back at least to Roman times, that every purchaser must examine, judge, and look for defects, and that the seller would not be held responsible for them.

C.C.A. Abbreviation for U.S. Circuit Court of Appeals.

cease and de·*sist*. An injunction from a court, or an order from an administrative agency, to immediately refrain from a specific activity that has been found to be illegal or objectionable. For example, a state health department may be empowered by statute to issue a *cease and desist* order to a restaurant that is being operated in an unsanitary condition.

cede. To yield over; to grant. Generally used in connection with the transfer of ownership and sovereignty of territory by one government to another. For instance the Federal government may *cede* jurisdiction over part of an installation to the state government.

cer·ti·fied. Guaranteed in writing. To vouch for in writing.

cer·ti·fied check. A check guaranteed by the bank on which drawn, both as to the amount and the authenticity of the signature of the maker. Once presented for certification by either the maker or a holder, the check becomes a direct obligation of the bank and not an order to pay from the account of the maker. When presented for certification for a set fee, the bank deducts the amount of the check from the maker's account and marks it *certified* or *accepted.* The drawer of a *certified check* cannot stop payment on it.

cer·ti·fied cop·y. A copy of a record or document certified and signed as a true copy by the official in whose custody the original is maintained.

cer·tio·ra·ri. (Latin–sur·shuh·*rare*·ee) Literally, *to search out the facts.* A writ or order that is part of the appeals procedure used by most

APPELLATE courts (review courts or higher courts). *Certiorari* is the name of the writ (order) issued by the higher court calling up the record of a proceeding or trial for appellate review of the higher court. Lawyers say "*Certiorari* is to perfect the record of appeal." It is to give the higher court enough information to determine whether an error was made by the lower tribunal. In some states this old legal term is no longer used—it is called a *writ of review* or *writ of error*.

ces·tui que trust. (French) *That one with a right to the trust.* The beneficiary of a TRUST.

chain of ti·tle. The history, or record of ownership, of TITLE to a piece of land, from the original grant to the present owner.

chal·lenge. A legal objection or exception. A *challenge to the array* is an objection or challenge to all those jurors that have been impanelled. A *challenge to the poll* is an exception to an individual juror. A *preemptory challenge* of a juror is that which one side to a trial may make without giving any reason.

cham·bers. The private rooms of offices of a judge in which the judge signs papers, hears motions, consults with attorneys, or transacts other legal business when not in open court. Matters handled in this manner are said to be done *in chambers*.

cham·per·ty. (Norman-French *champart*–the lord's share in the crop of a tenant's land; Latin *campi pars*—a field of land.) **(1)** An illegal sharing of the proceeds of a lawsuit by an outside party who has promoted it. **(2)** Sometimes used in the sense of an unjustified attempt to stir up a lawsuit by an attorney or by a third party who was not wronged. A so-called AMBULANCE CHASER may be guilty of *champerty.*

chan·ce·ry. Generally used synonymously with EQUITY, or equity court.

char·ac·ter. Those personal traits and habits that may be testified to by close associates in the event that an individual's *character* becomes in issue in either a criminal or civil trial.

charge. **(1)** A claim, INCUMBRANCE, or LIEN. Any financial claim. **(2)** To place a burden upon, or impose a duty. **(3)** A formal complaint or accusation made in a criminal matter. **(4)** The instructions given by the court (judge) to the jury on some particular point or question involved in the case, often in answer to an attorney's request. The *charge* may involve a summation and series of instructions to the jury at the end of the presentation of evidence, and before jury deliberation. **(5)** To purchase something on regular payments. **(6)** An individual is said to be a *public charge* when supported at public expense by reason of idiocy, disease, or poverty.

charge to the *ju·ry*. An address by a judge to a jury at the close of a trial. It usually includes instructions and advice.

Purpose of the *charge* is to instruct the jury about the law that applies to this particular case, and also instruct how the jury is required to act in giving consideration to specific parts of the evidence. Any number of *charges* may be given in concise written form. Some of these instructions are standard in form, and may be passed along from judge to judge and from trial to trial. In unusual situations, however, specific instructions will be needed about the law as it applies to the facts at hand. A careful defense attorney will review *charges to the jury,* hoping to find a prejudiced or inappropriate charge that could mislead the jury, serving as the basis for an appeal if the client is found guilty.

char·i·ta·ble trust. A trust with a charitable or public organization as beneficiary. It is characterized by a definite statement of charitable purpose, but the actual beneficiaries may not be designated by name. For example, a trust set up "for the orphans at the Masonic Home," or "for the sisters at St. Anne's."

char·ter. (1) A grant, guarantee of rights, franchises, or privileges from the sovereign power of a state or nation. (2) The authority by virtue of which a CORPORATION or organized body acts. (3) In mercantile law, the lease of a vessel or vehicle for transportation.

char·ter *par·ty*. A lease contract by which a ship, or some principal part thereof, is leased to another. Generally these leases are of three types: **(a)** voyage charter, in which the ship is engaged to carry cargo on one voyage only, with the vessel manned and navigated by the owner; **(b)** time charter, with the ship and crew committed for a definite period of time, regardless of the number of voyages involved; and **(c)** a demise charter, in which the charterer takes over the ship and supplies a crew for a set period of time.

chat·tel. Any kind of tangible personal property except real estate. Any type of property except: **(a)** intangible personal property, such as stocks and bonds (the paper is not value, it merely represents value), or **(b)** a freehold or ownership in land. Cattle and horses are *chattel*. In fact the term *chattel* derives from an old French word for cattle, an early symbol of wealth.

chat·tel *mort*·gage. A method for obtaining a loan on *chattels.* Laws of the various states use three legal viewpoints in the way mortgages of this kind are regarded: **(a)** The mortgage acts as an actual transfer, in whole or in part, of the property covered. **(b)** Ownership is not transferred at all, but the mortgage acts as a lien, or charge, against the property. Or, **(c)** The property is regarded as being placed in trust to a third party until the loan is satisfied. The laws of the states vary regarding the lender's legal remedies in the event of non-payment. In some states the foreclosure of a *chattel mortgage* can be effected only through court proceedings. In many states, the *chattel mortgage* must be recorded if the lender's rights are to be protected against other creditors of the borrower. Most states have laws making it a felony to remove mortgaged property out of state, or to deliberately sell or conceal the property. *Chattel mortgages* are usually limited to 3 or 4 years in duration by statute, becoming void automatically unless renewed. See CHATTEL; RECORDING; MORTGAGE; CONDITIONAL SALE CONTRACT.

check. A written order to a bank to pay the amount of money specified on the document from funds held by the bank. A *check* is a type of DRAFT, being distinguished by the fact that in a draft the DRAWER is a bank, while in a *check* the drawer is an individual. Both are NEGOTIABLE INSTRUMENTS, with a *check* being generally designed for immediate payment and not for circulation as money.

check ki·ting. See KITING.

chose in *ac*·tion. **(1)** The right to sue for damages; a right of action not reduced to possession, but recoverable in a lawsuit; a right to recover a debt, demand, or damages. **(2)** Sometimes the phrase includes not only the right of action, but also the thing that forms the subject matter of that right, such as stocks, bonds, or a written contract.

C.I.F. (also commonly written as "c. i. f." or "C. I. & F."). An abbreviation used in commercial contracts of sale to denote that the sale price includes the cost of the goods, insurance, and freight.

C.J. An abbreviation for chief justice of a court; may also be used as abbreviation for circuit judge.

cir·cuit. A geographical division of a state or nation covered by a court serving that area.

cir·cuit court. A court that serves an area comprised of several counties or several states. In state *circuit courts,* the tribunal's jurisdiction may extend over several districts or several counties, where sessions are held in such counties or districts alternately. The court may not sit at one location permanently, since there may not be enough cases in one locality to justify a permanent court. State *circuit courts* may have general ORIGINAL JURISDICTION, that is, the authority to try civil cases or criminal prosecutions. Federal circuit courts are not courts of original jurisdiction—they are APPELLATE COURTS that may serve a district comprised of several states or a large populated area. Federal circuit courts handle appeals from decisions handed down by the U.S. District Courts.

ci·*ta*·tion. An order, or writ, issued by a court, ordering someone to appear before the court at a specific date and time. **(2)** A notice of a failure to observe the law. For example, a *citation* issued by the building inspector to a contractor, pointing out that some phase of construction is not in conformance with the building code, and must be corrected under penalty of law. **(3)** The name and location, usually by volume and page numbers, of legal decisions and references that support legal pleadings or other legal papers.

cite. To order, or summon, an individual or the representative of a corporation to court. **(2)** To list legal decisions or authorities.

***civ*·il case.** A lawsuit or legal action undertaken in civil (not criminal) courts. It is usually filed to compel payment of money damages, seeking the correction, recovery, or establishment of private wrongs in a civil dispute (not a CRIME or a MISDEMEANOR). In some instances an injunction may be sought, along with monetary damages. An injunction is usually a court order directing the correction of wrongful acts or restricting the continuance of such action. (See INJUNCTION) A *civil case* is usually presented for trial by written allegations or claims made by the plaintiff (called a complaint), and denials or answers filed in written form by the defendant through legal counsel.

***civ*·il death.** When a criminal is sentenced to life imprisonment, most courts have ruled that the individual is *civilly dead*. This means that the convict has lost citizenship rights, such as the right to vote, to hold office, etc.

***civ*·il *rem*·e·dy.** Those legal actions that may be available to private individuals or interests, as opposed to a criminal prosecution.

***civ*·il rights.** Such rights as belong to every inhabitant of the United States, capable of being enforced or redressed in court action. These rights include protection of the laws, marriage, contract, the rights of property, and certain rights secured to all citizens of the U.S. by the

Constitution proper, the first ten amendments to the Constitution, rights secured in the Thirteenth and Fourteenth Amendments, and by acts of Congress made in pursuance of the Constitution.

claim. (1) Any legal demand asserted as a right. (2) To urge; to assert.

claim for re·*lief*. The original pleading filed by the PLAINTIFF in a lawsuit. This is a statement of those facts that go to show that the plaintiff has been wronged and that the court should enforce the plaintiff's claim against the DEFENDANT.

class *ac*·tion. See ACTION.

clean hands. The doctrine that any party seeking relief in a court of equity must come with *clean hands*. In other words, the plaintiff cannot expect justice unless the plaintiff is without substantial blame or fault.

clear and *pres*·ent *dan*·ger. The doctrine, or test, first applied by Justice Holmes of the U.S. Supreme Court to determine what restrictions may constitutionally be put on free speech and free press. By the terms of this test, an individual cannot be prohibited from making a speech unless it appears there is a *clear and present danger* that serious violence or RIOT would result from the speech. The fact that a speech creates public unrest, annoyance or inconvenience is not enough. Prohibited speech is that which stirs to action, in the immediate presence.

clear *ti*·tle. TITLE to property that is free from incumbrances, obstructions, or limitations of any kind. For example, a tract of land that has no mortgages, liens, or claims of any kind against it.

***clem*·en·cy.** A merciful or lenient act, especially in the sentencing of a criminal. In some instances *clemency* may mean lenient treatment of one already convicted.

close. An enclosed area of well-identified land, marked off by a fence, hedge, or field markers. The term was frequently used in old English property law, but has reduced usage in the U.S. today.

close cor·po··*ra*·tion. A CORPORATION in which the directors and officers have the power to fill vacancies in their own number, without allowing general stockholders to vote. This power, of course, is provided in the organizational charter. Most joint stock companies (corporations) are so-called *open* corporations, with directors being selected by stockholder vote.

closed cor·po·*ra*·tion. A CORPORATION that is effectively owned or controlled by a small number of individuals. Often, this is a family-owned corporation, that may or may not be listed on a stock exchange.

clo•**ture.** The parliamentary procedure for ending debate and taking an immediate vote on the matter under consideration. It is sometimes used in Congress or other legislative assemblies. For example, the newspapers may report that *the presiding officer of the Senate invoked cloture.*

cloud on *ti*•**tle.** Any outstanding incumbrance, claim or charge against a parcel of real estate. An unpaid tax lien, unsatisfied mortgage, or a previous deed granted for all or part of the property would constitute a *cloud on title.* See INCUMBRANCE.

code. A collection or compendium of existing laws. For example, the California Criminal Code would consist of all the California statutes (legislative enactments) that prohibit designated acts as criminal.

code *an*•**no**•**tat**•**ed.** A set of matching law books incorporating a code or collection of laws, along with appropriate commentary to explain or illustrate the meaning of individual laws. Legal *annotations* usually include the history of a specific statute, amendments or changes made to it, explanations, noteworthy court decisions and case citations interpreting that specific statute.

cod•**i**•**cil.** A written addendum or alteration, prepared to supplement or explain an individual's last will and testament. If legally prepared, the *codicil* is regarded as a legal part of the will.

cod•**i**•**fy.** To arrange the laws of a nation or a state into a CODE, or systematized collection.

cog•**ni**•**zance.** (1) The right and power to hear legal controversies. For example, we may say *the Supreme Court of the United States took cognizance of the dispute over Colorado River water between the states of California and Arizona, and settled the controversy.* (2) Taking judicial notice of a matter. For example, *the court took cognizance of the fact that June 4, 1978 fell on a Sunday.*

cog•*no*•**vit.** Written acknowledgement by a debtor of the justice of a claim against him or her, with written direction for the entry of a judgment against the debtor. The practical result of this is that it generally avoids the expense of a trial.

co•**hab**•**i**•*ta*•**tion.** The condition of living together in the manner of husband and wife. A great variety of legal problems arise in many states because of differences between *cohabitation* and a marriage relationship in regard to property acquired by cohabiting individuals, the legitimacy of offspring, inheritance of property, tax obligations, etc. Under the interpretation of most courts, *cohabitation* includes

43

sexual intercourse between the parties living together. But in some circumstances occasional acts of sexual intercourse may be insufficient to constitute *cohabitation.*

co·in·*sur*·ance. Insurance in which an individual insures property for less than the total value and must bear any loss that exceeds the insurance coverance.

col·*lat*·er·al. (1) SECURITIES, money, or property pledged by a borrower to protect the interests of a lender. (2) Additional, or auxiliary, accompanying as a co-ordinate.

col·*lat*·er·al at·*tack*. An effort to set aside an adverse court decision by beginning action in a different legal proceeding. Sometimes called an *indirect attack* in legal terminology, a *collateral attack* is an attempt to set aside a court's judgment in an incidental proceeding, in some type of action other than that provided by law for the express purpose of attacking the judgment.

col·*lat*·er·al de·*scent*. A line of descent connecting individuals who are not directly related to each other as ascendants and descendants, but whose kinship consists in common descent from the same ancestor.

col·*lat*·er·al es·*top*·pel. The principle that a LITIGANT will be barred (will be *estopped*) from making a claim in one court, if the issue was a necessary part of another matter previously decided in a court proceeding. It is the conclusiveness of judgment in a prior action which involved one of the same legal issues that is brought up in a subsequent lawsuit. For example, in a divorce action both parties made their assets known to the court, and it was determined at that time that the husband's life insurance policies had been paid for prior to marriage and were not community property. Later, when the husband died, the wife filed suit against his heirs, seeking to obtain half of the insurance, as her share of community property. The wife's suit was dismissed on the principle of *collateral estoppel,* arising from the decisions made in the divorce settlement.

col·*lat*·er·als. Relatives by blood who are not in the same line of descent. Examples would be uncles, aunts, nephews, or nieces of a given individual.

col·*lu*·sion. Cooperation between two or more individuals for an illegal or fraudulent purpose.

col·or of *ti*·tle. The appearance of TITLE, but which for some defect, in actuality falls short of establishing it.

col·or·**able.** That which is counterfeit, but is seemingly valid; that which gives appearance only, but is intended to deceive.

co-*mak*·**er.** One who signs an obligation such as a promissory note or check, being secondarily liable for payment after the original maker.

com·i·**ty.** The practice by which one court follows the decision of another court on the same set of facts.

com·*mer*·**cial acre.** In real estate law, that which remains of an acre of subdivided land after streets, sidewalks, curbs, etc. have been deducted from the full acre.

com·*mer*·**cial paper.** Bank checks, promissory notes, bills of exchange and other NEGOTIABLE INSTRUMENTS for the payment of money in commerce and trade.

com·*min*·**gle.** To combine money, properties, or commodities into a common fund, account, or stock. To put together into one mass or one fund. For example, mixing wheat shipments from two farmers is to *commingle the grain*. This practice makes it difficult to trace funds or commodities, which may lose legal identity when *commingling* takes place.

com·*mis*·**sion.** (1) A formal government or court grant of power to do various acts or duties. (2) A certificate conferring military rank and authority. (3) Authority to act for or in behalf of another, in conducting private business. This is a form of AGENCY. (4) The reward or pay to an agent, factor, salesman, broker, etc. calculated as a percentage of the money owing to the PRINCIPAL. (5) The perpetration of a criminal act. For example, we speak of the *commission* of a crime.

com·*mit*·**ment.** The writ (order) or warrant issued by a court or judge serving as authority either to hold an insane person or to place a convict in prison. It is the court order to receive the mental patient or convict into custody and to safely confine that individual.

com·**mon** car·ri·**er.** A company or individual in business to transport goods or passengers for anyone desiring such service. The *common carrier of goods* is legally responsible for any damage or loss of merchandise except those losses caused by enemy action in wartime or by an act of God, such as an earthquake or cyclone. The carrier's legal responsibility continues during transportation and for a reasonable time after the goods have arrived at their destination. Thereafter, the carrier may put the goods in a warehouse, and the carrier's liability is reduced to that of ordinary care. The *common carrier* cannot refuse service to anyone, but legal liability may be qualified by contract. *Common carriers* who transport passengers have the duty to exercise a high degree of watchfulness and care for the safety of their passengers, but they are not legally at fault when the injury is caused solely by the passenger's negligence.

com•**mon** *coun*•**cil.** The name sometimes given to the governing body of a city government. This group may also be called the *city council.*

com•**mon** *ju*•**ry.** The kind of JURY ordinarily used in a civil trial by which issues of fact are generally tried, as distinguished from a special jury.

com•**mon law.** That body of law and legal principles which originated with the judges of England and which has been adopted into the law of most peoples and governments in the new world that had Anglo-Saxon stock, except Louisiana. The *common law* is JUDGE-MADE LAW, based on custom and precedent, unwritten in statute and code. Much of this law was subsequently incorporated into state codes in those states that now follow codes only.

com•**mon law** *ac*•**tion.** The old forms of pleading that were used in law courts (not equity courts) in England. These were actions such as *trover,* a kind of legal petition or cause of action that was used to recover damages against a person who had found another's goods and wrongfully converted them to his or her own use. These old English courts would not allow a recovery unless the plaintiff's cause of action fell squarely within the narrow limits covered by *trover.* If the defendant had stolen, rather than found, the plaintiff's goods, another type of common law action would be used to get the matter before the courts. As business affairs became more complex, there simply were not enough of these old common law forms of action, and they were not flexible enough to cover many situations where the plaintiff had been seriously wronged. To keep law uniform, the hidebound English courts would not accept matters that did not fall into one of the common law action categories. Other high judges in the king's courts set up a separate category of courts, the so-called EQUITY courts or chancery courts, to handle the obvious injustices that were being ignored by the established law courts. In the early history of this country, both *law courts* and EQUITY COURTS were set up in most jurisdictions. Sometimes a single court would function as a *law court* one day, and a *court of equity* on the following day. Gradually, these distinctions have been done away with, though some vestiges of the old dual system remains. In most jurisdictions, any court follows the legal principles of both the law and equity, and there is no requirement that the exact language of the old *common law* pleadings must be used.

com·mon law *mar·*riage. A marriage not solemnized in the regular manner, but based on the parties' agreement to consider themselves married, followed by COHABITATION. The parties must usually hold themselves out to be married, with a public and continued recognition of such relationship, as distinguished from incidental or occasional recognition. By statute in some states, a *common law relationship* that lasts for a specified number of years is legally treated as a conventional marriage, provided the parties had the requisite legal capacity for a regular marriage.

com·*mu·*ni·ty *prop·*er·ty. Property acquired by husband and wife, or either, during marriage, when not acquired as the separate property of either. It is a kind of marital partnership, in which both own anything that is acquired through the work, business trades, or acumen of either spouse, or the savings that are accumulated during the marriage. To be claimed as separate property of one spouse, the courts generally put the burden on the spouse so claiming. Generally, money or property used by both is assumed by the courts to be *community property.* For example, if the husband is a cattle rancher who marries a woman who owned land and cattle, the offspring of the cattle would be community property, unless individual animals were clearly marked as separate property of one spouse or the other. Most western states in the U.S. follow *community property* law doctrines, and there seems to be a tendency for other states to adopt the ideas.

com·mu·*ta·*tion. A reduction of sentence for criminal punishment from a greater to a lesser penalty. For example, from hanging or electrocution to life imprisonment. *Commutations,* PARDONS and REPRIEVES are all granted at the discretion of the sovereign power (the President of the U.S. in federal crimes and the Governor in state crimes). A *commutation* is distinguished from a pardon, which terminates or avoids punishment, while the commutation reduces it. A reprieve is merely a postponement or suspension of the execution of sentence.

The sovereign power (President or Governor) can only reduce, not increase, the sentence received under the power of *commutation.*

47

A change from an existing sentence to a greater sentence or punishment is illegal under the *ex post facto* provisions of the U.S. Constitution (Art. 1, Sec. 10).

com·pact. An agreement or contract, usually used to mean an agreement or convention between independent nations or governments.

com·*par*·a·tive *rec*·ti·tude. The doctrine followed in divorce courts in some states granting the divorce to the spouse that appears to the court to be least at fault when both spouses have shown grounds for divorce.

com·*pen*·sa·to·ry *dam*·ag·es. An award of damages that will repay the money losses of the injured party, and nothing more. *Compensatory damages* are to be distinguished from EXEMPLARY DAMAGES, which are generally allowed by the courts as payment beyond actual monetary losses for wrongs done by violence, malice, fraud, oppression, or deliberately wicked conduct.

com·pe·tent. **(1)** Answering to all the legal requirements. **(2)** Sometimes used in the sense of mental qualifications. For example, to be *competent* for jury duty, an individual must have those mental qualifications that indicate full possession of mental faculties.

com·pe·tent *ev*·i·dence. That kind of EVIDENCE which is required by the very nature of the thing to be proved. That evidence which is relevant and admissible.

com·*plaint*. *Complaints* are filed in both CIVIL cases and CRIMINAL cases. In a civil case, the *complaint* is the first paper filed with the clerk of the court to begin a civil lawsuit. The *complaint* sets out the nature and specifics of the alleged civil wrong that is the basis for the action.

In a criminal case, a *complaint* is the charge filed before a magistrate or other designated official with authority to initiate a criminal prosecution. The *complaint* is then used as the basis for the issuance of an arrest warrant. In most jurisdictions, criminal prosecutions begin by the filing of a *complaint* by a police officer, investigator, or federal agent, or by the return of a grand jury indictment (see GRAND JURY; see INDICTMENT).

com·po·*si*·tion (sometimes known as com·po·*si*·tion with *cred*·i·tors). A settlement, agreed between a debtor and creditors, for a reduced amount from a debtor who cannot pay in full. This is an agreement (contract) made on consideration, for the sake of immediate or sooner payment, distributed PRO RATA among the creditors in discharge and satisfaction of the whole debt. A *composition* is usually an arrangement to avoid bankruptcy, with the creditors getting their *pro rata* part of the debtor's payments immediately. Creditors may also receive more in this kind of settlement, since the costs for administration of BANKRUPTCY can be avoided.

com·*pound*·ing crime. The criminal offense committed by an individual who, having been directly injured or victimized by the criminal, receives a bribe, reward, or reparation from the criminal in agreement not to prosecute.

com·*pound*·ing *fel*·o·ny. Same as COMPOUNDING CRIME.

com·*pul*·so·ry *proc*·ess. A legal process for compelling the attendance in court of an individual wanted there, either as a witness, under an attachment, or under a warrant of arrest. A subpoena for a witness to a criminal trial is a common example of *compulsory process.* It is that coercive power of the courts to have the sheriff or other officer bring in those who will not comply, and to place them under contempt.

com·*pur*·ga·tor. An individual who takes the witness stand and testifies as a character witness in favor of someone accused of crime, or for a defendant in a civil action.

con·*ceal*·ment. The improper suppression of a fact or circumstance by one party to a contract, which suppression ought to be known to the other party.

con·*clu*·sion of law. A conclusion arrived at by applying the law to the facts of a particular case. For example, an individual killed his neighbor in a premeditated way, without any provocation or excuse. As a *conclusion of law,* the jury could find the offender guilty of murder.

con·*cur*·rent. That which happens at the same time and place; acting in conjunction; running together. *Concurrent sentences* are prison sentences served at the same time.

con·*cur*·rent ju·ris·*dic*·tion. The power of differing courts to each deal with the same cases and subjects. For example, a Federal court may have the right to try an individual who violates the Federal Bank Robbery Statute, while a state court may have *concurrent jurisdiction* to try the violator under state statutes prohibiting armed robbery.

con·*cur*·rent *pow*·er. Political power exercised independently by both Federal and state governments in the same field of legislation. For example, both the Federal and the state governments have authority to impose an income tax on personal or corporate income, according to the holdings of the courts.

con·*cur*·ring o·*pin*·ion. A legal opinion by an appellate court judge who agrees with the conclusions or results of another opinion filed by the majority or by a dissenting judge, although reasons for reaching the opinion may differ.

con·*di*·tion·al es·*tate*. See ESTATE.

con·do·*na*·tion. The conditional forgiveness of one spouse of marital indiscretions of the other, that would constitute sufficient grounds for divorce; the condition being that the offense would not be repeated.

con·*fes*·sion. An acknowledgment of guilt in a criminal case. A *confession* may be either oral or written. When it is written and signed, it is usually called a *signed statement*. The term ADMISSION is usually applied to legal matters of a civil nature, while a *confession* is a statement of guilt in a criminal charge.

con·*fes*·sion and a·*void*·ance. Legal pleadings that admit the truth of the averments of fact by the other side to a lawsuit, but that obviate or neutralize the opponent's claims by raising new facts which obviate the ordinary legal effect of the opponent's original claims. Sometimes called an AFFIRMATIVE DEFENSE.

con·*fes*·sion of *judg*·ment. The act of a debtor in permitting a judgment to be entered against him or her for a specified sum of money, by a written statement to that effect, without going to the expense and trouble of defending against a lawsuit in court.

con·fis·cate. The seizure of private property by the state or national government without payment. For example, under federal law an automobile used to transport bootleg alcohol or narcotics may be seized by government agents, and used for transportation by those agents.

con·flict of laws. That branch of jurisprudence concerned with conflicting rights and obligations that arise from doing business or living in two or more states or nations. A contract may be made under the laws of one state, but enforcement of the contract may be sought in another state, where there may be differences in interpretation by the courts, where different statutes may be in force, and where legal procedures are at variance.

con·*sent judg*·ment. A judgment, the provisions and terms of which are agreed to by both parties to the action, and approved by the judge hearing the case. A *consent judgment* is, in effect, a contract for the settlement of a lawsuit, acknowledged in open court, and ordered to be recorded. It binds the parties as fully as any other judgment. See: JUDGMENT.

50

con·sid·er·*a*·tion. (1) Something of value given or promised to induce one of the parties to make a CONTRACT. The price, motive, or value inducement for a contract. The courts say no contract was made unless there is something done or promised by both sides to the agreement. If a farmer sells a cow to a butcher, who promises to pay $100, the promise of payment is the consideration. In some jurisdictions, *family love and affection* is regarded as sufficient consideration for a transfer of property, even though no actual payment of money took place. (2) The legal assessment of a case and the judicial determination given to it by a court or judicial body.

con·*sign*. To give in charge; to entrust; to transmit or send goods to a merchant, a factor, or an agent for sale.

con·sign·*ee*. One to whom a shipment (consignment) is directed.

con·sign·*or*. A shipper of goods; one who sends merchandise in a consignment.

con·*spir*·a·cy. A combination or agreement between two or more persons to violate the law. It is also a *conspiracy* if the parties seek to accomplish some lawful purpose by unlawful means. There must be a joint scheme or plan by the *conspirators,* but a single act by any one is sufficient to bring the crime into being after conspirators have agreed upon the plot. A criminal *conspiracy* may be a continuing one, with some actors dropping out and other new actors entering the scheme. A *conspiracy* is a partnership in criminal purpose.

Judges and lawyers frequently have differing opinions about the requirements of limits of a *conspiracy,* because of the broad nature of the crime. A *conspiracy* may involve both criminal and civil wrongs.

con·*struc*·tive *no*·tice. See NOTICE.

con·sum·mate. To complete.

con·*tin*·gent re·*tain*·er. An agreement retaining the services of an attorney, the fee usually being a set percentage of the recovery in a lawsuit.

con·*tin*·u·ance. The postponement or adjournment of the trial of a lawsuit or prosecutive action to a later date of the same term of court, or to a subsequent term.

con·tract. An agreement between two or more parties to do, or not to do, a particular thing. It is an agreement by which each party is bound to do or refrain from doing some act, and each acquires a right to what the other promises or performs. A one-sided agreement is not a contract, as it lacks CONSIDERATION. See CONSIDERATION.

con·tra·*ven*·tion. Something done in violation of the laws or in violation of a duty imposed by law. For example, setting fire to your neighbor's home is in *contravention* of state laws against arson.

con·*ver*·sion. The unauthorized appropriation of another's property for the use of the wrongdoer, or the destruction or alteration of the nature of the property.

con·*vey*·ance. (1) An instrument or document by which title to land is transferred. (2) The transfer of the title to land from one person or classes of persons to another.

con·*vic*·tion. A finding of guilty of a criminal offense.

cop·y·right. The exclusive right of the author or creator for publishing, printing, or copying artistic or literary work, along with the right of distribution. Books, paintings, sculptures, engravings, maps, music sheets, pamphlets, articles, or any other kind of writing may be given a *copyright* by the U.S. Copyright Office, Library of Congress, Washington, D.C. This right was set up by Federal law, and permits the holder to sue for damages for infringement. An INJUNCTION may also be given by a court, restraining future violations. The symbol for a copyright is © .

co·ram no·bis. (Latin–*ko*·ram *noe*·bis). An appeal procedure, or a writ to correct possible miscarriage of justice because of a mistake of fact in the trial court. As used in a criminal case, the defendant petitions the court that renders an adverse judgment, asking the court to again consider the matter on the basis that a mistake of fact occurred at the trial. The petition filed by the defendant must make a claim that the true facts were not known at the time of the defendant's trial. *Coram nobis* is usually an appeal seeking to set aside a guilty verdict on the basis of fraud, duress, or coercion that did not come to light until after the trial was over. *The attorney filed a writ of* CORAM NOBIS.

co·re·*spon*·dent. (1) An individual charged with having committed adultery with the defendant in a divorce action. (2) A person summoned by a court to answer a bill, petition, or libel.

cor·o·ner. Sometimes used synonymously with state or county medical officer. A state or county official charged with responsibility to inquire into the cause of death of persons dying from other than natural causes. In most jurisdictions a *coroner* holds an INQUEST before a jury at a Coroner's Court. The *coroner* usually has both ministerial and judicial duties, and can call witnesses and medical experts to testify about circumstances surrounding a questionable death. In a few jurisdictions, the *coroner* is required to be a medical doctor.

cor·o·ner's ju·ry. A JURY functioning under the authority of a medical examiner or CORONER inquiring into the cause of unexplained death. A verdict by the *coroner's jury* is not binding on anyone, nor does it convict anyone. But it performs a vital function. For example, a *coroner's jury* verdict may reach the conclusion that "death resulted from foul means, and not from natural causes." After a verdict of this kind is entered on the public record, an indecisive prosecuting attorney cannot very well refuse to prosecute persons who appear to be responsible for the death.

cor·po·rate veil. The legal principle that the acts of a CORPORATION are not to be regarded as acts of the individuals who own the corporation. Stockholders hide behind the *corporate veil,* so to speak, since they cannot be sued individually for the actions of the corporation. In the contemplation of the law, a corporation is a legal entity.

cor·po·ra·tion. An artificial being created under the laws of a state or nation; a body authorized and formed by law to act as a single person, although composed of several owners, which body has the right to do business according to the charter or franchise under which authorized. A *corporation* is treated as an entity, distinct from its members (stockholders), with rights and liabilities of its own. It may own property in its corporate name.

cor·po·re·al her·e·dit·a·ments. Any substantial or material kind of property that is subject to inheritance.

cor·pus de·lic·ti. (Latin–*kor·*pus dil·*ick·*tie) The essential elements, substance, or basic requirements of a crime. In a specific criminal violation there are certain basic proofs that must be presented to satisfy the requirements of conviction. The term *corpus delicti* is frequently misinterpreted, in that it is sometimes believed that the body of a murder victim must be produced or recovered before a murder conviction can be obtained. The term has no reference to a physical body, and a murder conviction may be obtained if there is proof of the wrongful death, whether or not the victim's body is ever found. An example would be the case of a sea captain pushed into the sea by rebellious seamen. The *corpus delicti* of the crime might consist of the testimony of seamen who refused to join the conspiracy, testifying that the rebels pushed the captain into the sea and that his body was never recovered.

costs. An allowance made by a judge or a court to a successful party to a civil lawsuit, to compensate for his expenses in conducting it. *Costs* are over and above a monetary award for damages. At the time the judgment against the loser is entered, the loser of a lawsuit is assessed the winner's expenses, as *costs.*

coun·sel, *coun*·sel·or, *coun*·sel·lor. A lawyer, attorney, legal pleader, legal advocate, or legal advisor. In the United States all of these terms are used interchangeably to mean a lawyer. In England and some other English-speaking countries, an ATTORNEY may draw up legal papers, prepare the testimony, and conduct legal matters out of court, while an ADVOCATE or BARRISTER conducts the actual trial of the case in court. In the United States there are no different classes of lawyers.

coun·ter·claim. A legal cause of action brought up by the defendant, which has the effect of a lawsuit by the DEFENDANT against the PLAINTIFF. It is not necessarily an offset to the plaintiff's original claim, and it is not necessarily confined or restricted to the justice of the plaintiff's claim. It can be based on facts not related to the plaintiff's case, and can result in the defendant recovering money from the plaintiff. See CROSS-CLAIM, from which a *counterclaim* is distinguished.

court, ap·*pel*·late. See APPELLATE COURT.

court *cal*·en·dar. See CALENDAR.

court of in·ter·*me*·di·ate re·*view*. APPELLATE COURTS that are between the COURT OF ORIGINAL JURISDICTION (trial court) and the court of LAST RESORT (highest court). The federal government and most states have a three-tiered court system, with the courts of intermediate review as the middle tier. Established to relieve congestion in the highest appellate court, the *courts of intermediate review* have appellate jurisdiction only, with limited power to issue limited types of writs, such as writs of CERTIORARI, HABEAS CORPUS, or MANDAMUS.

court of or·*ig*·i·nal ju·ris·*dic*·tion. A court that has the right to try a matter from the outset.

court of *rec*·ord. See RECORD (COURT OF).

cov·e·nant. A written agreement or restriction, usually incorporated into a deed, that protects the buyer against defects in the TITLE to the property. A WARRANTY DEED, for example, traditionally contains a *covenant* by the seller to protect the buyer against defects. The seller is liable for damages, if it should subsequently turn out that the title was bad.

cov·e·nant run·ning **with the land.** An agreement entered into by deed, whereby one of the parties promises the performance or non-performance of a specific act or series of acts in connection with the property, and which agreement extends to any subsequent buyer of the land. The agreement may be enforced by the courts against any purchaser, whether the latter was or was not a party to the original COVENANT. For example, a restriction in the deed to build only one mill on the streams running through the property can be enforced at any future time. Any covenant which is immoral, illegal, or against public policy, cannot be enforced. For example, a covenant to sell the property only to white protestant individuals of Anglo-Saxon parentage would be struck down by the courts as contrary to public policy.

cred·i·ble. Worthy of belief. *Credible evidence* is that which is trustworthy, or that merits belief by the jury.

cred·i·tor. An individual to whom a debt is owing by another person, called the debtor. See also SECURED CREDITOR.

crime. An act committed or omitted in violation of a public law. *Crimes* are those wrongs that the government regards as injurious to the public and punishes in what is called a criminal proceeding. Properly speaking, a "crime" and a "misdemeanor" are synonymous terms, but in common usage "crimes" denotes more serious offenses than relatively minor "misdemeanors."

crim·i·nal ac·tion. A criminal prosecution.

crim·i·nal con·ver·sa·tion. Sexual intercourse by an outsider with either husband or wife. Sometimes used interchangeably with ADULTERY.

cross-ac·tion. A COUNTERCLAIM, arising out of the same facts for which the plaintiff sues.

cross-bill. See CROSS-ACTION.

cross-claim. A claim brought in a lawsuit by a DEFENDANT against a PLAINTIFF or a co-defendant. It is brought on the same transaction or series of transactions on which the plaintiff's case is based, and is an off-set. It is a balance off from the same facts on which the plaintiff sues. A *cross-claim* is sometimes said to be distinguished from a COUNTERCLAIM, in that the counterclaim may be independent of the dispute on which the plaintiff originally filed suit. See COUNTERCLAIM.

cross-ex·am·i·na·tion. The questioning of a witness called by the opposing side in a trial. The purpose is to show inconsistencies or to otherwise discredit the witness. Under Article VII of the U.S. Constitution, the accused has the right "to be confronted with the witnesses against him. ..." This right to confront a witness includes the right to *cross-examine*. Most courts, however, permit *cross-examination* only on matters to which the witness has previously testified, or to matters that would show the witness is prejudiced against the other side in the controversy.

cul·pa·ble. Blameable; at fault; censurable. In a legal sense, *culpable* is not the equivalent of "guilty" or "criminal" since it implies blame but not necessarily criminal malice or guilty purpose.

cu·mu·la·tive *ev*·i·dence. That which goes to prove what has already been established by other EVIDENCE.

cu·mu·la·tive of·*fense*. A criminal offense which can be committed only by a repetition of acts of the same kind, repeated on different days. For example, to be charged as a "common seller of intoxicating liquors," it would be necessary for the offender to sell on more than one day.

cu·mu·la·tive *sen*·tence. An additional sentence or prison term imposed on an individual already sentenced for crime. The additional term is to be served after the termination of the prior sentence.

cu·*ra*·tor (or *cu*·ra·tor). A guardian appointed to care for an incompetent person, or to take care of property of another.

cus·to·dy. (1) Arrest or detention. (2) A rather elastic term to denote that an article or an individual is in the care or keeping of someone with authority. For example: *The recovered loot from the bank robbery was left in the custody of the United States Marshal.*

D

dam·ag·es. Compensation in money imposed by a court for loss or injury caused by the fault of another. See LIQUIDATED DAMAGES, UNLIQUIDATED DAMAGES, GENERAL DAMAGES, EXEMPLARY DAMAGES, NOMINAL DAMAGES.

dam·num. (Latin–*dam*·num) DAMAGES.

dam·num *abs*·que *in*·ju·ri·a. (Latin–*dam*·num *abs*·kwee in·*jew* ree uh) *Loss without real injury.* A loss, but of the type that cannot be redressed in the courts.

day *cer*·tain. Old legal term that is still used to mean a specified or designated day in the future.

day in court. (1) As commonly used, a fair and full opportunity to be heard by governmental administrative authorities or in the judicial or legal system to present one's case or viewpoint. (2) An opportunity to be cited or put on notice to appear and be heard in a lawsuit.

de·*ben*·ture. (1) A voucher or certificate acknowledging a debt. (2) An unsecured bond, issued by a corporation or agency of the government, backed only by the credit issuer. (3) A document issued by a customs collector, specifying that an importer is entitled to a refund for import duties paid on some items that are being delivered for exempt uses.

de bon·*is non* (or **de bon·*is non ad·min·is·tra·tis***). (Latin–dee *boe*·nis non add·min·is·*tray*·tis) *Of the goods not administered.* In the administration of the estate of a deceased, if the property is not completely settled by the first administrator appointed, a subsequent administrator is said to be appointed *administrator de bonis non,* or administrator of that which has not already been settled.

debt. Something owed, such as money, services, or goods. It involves an unconditional obligation to pay at a fixed time.

debt·or. One who owes something to another.

de·*ce*·dent. A dead person.

de·*ce*·dent's debts. The debts of a person who has died. The administrator or executor of the deceased's estate is required first to pay the just debts and then to make distribution to the heirs of the properties and monies that remain. Usually there are statutes that control, with property going to satisfy debts used in the following order: personal estate not specifically bequeathed, real estate designated to be sold for payment of debts, real estate not devised by will but not earmarked to pay debts, etc.

de·*ceit*. Trickery; fraudulent misrepresentation; cheating; connivance to defraud.

de·*ci*·sion. (1) A decree or judgment pronounced by a court in settlement of a controversy before that court. A *decision* of the court is its judgment, and the OPINION is the reason given for the judgment, or a statement of the views of the judge. (2) A *decision* may also represent the determination made by a quasi-judicial body or an administrative board, in settling a dispute before that board or body.

dec·la·*ra*·tion. A statement made out of court and not under oath. Ordinarily, a statement of this kind will not be admitted as evidence in a court trial unless it is: **(a)** a declaration against interest (a statement that hurts the speaker financially or in some other way, that would apparently not be made if it were not true); **(b)** or a dying declaration, made by someone facing impending death. (The theory here is that a person would not lie under such circumstances.) **(2)** The name given to the first pleadings filed by a plaintiff in a lawsuit. **(3)** A formal proclamation or statement issued by a government, association, or body.

dec·la·*ra*·tion of trust. The formal document that is frequently drawn up to set up a TRUST.

de·*clar*·a·to·ry *judg*·ment. A court judgment which merely states the rights of the parties, or gives the opinion of the court on a matter of law. A *declaratory judgment* merely sets forth the rights of the contestants. It does not order execution or performance from the defendant, such as ordering action or the payment of damages. It is to be pointed out, however, that the courts will not accept for adjudication, nor give an opinion in a theoretical matter. The courts will deal only with a matter of real fact, but it may be a situation where a money award is not involved.

de·*cree*. The judgment or sentence of a court; an order having the force of law.

de·*cree ni*·si. See NISI.

ded·i·*ca*·tion. The giving of land by the owner for some public use, or as part of a road or highway. An acceptance by or in behalf of the public is necessary, and is usually by deed.

deed. A legal document by which ownership of land is transferred from one owner or seller (the grantor) to a new owner. Buildings and items attached are transferred with the land. A *deed* is a conveyance of realty (real estate, not personal property or intangibles; normally, A BILL OF SALE or sales contract transfers ownership of personal items). The essential difference between a *deed* and a WILL is that the former transfers a present interest in property, while a will passes no interest until after the death of the maker. Old English law required the seller's signature and wax seal on the deed, but this has been generally abolished in the U.S. There are different kinds of *deeds,* some of which will pass only those rights to the new owner (buyer) that the grantor actually possessed at the time the deed was signed. When the term *deed* is used, it normally refers to a WARRANTY DEED. See BARGAIN AND SALE DEED, DEED OF GIFT, DEED OF TRUST, QUITCLAIM DEED, STATUTORY DEED, WARRANTY DEED.

deed of gift. A DEED that delivers and conveys property without the payment of CONSIDERATION. In old England a deed required payment of a consideration of at least nominal amount. Today, in the U.S. this is not required in most jurisdictions.

deed of trust. A legal arrangement by which property may be purchased on time payments. Under a *deed of trust,* ownership of the property is transferred to an independent TRUSTEE, who accepts and accounts for payments until the property is fully paid off. Three parties are involved in a deed of trust: the seller (lender), buyer (borrower), and the trustee. A deed of trust is, in effect, a MORTGAGE arrangement.

de *fac*·to. (Latin–dee·*fack*·toe) *In fact.* (1) As used legally, *de facto* refers to a condition that is an accomplished fact, but that does not have the sanction of legality. A dictator who seizes governmental power may be ruler *de facto,* but does not have lawful authority or backing. DE JURE is the antithesis of *de facto.* (2) The term is also used to mean *in actuality.* For example, a picket line around a business may be an obstruction *de facto,* rather than a mere paper obstruction.

de·fal·*ca*·tion. Failure to properly account for money or valuables that have been entrusted. The term "embezzlement" goes beyond *defalcation,* in that EMBEZZLEMENT involves a wrongful taking of money or valuables.

def·a·*ma*·tion. Libel or slander. The injury to an individual's character by malicious and false statements. *Defamation* is distinguished from *criticism,* as the latter deals with matters that invite public attention and does not follow the individual into private life or personal concerns. *Criticism* attacks the individual's work, and not the individual.

de·*fault*. (1) Failure to do something required by law, such as perform on a contract. (2) Failure to appear at the required time in a legal proceeding. (3) Failure to pay financial obligations.

de·*fault judg*·ment. A civil judgment rendered in consequence of the failure of a party to appear in court, or the failure to file pleadings within the required time set by law. In CRIMINAL prosecutions within the United States, the defendant (accused) cannot be convicted until after being brought into court and given an opportunity to defend. In a CIVIL trial, however, the defendant can lose the case without ever being present in court. When a civil lawsuit is filed against someone, a summons (writ) is delivered to the defendant in person by the sheriff or a process server. This summons informs the defendant of the legal action that has been filed, instructing the accused to show

59

up in court at a specific time and place, or risk losing the suit for failure to defend. The court has jurisdiction over the defendant when the summons is served, and can then proceed. If the court appearance is not made by the defendant, or legal papers disputing or answering the pleadings filed, a *default judgment* will be entered against the defendant. See SUMMONS.

de·*fea*·sance clause. A clause in a MORTGAGE providing that the mortgage is null and void if the indebtedness is paid.

de·*fen*·dant. The party against whom a lawsuit is filed; the individual or individuals required to give an answer in a legal action.

de·*fen*·dant in *er*·ror. See PARTIES.

de·*fense*. (1) The DEFENDANT and his or her legal counsel. (2) Those claims and reasons in law and in fact advanced by the DEFENDANT to show why the PLAINTIFF should not prevail in a lawsuit, or why the ACCUSED should not be convicted in a criminal prosecution.

de·*fi*·cien·cy *judg*·ment. See EXECUTION OF JUDGMENT.

de·*fraud*. To swindle, cheat, or trick.

de ju·re. (Latin-dee·*jour*·ee) *Of right.* That which is lawful and right. An officer who assumes a public office after an invalid election is a DE FACTO officer. Taking office after a legal election process, this same individual would be an officer *de jure.*

del cred·er·e. (Italian-dell·*cred*·uhr·ee, or *kree*·der·ee) An agreement by which an AGENT, for a higher commission, guarantees to reimburse the seller for goods sold on credit, if the buyer does not pay. An AGENT or FACTOR who makes this guarantee is sometimes called a *del credere agent,* and is a surety for the PRINCIPAL only in case of default.

de·*lict*·um. (Latin-dee·*lict*·um) A civil wrong, a TORT, or a crime.

de·*lin*·quen·cy. (1) An omission of duty, or a failure to perform that which is required. (2) The incorrigibility or lawless conduct of a minor.

de·*lin*·quent. (1) A debt that is due and unpaid at the time set by law. (2) A minor or underage child who is incorrigible or who is a law violator. (3) An individual who neglects or fails to do whatever is required by law or the obligations of morality.

de·*mand*. A formal request or requisition for a right, or for the fulfillment of an obligation legally due to the person making the *demand.* A *demand* is different from a claim, in that a *demand* presupposes there is no defense or doubt on the question of right.

de *min*·**i**·**mus.** (Latin) *Trifles.* Things that are too insignificant for the law to be concerned with.

de·*mise.* (1) The conveyance of an estate, or real property. (2) Death.

de·*mise char*·**ter.** See CHARTER PARTY.

de·*mon*·**stra·tive** *ev*·**i·dence.** Any kind of EVIDENCE, or legal proof, other than that given by oral testimony; evidence that is directed toward the senses, such as sight, touch, or smell. A knife found at the scene of a crime, a human hair caught in the fingernail of the slain victim, a fingerprint, are all examples of *demonstrative evidence.*

de·*mur*·**rage.** (1) In maritime or transportation law, the detention of a ship, railroad car, or other cargo conveyance during loading or unloading in excess of a specified period of time. (2) The monetary charge paid for this detention, usually paid by the day. *A warehouse paid two days demurrage on a railroad boxcar because there were no available freight handlers to unload it.*

de·*mur*·**rer.** A pleading by a party in a legal action, alleging that the pleadings of the opposite party are not sufficient to show a cause of action that will stand up in court. The *demurrer* does not admit the truth of the facts alleged by the other party. The *demurrer* says, in effect, "even if your facts were true, they do not contain the essential elements or legal requirements that would be necessary to spell out a case against me—therefore, you should not be allowed to proceed further." Put in other words, the *demurrer* says, "There are certain basic facts and elements of law that must be alleged in order to constitute a lawsuit. Some of these are missing from your pleadings, and the case should therefore be dismissed."

de·*ni*·**al.** A form of legal pleading, in which claims of the opposing party to a lawsuit are controverted or denied.

de no·**vo.** (Latin–dee *noe*·voe) *Completely new.* New from the start. A jury *de novo* is a completely new jury for a second trial.

de·*pen*·**dent.** (1) One who relies on another for monetary support. (2) Contingent upon something or someone else.

de·*ple*·**tion.** Using up, exhausting, or emptying of assets.

de·*ple*·**tion** al·*low*·**ance.** An allowance for the reduction of taxes to compensate for the wasting away or depletion of assets such as oil and gas, minerals, timber, or other natural resources.

de·*po*·**nent.** One who gives testimony under oath that is reduced to writing. In the United States the term is used interchangeably with AFFIANT. See AFFIDAVIT.

de·*pose*. (1) To give evidence for a lawsuit in the form of a *deposition,* taken out of court. (2) To remove or deprive a person of public office or employment against that individual's will.

de·*pre·*ci·a·tion. The reduction in value of an asset caused by usage, obsolescence, wear and tear, or because of the passage of time. The value of equipment or machinery may be *depreciated* under Federal income tax law.

de·*raign*. To trace, or to prove.

de·*riv·*a·tive *ac·*tion. A lawsuit brought by a stockholder for the benefit of all stockholders in a CORPORATION. A *derivative action* usually involves a suit against a director or officer of the corporation who is believed to be wrongfully dissipating corporate assets, or failing to act properly for the protection of corporate rights. If the court hearing the matter grants relief, the award will be in favor of all stockholders, not the individual stockholder who started the action.

de·*riv·*a·tive rule. The legal principle that evidence flowing from or derived out of an illegal act will be barred at the time of trial. Application of the rule is very complicated and it does not apply to all proceedings, hearings, or trials in either criminal or civil cases.

The terms *derivative rule* and EXCLUSIONARY RULE are sometimes used interchangeably by the court. The basic idea of law is: (1) Courts will refuse to allow illegally obtained evidence to be presented in a trial in court, and (2) any investigative leads or new facts flowing from or derived out of the illegal act will also be barred at the time of trial. Many situations of this kind arise from unlawful searches of a suspect in narcotics investigations. If an illegal search is made and narcotics are found, the *derivative rule* doctrine would not allow the narcotics to be presented in evidence. If a notebook was found on the suspect, with names and telephone numbers of contacts of the suspect, narcotics obtained from those contacts would likewise be barred as evidence.

This idea is sometimes described as the "fruit of the poisonous tree" doctrine, and some of the cases that discuss it include U.S. Supreme Court cases: Silverthorne Lumber Company v. United States, 251 U.S. 385 (decided in 1920) and Nardone v. United States, 308 U.S. 338 (1939).

de·*scent*. (1) Succession in the ownership of property or lands through hereditary derivation or lineage. (2) Obtaining ownership of property

or TITLE to lands by inheritance from forebearers, rather than receiving such things by gift or purchase.

de·*ser*·tion. (1) Voluntary separation from a spouse without justification,
and with no intention of returning or supporting the mate financially.
A wife may leave her husband without *desertion* if she fears that he
is going to do her bodily harm. *Desertion* may also consist of the
voluntary abandonment or separation from a child. See ABANDON-
MENT. (2) Under military law, a voluntary abandonment of a military
post or watch without permission.

de·*tain*·er. A hold order placed in a prisoner's jail or institutional file to
give custody to another jurisdiction on satisfaction of the sentence
being served.

  If a prison or jail inmate is wanted in another state or jurisdiction,
or has escaped from another institution, a *detainer* prevents release
without notification to the place where the prisoner is wanted. In
con-talk, a detainer is a *sticker*.

  By statute in many jurisdictions, a prison inmate is not eligible
for parole if a *detainer* has been lodged. As a result, prison-wise
individuals frequently seek to have all charges against them disposed
of at the time of sentencing, rather than lose the possibility of *good
time* or an opportunity for release on parole.

de·*ten*·tion. The keeping in custody or confinement, especially while
awaiting trial or undergoing questioning concerning involvement in
crime. If a criminal charge is not filed, the person being held may be
freed by the writ of HABEAS CORPUS.

de·*vest*. To deprive of rights of property, authority, or power.

de·vi·*a*·tion. (1) In maritime law, an unnecessary and deliberate departure
from the due course of a ship's voyage. (2) In contract law, it is a
change made from the original design, terms, or method agreed upon
in the contract.

de·*vise*. A gift of land or personal property by will.

de·vi·*see*. One to whom property is left in a will.

de·vi·*sor*. One who leaves property to another by will.

de·vo·*lu*·tion. (1) The passing to another of property, TITLE, legal rights,
or interests, by operation of the law or by legal processes. For example, title to a tract of land may pass by *devolution* upon the death
of the owner. (2) To delegate or pass on duties, authority, or office
to another.

dic·ta. (Latin–*dick*·tuh) The opinion of a judge on a legal point or issue other than the one squarely before the court for decision; a judicial opinion on a side issue of law other than the precise one involved in determining a case. For example, a judge may say that in a slightly different factual situation he would hold (decide) in favor of the plaintiff. This statement by the judge is *dicta*. It is not binding on anybody, because it was not the exact issue before the court. Lawyers point out that the judge may give an opinion on some possibility that may happen in the future. Since it has not yet happened, and is not in issue before the judge, then future courts or litigants are not bound by what the judge said. The court's opinion always applies only to the facts (legal problem) between the litigants. See DICTUM.

dic·tum. (Latin) Sometimes used as an abbreviated form of OBITER DICTUM. Dictum is the singular form of DICTA. It means a remark of statement by a judge, in passing. It is generally an opinion or application of law to some question suggested by the case at bar, but not necessarily essential to its determination. See DICTA.

di·gest. A type of law book used by attorneys. *Digests,* of course, vary in scope and treatment. They usually contain excerpts, condensations, or summaries of decided cases, that may be used to support the lawyer's own case. *Digests* are usually arranged by subject categories, without statements as to historical developments of legal principles, jurisdictional matters, or editorial comments.

dil·a·to·ry. Characterized by unnecessary delay or procrastination.

di·*min*·ished re·*spon*·si·bil·i·ty. A defense to a criminal charge allowed in some states, in which the defense admits that the accused is legally sane, but is substantially lacking in mental capacity. Under the *diminished responsibility* doctrine, the courts allow proof of mental derangement short of insanity as evidence of lack of PREMEDITATION or MALICE AFORETHOUGHT. This may be an important difference, since malice aforethought or premeditation is one of the elements that must be proved to convict for murder, while malice aforethought is not a necessary element in proving a conviction for manslaughter. Therefore, proof of mental impairment short of insanity may result in a conviction for MANSLAUGHTER, rather than MURDER.

di·*rect* ev·i·dence. Testimony from the witness stand of an individual under oath as to acts observed, words spoken, or things actually witnessed. Circumstantial evidence, as distinguished from *direct* *evidence,* involves testimony of facts that tend to prove the matter indirectly, or by inference.

di·*rect* ex·*am*·i·na·**tion.** The first questioning of a witness on the witness stand. Sometimes called examination-in-chief. *Direct examination* is conducted by the attorney for the side that called the witness to the stand. *Direct examination* is, of course, followed by CROSS-EXAMINA-TION by the attorney for the opposite side.

di·*rect tax*·es. Taxes assessed directly against the taxpayer, as against an indirect or hidden tax. An income tax is a *direct tax,* whereas a sales tax on an article is an indirect levy. When an indirect tax is levied, there is no certainty as to who will eventually pay for it.

di·*rect*·ed *ver*·dict. A verdict ordered by the judge, taking the decision out of the jury's hands. For example, in a criminal prosecution, it is the prosecution's responsibility to prove each of the essential elements of the case. If the prosecution fails to prove one of these essential elements by the introduction of evidence, the accused will be released as a matter of law. At that stage of the case, the judge will order the jury to enter a *directed verdict,* without taking a vote on guilt or innocence. This not only saves time, but there is always the possibility that the jury could not understand what has happened and might vote a guilty verdict on the basis of the evidence that was presented.

dis·a·*bil*·i·ty. A legal disqualification or incapacity. A want of legal authority or qualification to perform a specific act. For example an insane person is legally said to be under *disability* to make a will. A ten-year-old child is under *disability* to obtain a marriage license.

dis·af·*firm*·ance. To set aside, or repudiate. For example, a minor may *disaffirm* a contract on reaching legal age, refusing to honor the contract agreement.

dis·*bar*. To revoke the right to practice law, which right was granted by passage of the bar examination.

dis·*charge*. (1) A release from confinement, or from a prison sentence. (2) To dismiss a worker or employee. (3) To perform a specific obligation. (4) To cancel or annul an obligation, or end a contract by performance.

dis·*claim*·er. (1) The renouncing of one's rights or claim of a legal nature. (2) A clause in a contract or sales agreement, putting the buyer on notice that one party *disclaims* responsibility for specific contingencies.

dis·con·*tin*·u·ance. The termination of a lawsuit, either by dismissal or by a non-suit.

dis·*cov*·e·ry. (1) The right of a defendant in a criminal case to obtain exculpatory and mitigating evidence against the accused that may be in the prosecution's possession. Rights of *discovery* vary from jurisdiction to jurisdiction, but usually give the defendant's attorney the right to examine signed statements given to authorities, and in some instances to examine the physical evidence against the accused. (2) A disclosure by the defendant in a civil matter of land titles, documents, other documents, or facts that may be under the exclusive control of the defendant, and that are necessary to the party seeking the *discovery* as a part of the action. For example, "A" made a contract with "B," whereby "B" was to erect a building. "B" took no action to fulfill the contract. The contract was signed before witnesses, and "B" cannot very well claim that it does not exist. "A's" copy of the contract was destroyed by fire. As part of a lawsuit for breach of contract, "A" could file a *bill of discovery* asking for "B" to be ordered to produce the contract for "A" to use in the lawsuit. DEPOSITIONS and INTERROGATORIES from individuals with knowledge of the facts are techniques frequently used by lawyers as a type of *discovery.*

dis·crim·i·*na*·tion. A failure to treat all equally; differential based on race, color, ethnic distinctions, or class.

dis·*fran*·chise. To take away the right of citizenship, especially the right to vote.

dis·*hon*·or. To refuse to accept or pay a negotiable instrument that has become due.

dis·*or*·der·ly *con*·duct. Any kind of action that disturbs the public order, or shocks the public sense of morality. Conduct that is indecent, riotous, or turbulent. Some modern statutes have attempted to define *disorderly conduct,* but the meaning is frequently somewhat indefinite.

dis·*or*·der·ly house. Any house whose occupants behave so badly as to be regarded as a neighborhood nuisance. The term has a wide range of meaning, including gambling houses, houses of prostitution, or even a college fraternity house if students regularly disturb the neighborhood.

dis·pos·*sess* ac·tion. A legal action to remove an occupant from real property. It may be brought under the terms of a LEASE, when the lease states that breach of a covenant automatically terminates the lease. Under an action of EJECTMENT, the landlord usually is suing on a covenant that merely gives the landlord the right of re-entry, and the breach does not automatically terminate the lease. See EVICTION; EJECTMENT.

dis·qual·i·fi·*ca*·tion. That which renders ineligible or incapacitates. The judge's act in removing himself or herself from a case in which there is a personal interest would be one type of *disqualification*. It may involve a situation in which the judge has a business or family relationship with either side in a legal case. If a criminal defendant, for example, is represented by a defense attorney who was the judge's former law partner, then the judge should *disqualify* himself or herself. This is not to infer that the judge might not be fair, but might be unduly influenced. *Disqualification* of such a judge helps keep the court system above suspicion. Jurors and others involved in the trial of a case may be *disqualified* to serve. A juror, for example, will be *disqualified* by the trial judge if the juror indicates a fixed, preconceived opinion.

dis·*sent*. The disagreement of one or more judges or justices with the majority opinion, in a case where the case is being considered. Disagreeing judges may or may not submit a *dissenting opinion* in writing.

dis·so·*lu*·tion. The termination or break up of a legal relationship. For example, the *dissolution* of a contract could arise by mutual consent of the parties. The *dissolution* of a corporation is the termination of legal existence. DIVORCE, but not ANNULMENT, is the *dissolution* of a marriage.

dis·*train*. To seize personal property belonging to another, to compel payment of a debt, or to compel payment for a wrong done. The seizure may be either lawful or unlawful.

dis·*train* for rent in ar·*rears*. Action permitted by the landlord in some states, to seize the tenant's personal belongings or goods to be held as SECURITY for the payment of past due rent. Under most statutes, the landlord can take action the day after the rent is due. If the landlord has allowed the tenant to be habitually late, the action cannot be taken without advising the tenant in advance that punctual payments must be made in the future.

dis·*tress*. The holding of personal property of another after it has been *distrained*. See DISTRAIN.

dis·tri·*bu*·tion. In PROBATE law, the division and apportionment of the property of a deceased individual, under the supervision of the probate court.

dis·*tur*·bance of the peace. Any activity that throws the community or neighborhood into disorder; causing annoyance, agitation, disquiet, or derangement to others, particularly by unnecessary noise or harassment.

di·*ver*·sion. An altering or turning aside, as a *diversion* of company funds by an embezzler.

di·*vest*. See DEVEST.

di·*vid*·ed *dam*·a·ges. The legal principle or doctrine followed in Admiralty law that divides damages equally where both vessels are at fault in a collision. Under the old rule of contributory negligence, recovery would be barred for either party where both were negligent. Perhaps most maritime nations follow still another approach. Under the terms of the Brussels Collision Convention of 1910, many nations require their courts to award damages in proportion to the degree of fault—the party 90% at fault should pay for 90% of the damages. Of course, it is sometimes difficult to ascertain the percentage of fault.

***div*·i·dend.** A share of profits received by a stockholder of a corporation, or by a policyholder in a mutual insurance company. The declaration of a *dividend,* as well as the amount to be paid, is usually within the authority of the board of directors of a corporation.

di·*vorce*. The legal termination of a marriage through court order. *Divorce* is distinguished from an ANNULMENT, since an annulment regards the marriage as never having existed. A divorce is also legally different from a *divorce a mensa et thoro* (divorce from bed and board), a limited kind of termination of the marriage arrangement that puts an end to cohabitation and living together, but does not permit either to remarry.

dock. (1) The enclosed area or cage in a criminal courtroom where the accused stands or sits when brought for trial. (2) To deduct a part from salary or wages. (3) In maritime law, a pier or wharf.

dock•et. A book maintained by the clerk of a court, containing entries and legal papers for the court. The entries reflect all important acts done in court in the conduct of each case, from inception to the final judgment or sentence. Different types of *dockets* may be maintained for some courts, such as an "appearance docket," a "bar docket," an "execution docket," and a "judgment docket." A *judgment docket,* for example, would contain a listing of each judgment entered against a defendant in a given term of court, open to public inspection, and designed to afford official notice to interested individuals of details thereof.

doc•trine. A rule, theory, or tenet of law; a legal principle.

doc•u•*men*•ta•ry *ev*•i•dence. Evidence supplied by writings, printings, or documents of every kind. It is distinguished from "oral" evidence, or that delivered by human beings by voice.

do•*main.* The absolute ownership and right to dispose of property. *Domain* is distinguished from property, in that *domain* is the active right to dispose, while the other is a passive quality which follows the thing and places it at the disposal of the owner.

do•*mes*•tic cor•po•*ra*•tion. A CORPORATION organized or receiving a charter under the laws of the state which is the corporation's principal place of business. A *domestic corporation* is distinguished from a FOREIGN CORPORATION, which is organized or chartered under the laws of an outside state.

dom•i•cile. An individual's true, fixed, and permanent residence. Any person can have only one domicile, which is the location intended as a permanent home for an unlimited or indefinite period. A *domicile* is not necessarily the same as a RESIDENCE.

dom•i•*cil*•i•ar•y. That which pertains to the home, or to the *domicile.*

dom•i•*cil*•i•ar•y ad•min•is•*tra*•tion. In settling an estate, the principal or primary place of administration is the state where the deceased was DOMICILED at the time of death. This administrative process is called *domiciliary administration.*

dom•i•nant es•*tate.* See SERVITUDE.

do•na•tive trust (or *don*•a•tive trust). A TRUST set up as a gift to an individual or organization. Payment of CONSIDERATION by the beneficiary is not required.

do•*nee.* One who is the recipient of a gift.

do·nor. One who makes a gift.

dor·mant claim. A claim which is inactive, or in abeyance.

dor·mant part·ner. A concealed or silent partner, who owns part of a business but who is not openly involved in operation of it.

dou·ble jeop·ar·dy. A second prosecution after a prior trial for the same offense. (Prohibited by Fifth Amendment to the U.S. Constitution.)

dow·er. The right of a wife to at least part of her deceased husband's estate, at least during her lifetime. *Dower* provisions were recognized hundreds of years ago, to leave the widow some property for her subsistence. *Dower* rights have been changed by statutes, or by operation of community property laws in most jurisdictions.

Dra·co·ni·an law. Any unusually harsh or severe law. The term is taken from *Draco,* Athenian lawgiver whose code in 621 B.C. was regarded as unusually severe.

draft. (1) An order for the payment of money drawn by one individual on another. A *draft* is the most common form of a BILL OF EXCHANGE, and a check is the most common kind of *draft.* Both are NEGOTIABLE INSTRUMENTS. (2) A tentative writing of a legal document, such as a lease, contract, legislative bill, etc.

drafts·man. An individual who prepares or draws up a legal document. An attorney, for example, may be the *draftsman* of a client's will or deed of conveyance of land.

draw·ee. The person or institution to whom a bill of exchange is addressed, and who is expected to pay. As an example of a BILL OF EXCHANGE, a check is sent by the bank depositor to the bank (*drawee*) to be cashed.

draw·er. The individual who draws or drafts an order for the payment of money. The *drawer* of a check, for example, is the individual who has an account at the bank and issues and signs a check on the account.

droit. (French) *Right.* Justice; law. That which is opposed to wrong, injustice, or the absence of law.

du·ces te·cum. (Latin) *"Bring with you."* See SUBPOENA DUCES TECUM.

due. (1) Payable immediately or on demand. (2) The amount still owed on a debt. (3) That which is attributable to. (4) Appropriate or warranted care; fitting; reasonable.

due *proc•ess* of law. The application and administration of law in its regular course through the courts of justice. This includes notice and the opportunity to be heard and to defend in orderly proceedings adopted to the nature of the case. In other language: a legal procedure which hears before it condemns, which proceeds on inquiry, and renders judgment only after trial. Under *due process,* no one may be deprived of life, liberty or property without first having notice. This includes the right to be heard by testimony or other accepted presentation of evidence, and to have all legal safeguards for the protection of individual rights, in either criminal or property matters. The Supreme Court of the United States has changed the legal requirements of *due process* from time to time, but the basic principle laid down by the Supreme Court is that ''law shall not be unreasonable, arbitrary, or capricious, and that the means selected shall have real and substantial relation to the object.'' Nebbia v. New York, 291 US 502.

*du•*ress.** The use of force to compel someone to do what would not otherwise have been done. A physical restraint may constitute *duress,* in addition to the use of threats or force.

*du•*ty.** (1) A legal or moral obligation. (2) The obligation to follow all laws or court directives. (3) The obligation to refrain from interfering with rights of others that have been established by law or the court processes. (4) A tax imposed on the import or export of goods or personal items. The terms TARIFF and *duty* are sometimes used interchangeably, but the *duty* is the actual tax collected or imposed, while the tariff is the schedule of duties.

*dy•*ing dec•la•*ra•*tion.** A statement made by one injured by another, who is aware that death is impending as a result of this injury. A statement of this kind is concerned with the circumstances of the injury, and the person or persons who caused it. Ordinarily a statement of this kind would not be permitted as evidence because it would be hearsay when repeated in court by the individual who heard the dying person's statement. This is an exception to the HEARSAY EVIDENCE RULE, however, and would be allowed in a criminal prosecution. The courts have always reasoned that the knowledge of impending death is a sufficient guarantee of trustworthiness, and substantial justice requires the availability of such evidence.

E

ear·nest *mon·ey.* The payment of part of the purchase price for real estate to bind the sale. This payment is also sometimes called a binder. The *earnest money* is retained by the seller if the buyer backs out. If the buyer does produce the rest of the purchase price and meet other terms of the sale, the *earnest money* is applied as part payment of the purchase price. Forfeited *earnest money* is compensation to the seller for losses and expenses that would be sustained for failure to go through with the deal.

ease·ment. An interest in land owned by another that allows the holder to make a specific limited use of the land. For example, a man may own two lots, one of which does not have access to a public road. He may sell the lot without access, granting an *easement* across his other lot to the buyer. This would allow the buyer to drive across the other lot in order to reach the street. If the owner should eventually sell the remaining lot, the *easement* would continue. Some *easements* are granted to public service companies, such as an *easement* for the erection and maintenance of power poles for the installation of an electric line. An *easement* may be created by an express grant in a deed or other contract. If trespassers are allowed to cross over property as a regular practice, the owner may not be able to prohibit the general public from making use of the land in this manner. Laws in this regard vary from state to state.

edict. Any public proclamation that carries the force of law. It is usually a decree or command issued by a dictator or absolute ruler. A *public proclamation* is a similar statement, except that it does not carry the force of law.

ef·*fects.* **(1)** Personal property of all kinds. A term frequently used in wills by individuals intending to dispose of all their personal possessions. Sometimes used synonymously with *worldly goods.* The terms *effects* and *worldly goods* denote the whole of one's personal estate, rather than an individual's mere goods in the commercial sense. *Personal effects* or *worldly goods* would therefore include the right to sue (a chose in action). **(2)** *Effects* is sometimes construed by the courts to mean all one's property of any kind, both real and personal.

e.g. (Latin) Abbreviation for *exempli gratia,* meaning *for example.*

e·*ject*·ment. An old form of lawsuit used in the English courts to try titles to land. By a fiction of law considered necessary by early-day courts, the action was filed against a fictitious defendant called the casual ejector. This kind of a lawsuit has been replaced completely in many states. In other states, *ejectment* has been materially modified but still retains the same name.

e·*lec*·tion. **(1)** The process of choosing between a number of legal rights that may be available. For example, an insurance contract may make a surviving wife eligible to make an *election* between $10,000 in cash, or a fixed income per month for life. **(2)** The act of choosing by vote from among the candidates to fill an office or position. **(3)** In a criminal prosecution, the choice of counts under which the prosecution may proceed.

e·*lec*·tor. **(1)** Any qualified voter; one who elects. **(2)** A special name given to *Presidential Electors,* or members of the *Electoral College of the United States,* those individuals chosen by state elections to select the President of the United States.

e·*lec*·tor·al *col*·lege. See ELECTOR.

el·ee·*mos*·y·nar·y. Of, or pertaining to charity. For example, an orphanage is an *eleemosynary* institution that may be designated as the beneficiary of a CHARITABLE TRUST.

el·i·gi·*bil*·i·ty. One who is qualified for an office, position, or a specific status. As used in legal terms, the word usually means legally qualified. For example, an individual who is 21 years of age, of sound mind, of U.S. citizenship, who has not been convicted of a crime, is *eligible* to hold most elective governmental offices in the United States.

e·man·ci·*pa*·tion. The act of freeing from control or bondage. A slave becomes a free person through *emancipation.* A minor child is *emancipated* upon reaching legal age—a time when the parent is no longer obligated to furnish support or receive the wages of the offspring.

em·*bar*·go. **(1)** A governmental prohibition against shipping out specific items or types of merchandise from the country. **(2)** A suspension of incoming foreign trade completely, or incoming and outgoing trade in a particular commodity.

em·*bez*·zle·ment. The fraudulent appropriation of property or money entrusted to one's own use or benefit. In other terms, the unlawful appropriation of personal property of another by an individual who has gained rightful possession because of employment or by a trust relationship with the owner. The distinction between LARCENY (THEFT, or STEALING) from *embezzlement* is that in *embezzlement* the money is in the rightful possession, but not ownership, of the guilty individual. In LARCENY, the wrongdoer takes that which is in the possession or control of somebody else. In *embezzlement,* the wrongdoer takes that which is under the wrongdoer's control or custody.

em·ble·ments. Crops produced on land by labor and industry, which crops legally belong to the tenant working the land. Growing crops are usually regarded as real property until severed, and as personal property thereafter. *Emblements* are cultivated crops, and not grass growing in a pasture. In most states, the tenant has the right to the crop upon the ground and unharvested at the termination of the lease. This usually includes the right to come back later and make a reasonable entry on the land for harvesting. If the crop needs attention between the termination of the lease and harvest time, the tenant can also make reasonable entries to cultivate or take necessary steps to protect the crop.

em·*brac*·er. See EMBRACEOR.

em·*brace*·or. One who attempts to influence a court illegally. See EMBRACERY.

em·*brace*·ry. The attempt to influence a judge or jury by any corrupt means, usually bribery. Promises, persuasions, entreaties, entertainment, or any kind of influence on a judge or jury is sufficient to constitute the crime. There is no such crime as an attempt to commit *embracery*—the attempt is the crime itself.

em·i·nent do·*main*. The right of the government, either state or federal, to take private property for public use. The courts grant this need only for public exigency and for the public good. The property must, of course, be paid for, and most states allow the price to be fixed by a jury after testimony about property values.

e·*mol*·u·ment. The salary, wage, or pay from an office held, or from employment.

em·*pan*·el. To bring together individuals to act as a jury, or to select individuals to act in such capacity. Used synonymously with IMPANEL.

en·*a*·bling clause. That clause in a statutory enactment that gives administrators or officials the authority to put the law into effect and administer or enforce it.

en·*a*·bling leg·*is*·la·tion (or enabling statute). A statute that confers new power or authority to the government or to a public official.

en·*act*. To make a bill into a law (statute) by legislative process.

en banc. (French) *On the bench.* All the judges or justices of a court, hearing a matter together.

en·*croach*. To make an unlawful entry into the lands, property, or authority of another; to TRESPASS.

en·*cum*·ber. See INCUMBER.

en·*cum*·bered *as*·sets. Any property against which there is a recorded lien or claim, such as a mortgage, deed of trust, tax lien, mechanic's lien, or any other security arrangement.

en·*cum*·brance. See INCUMBRANCE.

en·*dow*·ment. **(1)** Funds or property given to an institution or charitable organization for its maintenance or use. **(2)** A type of life insurance that is payable in cash when the insured reaches a specified age, or when the insured dies.

en·*fran*·chise. **(1)** To give someone the right to vote. **(2)** To set free, as from slavery. **(3)** To bestow a right or privilege upon someone.

en·*join*. To prohibit or forbid by court order. For example, the courts will *enjoin* the director of a corporation from selling property of the corporation as his or her own. The term is commonly used along with the issuance of an INJUNCTION by a court.

en·*joy*·ment. The use of a right; the possession of something beneficial or pleasurable that arises out of the ownership and use of property.

en legis. (Latin–en·*lay*·jis) *Being of the law.* A fictitious being created by the law, such as a CORPORATION.

en·*tail*. A restriction on the ownership of property by limiting the inheritance to the owner's lineal descendants, or to a particular class of descendants, such as male offspring only.

***en*·ter.** **(1)** In real property law, to go upon a tract of land in order to take possession of it. **(2)** To place something before a court, or into the court record, such as to *enter a judgment,* or to *enter an appearance.* **(3)** To become a part of an enterprise or activity, such as to *enter* a law firm as a partner.

***en*·ter·ing *judg*·ment.** The clerical act by which a court's judgment is recorded in the court's official records, maintained by the clerk of the court. Normally, an appeal or an action on the judgment cannot be taken until the judgment is recorded, even though it has been rendered. The *rendition of judgment* is the judicial decision reached by the judge, while the *entry of judgment* is the recording of the rendition.

en·*tire*·ty. The whole, as contrasted to a part. For example, if land is conveyed by deed to a husband and wife, they take by the *entirety.* The property is one whole, and is not partitioned into half the parcel for each.

en·**ti·ty.** Something that has distinct and separate existence.

en·*trap*·ment. The act of police officers or agents of the government in leading or inducing a person to commit a crime not contemplated by the accused. The test of *entrapment* is whether the officer plants the idea in the mind of the criminal, and if so, this is *entrapment.* If the criminal has laid plans for the crime and the officer discovers the plans and becomes involved in developing it, then the officer may continue for the purpose of bringing the wrongdoer to task. In some states *entrapment* is not recognized as a defense to crime, while in other states *entrapment* will excuse if it can be proved.

en·**try.** **(1)** The record of a transaction or occurrence, such as a book-keeping entry. **(2)** Going on to property to take possession of it. **(3)** The passageway leading into any structure. **(4)** The filing of a claim to hold land in connection with a mining claim on public domain. **(5)** In criminal law, the unlawful going into a dwelling or other structure for the purpose of committing a crime therein (usually classified as BURGLARY). **(6)** The formal *entering* into the records of a court of motions, proceedings, notices, or notes that pertain to a lawsuit or other legal proceedings.

e·**qual pro·*tec*·tion of the laws.** The requirement in the U.S. Constitution that both the Federal and state governments must extend equal legal facilities and protection to all. This means courts must be open to everyone on the same conditions, with like rules of evidence and method of procedure in all kinds of cases. *Equal protection* and security must be extended for the enforcement and redress of wrongs and the enforcement of contracts. There shall be no discrimination in the acquisition of property, the enjoyment of personal liberty, or the right to pursue individual happiness, so long as the rights of the general public are not affected. Individuals shall not be liable for greater burdens or charges than such as are placed on all others. In addition, no greater or different punishment shall be imposed for violations of criminal laws.

eq·ui·ta·ble. (1) Right and just. (2) Pertaining to a court of equity, as distinguished from a court of law. See EQUITY.

eq·ui·ty. (1) In a broad sense, *equity* denotes that which is fair, just, and right. (2) In another sense, *equity* denotes equal or impartial justice as between two or more individuals whose claims or legal rights are in conflict. (3) In another sense, *equity* is a system of jurisprudence that is collateral to, or existing alongside, the system of jurisprudence based on the COMMON LAW (established body of civil law). At an early time in England the common law became very strict and narrow. An individual desiring to file a lawsuit could not do so unless it fell within one of the recognized writs, or technical forms of action. This frequently left the injured party without any legal recourse in the courts. In addition, common law courts had no provision for preventing a wrong that was about to happen. (They could not issue INJUNCTIONS restraining someone who was about to commit a wrong.) To correct these injustices, English Chancery courts began to step in and take over cases where it was obvious justice could not be done by the regular (common law) courts. For a time there were two systems of jurisprudence in England operating side by side. But since 1875, the law courts and chancery, or *equity,* courts, have merged. Some of the American colonies brought these separate courts into their system of jurisprudence. Some states still have distinct courts of law and *equity;* other states have law and *equity* administered by the same judges and courts. *Equity* was designed to work out substantial justice where that could not normally be obtained because of some of the "hide bound rules" followed without exception by the law courts. In some states, at the outset of the trial the judge may state that the court is sitting as a *law court,* or as a *court of equity.* (4) The surplus of value of property that may remain after charges or liens against the property are all paid.

eq·ui·ty of re·demp·tion. The right of an individual (MORTGAGOR) whose property has been foreclosed to obtain a return of the property by paying off the whole MORTGAGE in addition to the costs of foreclosure. Historically, in English courts, if the debtor did not pay the mortgage payment on or before the day when payment fell due (known as the "law day"), the creditor would become the absolute owner of the land. Because this worked a great injustice in many cases, the *equity of redemption* principle was eventually worked out by British courts and has been followed in U.S. law.

er•**go**. (Latin) Hence, because, or therefore.

er•*rat*•**um**. (Latin) *Error.*

er•**ror**. A mistake in judgment in the proceedings of a court of record in a matter of law or of fact. A wrongful application of law to the facts of a cause for judicial determination. The claim of *error* allows the losing side to have a matter reviewed by an APPELLATE COURT. The finding of *substantial error* may lead to a reversal or retrial of a case. But if the error is considered by the appellate court not likely to have prejudiced the party complaining, the matter is said to be *harmless error,* and will not be allowed as the basis for reversal, dismissal, or a new trial.

es•**ca**•**la**•**tor clause**. A clause in a contract providing for upward or downward adjustments, as in wages, benefits, production costs, or prices, depending on specified contingencies.

es•*cheat*. The reverting of land to the state. When a landowner does not bequeath property by will, and when there are no heirs to inherit, ownership of the land passes to the state.

es•**crow**. A conditional delivery of something to a third party, to be held until the happening of some event or the performance of some designated act. Perhaps the most common *escrow* situation involves the delivery of a deed to property to a trust company until the person buying the property (GRANTEE) makes certain payments on the purchase price. When the payments are made, the trust company delivers the deed to the grantee.

es•**pi**•**o**•**nage**. The criminal offense, as defined in Federal laws, of gathering or transmitting information relating to the national defense of the United States, with intent or reason to believe that the information will be used to the harm of the United States or to the advantage of any foreign nation.

es•*tate*. **(1)** The interest which one has in lands or any other kind of property. **(2)** In another sense, the term *estate* refers to the subject matter of ownership—to the property itself. *Estates* may be either absolute or conditional. An *absolute estate* is a full and complete estate in lands, not subject to be defeated upon any conditions. The existence of a *conditional estate* depends upon the happening or not happening of some uncertain event. For example, a grandfather could leave a *conditional estate* in land to his only son, with title to pass to the son upon the birth of a male descendant of the son.

es·*tate* at will. An *estate at will* is a tenancy created with the consent of the landlord that is to exist or continue for an indefinite period, depending on the happening of a specified event. For example, an *estate at will* could consist of a lease beginning in 1940 and ending sixty days after the signing of the treaty of peace on the close of war with either Germany or Japan, whichever was to take place first.

es·*tate* in fee *sim*·ple. An absolute estate, full and complete, and not subject to be defeated upon any condition. Ownership with no restriction of any kind.

es·*tate* of in·*her*·i·tance. Another name for an *estate in fee simple.* See *FEE SIMPLE;* see *ESTATE.*

es·*tate* tax. A tax that is required to be paid on the entire net ESTATE, before it is divided for distribution to the heirs. This is not the same as an INHERITANCE TAX, which is paid by each heir on the part that heir inherits.

es·*top*·pel. The legal doctrine that one cannot allege or deny a fact when one's previous actions or words have been to the exact opposite. It is a prohibition which does not allow one to speak against one's own act or deed in a business transaction. The elements or essentials of *estoppel* include a change of position of the parties, so that the party against whom *estoppel* is invoked has received a profit or benefit, or the party invoking *estoppel* has changed his position to his detriment in reliance on words or acts of the other party. For example, A could say to B, "On your lunch hour go buy me a model 7B generator for my automobile, and I will pay your costs plus $10." Relying on this promise, B went to considerable trouble to buy the model 7B generator. When B attempted to deliver the generator, A stated, "I have decided I don't want to fix up my car, so I will not take the generator." The courts would say that A is *estopped* from denying that he wants the generator, and must pay, since B relied on A's statement, to B's own detriment. The *estoppel* principle would apply, whether or not there is a valid contract between the parties.

es·*top*·pel by *judg*·ment. The legal principle that a specific issue cannot be raised in court, because a court has previously adjudicated that issue between the two parties.

et al. (Latin abbreviation for *Et alii—and others*) A term added to the name of the individual first listed when there are others involved. For example, a lawsuit might be filed by one Henry Wain against Manuel

King and ten of King's business associates. All of these ten associates would be named individually in the original pleadings filed by Wain. Thereafter, the case would be known as Wain vs. King, et. al.

et ano. (Latin–*and one other*) A method for abbreviating the title of a case (title of a lawsuit) where there are two plaintiffs or two defendants.

et seq. (Latin–abbreviation for *et sequentes* or *et sequentia,* meaning *and the following*)

et ux. (Latin–abbreviation for *et uxor–and wife*) An abbreviation sometimes used in a deed, to show that it is a conveyance of land by both the husband and wife.

e·*vic*·tion. The forcing out or dispossession of a tenant by a landlord. If the landlord is putting out the tenant, it can be by self help or by going to court and having the actual act done by the sheriff. There are two basic forms of eviction: **(a)** actual eviction, in which the owner or agent forces the tenant to give up the property prior to the termination of the lease, and **(b)** construction, in which the tenant must give up the occupancy because the property has become uninhabitable, or can no longer be used for the purpose for which it was leased. See EJECTMENT; see DISPOSSESS ACTION.

ev·i·dence. Any kind of proof that will be accepted by the court to show the truth or untruth of a matter on dispute.

Taking a wide variety of forms, *evidence* may consist of verbal testimony, weapons or items used to commit a crime, or physical items from which an inference may be drawn. Frequently *evidence* may consist of testimony about what a witness saw, heard, or learned through any of the physical senses.

ex·am·i·*na*·tion. **(1)** The legal process by which witnesses are questioned under oath, such as in the taking of a DEPOSITION. **(2)** In criminal law, an investigation by a committing magistrate of an individual who has been arrested on a criminal charge, to ascertain whether there are sufficient grounds to bind over for trial. **(3)** In real property law, the investigation made by one intending to purchase real estate, in a *examination* of title. This is to ascertain whether there is any CLOUD ON THE TITLE, such as a MORTGAGE, LIEN, or other INCUMBRANCE.

ex·am·i·*na*·tion-in-chief. See DIRECT EXAMINATION.

ex·*am*·in·er. (1) An officer sometimes designated by a chancery (EQUITY) court in cases pending before that court. (2) The name given to some administrative judges or officials, as in the U.S. Patent Office or Bureau of Immigration and Naturalization.

ex·*cep*·tion. (1) In real property law, a clause by which a grantor withdraws something out of that which was granted by deed, and which would otherwise be conveyed to the grantee. (2) In an insurance contract or policy, an exclusion of specified risks. (3) A formal statement of objection to a judge's ruling during the trial of a lawsuit in overruling an objection or refusing a request, which objection may be claimed as a prejudicial error on appeal. (4) In statutory law, a clause in the enactment that exempts certain classes of persons or things from the operation of the law.

ex·cise **(or *ex*·cise tax).** An internal tax imposed on the manufacture, sale or consumption of an item within a country, or paid for a license to carry on certain callings or occupations. For example, a tax on the manufacture of a package of cigarettes is an *excise tax.* While there is no hard and fast rule, *excise taxes* are not generally levied on items that are considered necessities.

ex·*clu*·sion (rule of). The legal principle that a witness may not testify to his or her uncommunicated intent, even though this intent may be material to the question in issue.

ex·*clu*·sion·a·ry rule. The legal principle that illegally obtained evidence will not be allowed as evidence in a criminal prosecution. In the usual situation of this kind, police officers must make an arrest prior to obtaining a warrant to prevent the escape of a suspect. In making this arrest, the suspect is searched and damaging evidence obtained, although the officer did not have sufficient evidence for probable cause until this evidence was found. The usual technique is for the defense attorney to object to this evidence in a pre-trial hearing. If, at this hearing, the evidence is held to have been illegally obtained, it cannot be used in the trial, under the *exclusionary rule.*

ex·*clu*·sive ju·ris·*dic*·tion. JURISDICTION that belongs to one court, or to one class of courts alone. If JURISDICTION is assigned to a class of so-called lower courts or trial courts by statute, then APPELLATE COURTS have the right to handle appeals in such cases. The Constitution of the United States gives the Supreme Court exclusive JURISDICTION

81

over disputes between the various states. That means that the Supreme Court acts as both a trial court and an appeals COURT OF LAST RESORT in these cases.

ex·cul·pate, ex·cul·pate. To clear from alleged guilt or fault.

ex·*cul*·pa·to·ry clause. A clause in a TRUST agreement that relieves the TRUSTEE of all civil responsibility for losses or poor investments of trust assets, so long as the trustee acts in good faith.

ex cu·ri·a. (Latin–ex·*cue*·ree·uh) Away from the court, or out of court.

ex·*cus*·a·ble. Legally forgiveable, or admitting of palliation or excuse because of the attendant circumstances. An act or omission that is on its face unlawful, wrong, or liable to involve loss or blame on the individual chargeable, but with surrounding facts that offer a legal excuse or reason for withholding punishment or liability. For example, a woodchopper cut down a tree in such a way that it fell and killed a co-worker. So long as the death resulted from mere accident and not wilful design, it would be legally *excusable* (*excusable homicide*).

ex de·lic·to. (Latin–ex·duh·*lick*·toe, arising out of tort or crime) A legal cause of action arising out of a TORT or a crime by the opposite party. All legal causes of action (rights to sue) arise out of a breach of contract or out of a tort, which may or may not be a crime. An action *ex delicto* is one based on activities of an individual who commits a tort (TORTFEASOR).

ex·e·cute. **(1)** To make or to complete. **(2)** To sign a deed, a contract, or other legal instrument.

ex·e·*cu*·tion. **(1)** A judicial writ empowering the sheriff or some other officer to carry out a judgment. **(2)** Putting something into operation and effect. Taking a matter or course of conduct to its completion. **(3)** Signing, and in some cases delivering, a legal instrument or document, such as a deed of conveyance. **(4)** A putting to death as a legal penalty for crime.

ex·e·*cu*·tion of *judg*·ment. The process to put into effect the judgment of a court. For example, when a merchant wins a suit against a customer who fails to pay debts, the merchant goes into court and obtains a judgment against the debtor. If the customer refuses, or cannot pay the judgment, the merchant can instruct his attorney to apply to the court for an order (writ of execution), directing the sheriff or other court officer to seize the customer's property. In some jurisdictions an attorney can issue the writ without going to the court. The seized property is then sold at a sheriff's sale, constituting an *execution of judgment.* The merchant is then paid out of the proceeds of the sale, the sheriff retains some set fees as costs, and the remainder of the sale price goes to the customer. If there is a deficiency, and the debt is not fully satisfied, the merchant may obtain one or more *executions* until the judgment is paid in full. Lawyers frequently speak of the amount still due after a return of execution as the *deficiency judgment,* but the term is not commonly used by the courts.

ex·ec·u·tive. (1) A high official in government, business, or other organization. (2) One of the three branches of government (*executive,* LEGISLATIVE, JUDICIAL) that has to do with the execution of laws and the conduct of national and public affairs.

ex·ec·u·tive or·der. An administrative order issued by the head of state (the President or the governor of a state) that has the force of law. While the EXECUTIVE branch of government does not have the power to make laws, the legislature may pass enactments providing that the executive shall issue orders regulating a specific matter. When such an *executive order* is issued, it has the same authority of law as if passed individually by the legislature. For example, under authority of Congress, the President of the United States may issue an *executive order* that guns may not be carried on commercial airlines, except by specified Federal officers.

ex·ec·u·tor. (1) The individual appointed by one making a will to dispose of his or her property after death in accordance with the terms of the will. (2) An administrative or ministerial officer appointed by a court to carry out the judgment or orders of the court.

ex·ec·u·to·ry. That which has not yet been carried out, or executed. That which depends on a future contingency or event.

ex·em·pla·ry dam·ag·es. Damages awarded to the plaintiff beyond those needed to reimburse for the actual loss. *Exemplary damages* are granted as punishment, or to make an example of the defendant. See COMPENSATORY DAMAGES, from which *exemplary damages* is distinguished.

ex·em·pli·fi·ca·tion. An official copy or transcript of a public document intended to be used as evidence. To be admitted as evidence, the record must be authenticated as a true copy by the official who has custody of the document.

ex·*emp*·tion. Freedom from requirements or liabilities to which others are subjected. Immunity from taxes, charges, or other impositions.

ex·e·*qua*·tur. (Latin–ecks·uh·*kway*·ter, *Let it be executed*) A certificate used in international law that validates a judgment in one country so it will be recognized and EXECUTED in another country.

ex·er·cise. To put in action or practice some power or right that belongs to the holder. For example, a prospective purchaser may obtain an option to purchase a tract of land. In following through on this transaction, we say the purchaser will *exercise the option* by buying the land. Similarly, a citizen may *exercise the right to vote* by voting.

ex. gr. See E.G.

ex·*haus*·tion of ad·*min*·is·tra·tive *rem*·e·dies. The legal doctrine that where *administrative remedies* are available by statute, these remedies must first be exhausted before the courts will assume jurisdiction of the matter.

ex·*hib*·it. (1) A document or supporting papers filed with legal pleadings. (2) An INSTRUMENT, document, or paper produced during a court trial or hearing or in administrative or quasi-judicial hearings in proof of the facts, or as bearing on the subject under dispute. After being accepted by the court, the paper in question is marked as an *exhibit,* given an identifying number, and placed in the court records concerning the case. (3) To display or offer for inspection; to present publicly.

ex of·fi·ci·o. (Latin–ecks·uh·*fish*·ee·oh) By virtue of the office; by power that is incidental to the responsibility of the office.

ex·on·er·*a*·tion. (1) The right (sometimes called *right of exoneration*) which an individual has against a defaulter, when required to pay that which the defaulter should have paid. It is the right, or EQUITY, which exists between individuals who are successively liable for the same debt. For example, one who endorses a check and negotiates it at a grocery store will be held liable by the grocery store if the check is not good. The person passing the check is then entitled to *exoneration* against the prior endorsers or the original maker of the check. *Exoneration* is the right of a SURETY who signs a promissory note as an accomodation for a friend who subsequently defaults in payment. (2) The right to be liberated from an obligation to pay. (3) To be cleared of an accusation of crime.

ex par•te. (Latin–ecks *par*•tee–by or for one party only) A judicial proceeding, order, or injunction is said to be *ex parte* when it is granted
at the instance and for the benefit of one side in the legal dispute
without notice to the other party adversely involved. It is to be noted
that some judicial proceedings are proper and legal whether or not
the adverse party has been informed or is present.

ex•*pa•*tri•a•tion.** Voluntary renunciation of citizenship.

ex•pert *wit•*ness. Normally, a witness may not be allowed to testify in a
criminal trial, unless that individual saw or heard something pertinent, or can produce some piece of evidence. An *expert witness,*
however, may not have anything of a direct nature to offer.

The *expert witness* is allowed to give an individual opinion about
the nature or meaning of physical evidence or conditions that may be
in issue during a trial. The *expert witness* may be a scientist with
unusual technical education or scientific background. On the other
hand, unusual experience in an uncommon field of work may serve
to qualify. It is left to the trial judge's sole discretion whether the
proposed *expert witness* has the unusual qualifications that will
stamp that individual as an expert in the matter in dispute. An AP-
PELLATE COURT will not question the judge's opinion about qualifications of an expert, unless there is a clear showing of abuse by the
judge.

ex•*pos•*i•to•ry *stat•*ute.** A statute passed for the express purpose of clari-
fying a law already on the statute books.

ex post *fac•*to. (Latin–*after the fact*) There are three types of laws that
are said to be *ex post facto* laws, forbidden by the Constitution of the
United States, and therefore illegal in all jurisdictions in this country:
(1) laws that seek to punish an act that was not criminal at the time
the act was committed (acts committed prior to passage of the law);
(2) laws that increase the punishment for acts committed before the
enactment of the increased penalty; **(3)** laws that change the rules of
evidence to make it easier to prove a violation that occurred in the
past.

ex•*pro•*pri•ate.** **(1)** The act of voluntarily giving up that which was previously claimed as one's own. **(2)** As used in international law, this
term means the appropriation or taking of property without consent
of the rightful owner, at a price set by the appropriating government.

(Note that this is a completely unrelated meaning to the established legal meaning in the definition above.) The excuse usually given by foreign governments that *expropriate* the property of American countries is that the foreign government needs to *nationalize* that type of industry or business.

ex·*punge*. To strike out; delete; or obliterate.

ex rel. (ecks rel.) Abbreviation for *ex relatione*.

ex rel·at·i·o·ne. (Latin–ecks·rel·ah·see·*own*·ee) *On relation.* A legal proceeding begun by the ATTORNEY GENERAL or other official, in the name and in behalf of the state, and at the request of an individual who has a private interest in the matter. For example, the title of a case would be *Arizona ex rel. Smith v. Jones.*

ex tem·po·re. (Latin–ecks *tem*·por·ee) *From the lapse of time.*

ex·*ten*·sion. (1) An addition to the period of time in which a debt or payment must be made. Usually there must be an agreement between the debtor and creditor, supported by consideration, before such an arrangement is legal. (2) A prolongation of an existing lease at the same rate of payment.

ex·*ten*·u·at·ing *cir*·cum·stan·ces. Circumstances associated with the perpetration of a crime that serve to lessen the blame, make the offense less aggravated, or that palliate to some extent. For example, a starving man would be considered less blameworthy than a banker who stole a loaf of bread, since hunger could be an *extenuating circumstance.*

ex·*tin*·guish·ment. The nullification or destruction of some legal right.

ex·*tort*. (1) To obtain from an individual by force. (2) To obtain from an individual by threats to do bodily harm, to destry property, or to ruin reputation by exposing some fact in the victim's background that is not generally known. A professional mobster may *extort* money, for example by beating up the owner of a small shop, and by thereafter threatening to again resort to violence.

ex·*tor*·tion. Criminal laws usually classify *extortion* as the crime of obtaining money in any of three different situations: (1) by force that is less than the great bodily force required for robbery; (2) by threats to use force, to harm property, or to expose crime or misconduct; or (3) by demanding a fee or compensation for a service that should be done gratuitously. For example, a public official demanding payment for permitting individuals to inspect public records that are available to all.

ex·tra·*di*·tion. The surrender of a wanted individual by authorities of one
state to those having jurisdiction to try the offender.

ex·tra·ju·*di*·cial. That which is outside the scope of regular judicial proceedings.

ex·tra·ter·ri·*to*·ri·al·ly. The operation of laws beyond the usual territorial application. For example, U.S. courts have always permitted
U.S. military personnel to be brought to trial and punished for offenses committed on a U.S. military base. By the usual tests of territorial jurisdiction, this would be outside jurisdictional limits of this
country, and not subject to trial or punishment by any tribunal of the
U.S. government.

ex·*trem*·is. (Latin) *In the last illness.* The condition of being near death,
and beyond hope of recovery.

ex·*trin*·sic *ev*·i·dence. Evidence or facts that are outside the actual
document, INSTRUMENT, contract, etc. that is being adjudicated;
matters that are foreign to the *face* of the document. The instrument
may be valid on its face, but *extrinsic evidence* may alter the legal
relationship. For example, a man may have obtained a bill of sale for
an automobile, but it will be held invalid if *extrinsic evidence* shows
that the bill of sale was obtained at the point of a gun.

eye·*wit*·ness. A witness who actually observed what transpired, and can
testify to those facts. Usually, *eyewitness* is used to mean any witness
who can testify as to what was experienced by any of the physical
senses, either seeing, hearing, or smelling. Sometimes an *eyewitness*
is called an *eyeball witness* in the slang of law enforcement.

F

face a·*mount*. The amount of money written on the face of a document,
not including interest.

fac·*sim*·i·le. An exactly reproduced duplicate.

fact. An actual occurrence; an event, a happening. *Fact* is frequently
mentioned as different from *law,* in jurisprudence. Questions of fact
are for the jury to decide, after hearing all the evidence. Questions of
law are for the court (judge) to decide. Fact is that out of which a

point of *law* arises—that which is proved to be or not to be for the purpose of applying, or refusing to apply a rule of *law. Fact* is actual, and *law* is a principle. There is no appeal from the jury's decision or findings on the *facts.* Appeals arise out of misapplications of the *law* to the *facts* of the case.

fac·**tor.** An individual who receives goods for sale, getting a commission for transactions made.

fac·**tum.** (Latin) *Fact.*

fail·**ure of con**·**sid**·**er**·*a*·**tion.** A term used in contract law to describe a situation in which the event or condition on which the contract was based never took place or failed to exist. When there is a *failure of consideration,* the contract is not enforceable. For example, a widowed daughter was promised $40,000 in her father's will if she would take care of the father for the remainder of his life. The daughter lived with her father for a month, remarried, and declined to take care of the father any longer. The courts say that in a situation of this kind there was no contract because of *failure of consideration.*

fail·**ure of** *is*·**sue.** Dying without offspring who would succeed as heirs.

fair *mar*·**ket** *val*·**ue.** Price at which both a willing seller and a willing buyer will agree to transact business.

fair on its face. A document or a transaction that appears to be perfectly legal, except for the introduction of extraneous evidence. For example, a written contract in itself may appear to be proper, but it may be proved by extraneous evidence that one party to the agreement was forced to sign at gunpoint.

fair trade. A retail price restriction set by the manufacturer, requiring all retailers to sell only at the pre-set price. *Fair trade* restrictions on retailers are illegal in some jurisdictions.

fair *tri*·**al.** A hearing or proceeding which hears before it condemns, which proceeds upon inquiry of all pertinent facts, and renders judgment only after trial; a trial before an impartial judge and jury, in an atmosphere of judicial calm, in which witnesses can deliver their testimony without fear and intimidation, in which attorneys can assert defendant's rights, and in which truth may be received and given credence without fear or violence.

false. (1) That which is not true; artificial. (2) That which is deliberately untrue. (The word is used with both meanings).

false ar·*rest.* An unlawful or unjustifiable arrest, physical restraint, or detention. It makes no difference whether the person restrained was held in prison or any other place. From a legal standpoint, KIDNAPPING is usually regarded as including false arrest, or holding for ransom or reward. False arrest may be a crime as well as a TORT (civil wrong).

fal·sus in uno. (Latin-sometimes given as "falsus in uno, falsus in omnibus"-*false in one thing, false in everything*) The principle of law that a jury may disregard everything that a witness says, if any part of the witness's testimony is obviously false.

fam·i·ly car *prin*·ci·ple (or family car doctrine; family automobile doctrine; family purpose doctrine). The legal principle followed in a number of jurisdictions that the owner of a car will be civilly liable for injury or damage done by any member of the family in the use of this vehicle. Tort liability, but not criminal liability such as for negligent manslaughter, is attributed to the owner of the family car. The theory of this family doctrine is that any member of the family driving the car is the father's AGENT.

feas·or. A maker, or doer. For example, a tort-feasor is an individual who commits a tortious act.

fed·er·al *ques*·tion. A matter involving the U.S. Constitution or statutes. Usually, a Federal, or Constitutional, question must be involved before a matter can be APPEALED from the state courts to the U.S. Supreme Court.

fed·er·*a*·tion. Any group of individuals or organizations, usually unincorporated, joined together for a common aim.

fee. A charge for services. Most fees charged for legal filings, registrations, or postings are set by law.

fee *sim*·ple. The absolute ownership of real estate or real property. Ownership without any restrictions or limitations on how the owner may dispose of the property. See: LIFE ESTATE.

fee tail. An estate in land limited in inheritance to a specified individual, group, or class of heirs.

fel·on. (1) One who has committed a FELONY, and has not yet been discharged by completion of sentence. Generally, the term is no longer used after the convicted individual has paid his or her *debt to society.*
(2) Sometimes used improperly to describe any evildoer or villain.

fe·*lo*·ni·ous. (1) A technical term, referring to the mental intent (MENS REA, or criminal intent) of one who commits a criminal act. If an assault is committed in a *felonious manner,* it is done from an evil heart or purpose, wickedly, unlawfully, and with criminal intent. In bringing criminal charges, the prosecutor frequently alleges that an act was committed in a *felonious and unlawful* manner. (2) In larceny violations, the term *felonious* is used synonymously with the term *fraudulent.* If the prosecutor alleges that something was stolen with *felonious intent,* it means that the accused had the intent to steal.

fel·o·ny. (1) The definition varies. Under Federal law, a *felony* is a criminal offense punishable by death or by imprisonment for a term exceeding one year. (That is why a Federal judge may sentence to *a year and a day,* rather than one year–to make certain the record shows a *felony conviction.*) The Federal definition is used in a number of the states. In a number of other states, however, a *felony* is a crime punishable by death or by imprisonment in the state prison, regardless of length of time. In the latter states, an individual may have been convicted for a *felony,* although serving only six months in the state prison. (2) Any serious crime is commonly referred to as a *felony,* even though this definition may be technically incorrect under the conditions outlined in the first part of this definition.

fel·o·ny mur·der **rule.** The rule that an accidental killing during the commission of another FELONY makes that killing a murder, rather than manslaughter. The courts say that the requirement or element of legal malice, or intent, is supplied from the commission of the intended felony. This legal principle has been followed in most jurisdictions, either by statute or by following the COMMON LAW. A typical situation of this kind would occur when an armed robber has no intent to murder, but the gun is accidentally discharged and a store clerk killed. The courts say that the lack of intent to murder is immaterial. The rule is not used universally, however. A number of courts hold that the killing must actually take place during the commission of the original felony, and does not apply to an accidental killing of a third person by the getaway automobile. There is also a difference in opinion as to whether a killing of a third person by one attempting to defend himself or herself during the felony can be attributed to the criminals.

feme *cov·ert.* (Latin–a married woman) This term is generally used in the old English legal meaning, as a female who was legally dependent on her husband, and did not have equal rights to hold property, to inherit, etc. See FEME SOLE.

feme sole. (Latin–a single woman) See FEME COVERT.

fi·at. (Latin) *Let it be done.* A command to act; an order. *Government by fiat* means government by decree, as by the command of a dictator.

fic·*ti*·tious. That which is false, not genuine, not real, feigned, or imaginary. That which is based on fiction.

fi·*del*·i·ty bond. An insurance policy to repay funds or property stolen by the individual covered in the bond. This is the type of insurance coverage provided when it is said that employees are *bonded.*

fi·*du*·ci·ar·y. An individual or corporation having a duty, created by that party's undertaking, to act primarily for the benefit of another in that undertaking; one who holds the character of a TRUSTEE and who must act with utmost good faith for the benefit of another, placing the other's interest ahead of those of the *fiduciary.* GUARDIANS, ATTORNEYS, conservators and TRUSTEES must all operate in a *fiduciary* capacity.

fi·*er*·i *fac*·ias. (Latin) *You cause to be made.* An old name for a WRIT OF EXECUTION, ordering the sheriff to levy and make good a judgment on chattels or goods of the debtor.

Fifth Amend·ment. See TAKING THE FIFTH AMENDMENT.

file. (1) The court record in a lawsuit or other proceeding. (2) The delivery of papers to a custodian for retention and to complete the record for future use. (3) The practice of individuals, firms, or organizations in laying away papers, documents, and correspondence, and the device by which they are kept in order. (4) To submit the first papers in a lawsuit, or as a prerequisite for legal or business procedures, such as *filing* as a candidate for public office, to obtain a divorce, etc.

fil·i·*a*·tion pro·*ceed*·ing. Used synonymously with PATERNITY SUIT.

***find*·ing.** The result of a judicial inquiry or examination, or of the deliberations of a jury. The word frequently refers to the result reached by a judge, or to a recital of the facts as found by a jury.

***fix*·ture.** Anything of an accessory character affixed to the land or building, so that it becomes a part of the building. A *fixture* was originally a CHATTEL, but the legal nature changed when it became permanently affixed to the land or to a structure. A built-in kitchen cabinet is a *fixture.* So too is a fence, unless it is of a portable nature. The general common law rule is that a *fixture* affixed to land or building becomes a part of the land, and cannot be removed except by the individual owning the land. There are statutory variations of this rule in almost all states. Generally, five tests are applied as to whether a thing is a *fixture:* (a) the agreement of the parties, (b) the relationship of the parties, (c) the intent of the party affixing, (d) the nature of the article, and its adaptability to use generally at other locations; (d) way in which it is affixed or annexed.

flag·*ran*·te del·*ic*·to. (Latin) *In the very act of committing the crime.*

float·ing lien. An agreement by which property purchased later will serve as SECURITY, along with property already owned that is currently subject to being called to account to the CREDITOR as a secured debt or lien.

force. (1) Illegal or unlawful violence. The use of *force* in making a TRESPASS on to the property of another may not involve actual physical violence against persons or property. Simple entering in an unlawful way may be enough in the eyes of the law. (2) The term *in force* may mean in considerable numbers or in considerable strength. (3) *In force* may also mean in effect, or in operation.

force·a·ble de·*tain*·er. See FORCIBLE DETAINER.

forced sale. A sale made under foreclosure laws or other regulations set up by the courts. It is a sale against the consent of the owner, and for the benefit of a CREDITOR whose rights have been established in the courts.

force ma·*jeure*. (French-muh·*zhoor*) An unexpected or uncontrolled force that relieves liability from damages; an "act of God." An earthquake or cyclone, for example, involves a *force majeure.*

for·ci·ble de·*tain*·er. The refusal to surrender possession of lands or property that was entered rightfully, but is being wrongfully held. For example, when a renter refuses to leave after the rental term has expired, the renter is holding possession by *forcible detainer.*

for·ci·ble *en*·try. Entry into possession of land or property illegally, by threats or FORCE, and against the will of those entitled to possession.

for·ci·ble *en*·try and de·*tain*·er. A legal procedure to restore to possession one who has been wrongfully deprived of possession of land or property. Where used by the courts, this type of action does not attempt to settle ownership. It gives possession to the party entitled to that possession in order to prevent the disturbance of the public peace by the forcible assertion of a private right that should be pursued in a court.

fore·*bear*·ance. (1) The act of refraining from the enforcement of something, such as the right to collect an obligation. Granting an indulgence to a debtor. (2) The act of holding up, or failing to press, an action, especially an action to enforce a legal right. For example, a landlord could show *forebearance* by not evicting a noisy tenant who violated some of the terms of the lease, but who always paid on time.

fore·*clo*·sure. A legal proceeding that extinguishes a MORTGAGOR'S right of redeeming mortgaged property. If the mortgagor falls behind in payments, the *foreclosure* ends the owner's rights in the property and sells the property to pay off the mortgage debt. In most states this is done by a lawsuit.

for·**eign cor**·**po**·*ra*·**tion.** See DOMESTIC CORPORATION.

fore·**man.** The presiding member of a PETIT (TRIAL) JURY or GRAND JURY. The foreman, who may be a woman, coordinates deliberations and serves as spokesman to the court, although individual jurors can also communicate verbally with the judge when conditions are proper.

fo·*ren*·**sic** *med*·**i**·**cine.** Medical JURISPRUDENCE. The application of medical knowledge for the purposes of the law. In many cases, information from the sciences is needed to enable a court of law to reach a proper conclusion on a question affecting the cause of death or affecting property. The CORONER or medical examiner frequently makes use of his knowledge of *forensic medicine.*

for·**fei**·**ture.** A loss or punishment annexed by law to some illegal act, negligence, or legal duty; a penalty assessed as a consequence of having done or failed to do a certain act. For example, Federal laws for the filing of a mining claim on public lands require the claim to be worked on an annual basis. Failing to perform the required amount of work would result in *forfeiture.*

for·**ger**·**y.** (1) The crime of falsely making or altering a document, instrument, or writing. For example, a person committing *forgery* may cash a check after tracing a bank customer's name to it as maker, and presenting it for payment. In recent years, *forgery* has been extended to include the duplication of masterworks of art. The crime of *forgery* is not complete until the false maker attempts to use the falsely made item in cheating someone. (2) In evidence law, *forgery* is the altering or manipulation of evidence or physical objects in such a way as to create an erroneous impression, or to create a false idea in the mind of the observer.

for·**mal** *par*·**ty.** A party whose name is listed as one of the contestants in a lawsuit for technical reasons only, and who usually has no more than a passing interest in the outcome.

formed de·*sign.* This is the language sometimes used to describe the premeditation of a criminal. For example, a murderer had a *formed design,* or preconceived intent to kill the victim. This *formed design* need exist for only an instant in the mind of the perpetrator, to make this crime MURDER rather than MANSLAUGHTER.

forms of ac·tion. The old, technical categories of cases that could be brought in an English law court as the basis for a lawsuit. To get action, the plaintiff had to present a case that exactly corresponded to the narrow limits of one of these forms of action. These had such names as *trover, replevin, assumpsit,* and *trespass.* Cases that did not fit into one of these technical "pigeonholes" would not be considered in the English law courts. Gradually, the English chancery courts, or EQUITY courts, as they came to be called, began to accept injustices that could not qualify as a *form of action.* These old technical names were abolished in England by 1875, and in most states of the United States. But many of the principles regulating these common-law actions are still followed by the courts in some jurisdictions in the United States. See EQUITY for some background between law courts and equity courts.

for·ni·*ca*·tion. Unlawful sexual intercourse between two unmarried persons. Further, if one of the persons is married and the other not, the conduct is *fornication* on the part of the latter, while it is ADULTERY by the former. By statute in some states, however, the conduct is adultery on the part of both individuals if the woman is married, regardless of the marital status of the man. See ADULTERY.

for·*swear*. To swear to something that is known to be untrue. This is an all-inclusive kind of false swearing, and is not the same as PERJURY. To be guilty of PERJURY, the individual swearing falsely must: **(a)** be under oath as a witness at court, or under oath before a court officer, and **(b)** must swear falsely on an issue that is *material* to a pending court trial. To *forswear* may constitute PERJURY, but may also include false swearing under oath circumstances. For example, a witness to an armed robbery testified under oath in court that he observed the bandit rob the victim at gunpoint in a bar. The witness, a married man, testified that he was alone, drinking in the bar when the robbery occurred. In fact, the witness was drinking with three women when the crime occurred. The witness did not swear falsely to the material facts concerning the armed robbery, and therefore did not commit perjury, but did forswear concerning his companions in the bar. PERJURY is usually a serious crime, whereas *forswearing* is comparatively minor when prohibited by criminal laws.

fo·rum. (Latin) *A court of justice.* A place where justice is dispensed; where trials and legal matters are adjudicated.

fo·rum non con·ven·i·ens. (Latin–*foe*·rum non kon·*veen*·ee·ens) *Incon-*

venient court. The legal principle that a court has discretion to decline to hear a case where another court clearly has JURISDICTION, and where basic convenience and fairness to the PARTIES and the public requires that the matter should be heard in the second court.

for·**ward**·**ing fee.** The money paid to an attorney who lines up another attorney who can handle the special legal needs of the client. For example, a client may come to an attorney in New Jersey, asking for legal help. The problem involved, however, may need legal work done in Oregon.

fran·**chise.** **(1)** The right granted to an individual or group to sell the products or services of a parent firm in a particular territory. Usually the parent firm is national in scope or has a well-known product or service. **(2)** A special right or privilege granted by the government to an individual or group, which right is not available to citizens in general. This type of *franchise* was common with the English royalty, where the king sold some royal privilege to a subject, such as a right to prepare chinaware for the royal household. **(3)** The exercise of constitutional and statutory rights of citizenship, such as the right to vote.

fraud. Deceit, trickery, or deliberate perversion of the truth in order to induce someone to part with something of value, or to give up a legal right; misrepresentation, concealment, or deliberate nondisclosure of a material fact to induce another to enter a contract or a business deal that will work to a disadvantage.

fraud·**u**·**lent.** Based on deceit, trickery, or misrepresentation. For example, a transaction set up for the purpose of committing a swindle is *fraudulent.*

free·**hold** **es**·*tate.* An estate in fee simple. See FEE SIMPLE and LIFE ESTATE.

freight. **(1)** The carrying of goods or merchandise by a commercial carrier, as distinguished from mail, baggage, or express. **(2)** The goods themselves are sometimes referred to as *freight.* **(3)** The funds paid to the owner of a vessel for transporting goods, under admiralty law.

fresh pur·*suit.* The immediate and continuous pursuit of a criminal by a peace officer is said to be *fresh pursuit.* If the chase is discontinued at any time, or pursuit is lost, the principle no longer applies. Under this legal idea, a peace officer may continue into another state to arrest, even though the officer normally has no arrest power in the second state. This kind of authority is sometimes provided by statute, and frequently by reciprocal agreement between adjoining states.

friend·**ly suit.** A lawsuit instituted by arrangement between the parties, to obtain a legal judgment on a disputed question of interest to both. The courts do not look with favor on a contrived lawsuit, as judges feel their time could be more profitably used in settling legitimate legal disputes.

friend of the court. See AMICUS CURIAE.

frisk. In criminal law, rapidly running hands over a suspect's person, as distinguished from a full search. A "stop and frisk" examination of a suspect is usually regarded by the courts as a permissible form of search for a suspect encountered on the street by a police patrol officer. It is not a full search, and is permitted on the theory that an officer can "frisk" and immediately tell whether the suspect is carrying a gun or other weapon that may be used against the officer.

friv·o·lous. That which is lacking in legal seriousness, or that carries no weight. A "frivolous appeal" is one that is so lacking in merit that it is recognizable on its face as deserving no consideration.

fu·gi·tive from jus·tice. One who, after having committed a crime, hides out to avoid arrest by local officers, or flees to another state.

full faith and *cred·it*. The provision in the United States Constitution (Art. IV, S.1) that each state shall accept the public acts, records, and judicial proceedings of every other state. For example, a judgment handed down in a state court that has JURISDICTION over the subject matter or person involved is binding and conclusive in the courts of every other state, even though the judgment appears to be totally erroneous. If one state does not give *full faith and credit* to the acts of another state, then the first state cannot expect its own acts to be honored.

fund. (1) A sum of money or other resources, set apart for a specific purpose. (2) Assets, stocks and bonds, and revenues are sometimes termed "funds."

fun·da·*men*·tal law. That basic law which sets up the governmental organization and operation of a nation or state. In the case of the United States, the *fundamental law* is the United States Constitution.

fun·gi·bles. Movable substances or goods that are replaceable or indistinguishable as to individual parts in quantity. One unit is like every other unit. *Fungibles* are things that do not need to be dealt with individually (in specie). For example, one bushel in a carload of wheat would be indistinguishable from another bushel in the same carload. A shipment of horses, however, would not be a shipment of *fungibles,* since each of the horses has individual characteristics and values. In property law, rights often turn on whether or not goods are *fungibles*. If a farmer delivers grain (*fungible goods*) to an elevator, with an option to later receive an equal amount of grain of that grade, the transaction is a bailment. The farmer still owns the grain and must bear the loss in case fire destroys the grain elevator. But if the farmer delivers six sheep to a breeder, and the breeder promises to return six sheep of equal value (but not the same sheep), the transaction is a barter and sale, rather than a BAILMENT. In case of the sheep, they are distinguishable and are not *fungible goods;* TITLE passes to the breeder, and the latter must bear the loss if the sheep die. Whether or not goods are *fungibles,* and the options of the parties, determines whether there was a transfer of TITLE (a BAILMENT or a sale). This difference between a bailment and a sale will determine where the risk of loss rests, whose creditors may attach the goods, whether an innocent third party buying the goods can get good title, and who is liable for taxes on the property.

fu•ture ac•*quired prop*•er•ty. MORTGAGES are sometimes written to include presently owned property, and any property obtained in the future. An arrangement of this kind, covering future acquired property, enables a railroad to replace worn out boxcars with good rolling stock, without paying off old obligations and writing new mortgages on each unit.

fu•tures. Speculative transactions, such as on bulk commodities, bought for future acceptance or sold for future delivery. This may be done as a hedge against market price changes, or as a highly fluctuating type of investment.

G

gar•nish•*ee.* (1) An individual who holds money or property owing to another that is subject to GARNISHMENT. (2) To serve with a garnishment to attach a debtor's wages.

gar•nish•ment. A statutory proceeding whereby a debtor's wages, property, money, or credits are taken and applied as payment toward satisfaction of the debt.

gen•er•al as•*sign*•ment for *cred•i•*tors **(or general assignment for benefit of creditors).** A transfer of all a debtor's money, property, rights, or other assets to a TRUSTEE, to liquidate the debtor's affairs and pay off the creditors.

gen•er•al av•er•age con•tri•*bu•*tion **(or general average loss).** In maritime law, a loss that must be shared by all those involved in the shipment of cargo on a vessel when the vessel must be lightened by throwing some cargo overboard to save the whole.

*gen•er•al cred•i•*tor. A CREDITOR to whom money is owed, but who has no special security that gives preference over the claims of other creditors, such as a LIEN, MORTGAGE, etc.

*gen•er•al dam•a•*ges. Used synonymously with DAMAGES.

gen•er•al ex•e•*cu•*tion. A court writ, directing the sheriff or other officer to satisfy a judgment out of any personal property owned by the defendant. A *general execution* is distinguished from a SPECIAL EXECUTION, which authorizes a levy on only certain specified property.

gen•er•al **term.** See TERM OF COURT.

*gen•er•al ver•*dict. Same as VERDICT.

*gen•er•al war•*ran•ty **deed.** Same as a WARRANTY DEED.

ger•ry•man•der. To divide a state or territory into election districts so as to give one political party an unfair advantage by juggling areas with known political party preferences into groupings where the vote would be most advantageous. The word originated from combining the name of former Massachusetts Governor Elbridge Gerry and the word *salamander,* since a re-districted area in Massachusetts resembled the shape of a salamander.

gift. A voluntary conveyance of land, or the transfer of ownership of money or property, gratuitously and without any legal consideration. Legal requirements for a *gift* include the capacity and intent of the donor, a completed delivery to the DONEE (recipient), and the acceptance by the donee. If the gift is given a short time before the death of the donor, state statutes and Federal tax regulations may require the payment of gift or INHERITANCE TAXES. The difference between a *gift* and a *voluntary trust* is that the *gift* itself passes to the donee, while in the voluntary trust situation the beneficial or actual title passes to the donee, while the legal title is transferred to a third person (TRUSTEE) or is retained by the person creating the trust. (donor).

gift deed. A deed transferring ownership or title of real estate in consideration of love or affection. To satisfy old legal requirements, deeds of this kind are given for a nominal sum, such as one dollar. TITLE passes as completed as if there had been a sale involving monetary consideration.

go·ing *pub*·lic. The procedure whereby corporate shares are placed on the general market. This usually means having the stock traded on a stock exchange.

good. Sound; praiseworthy; for the public welfare; valid; reliable; solvent.

good be·*hav*·ior. A term with imprecise meanings; usually meaning lawful, responsible, peaceable conduct.

good cause. Valid or substantial reason. In discharging an employee for *good cause,* it has been held to be any ground put forward by authorities in good faith that is not unreasonable, arbitrary, irrelevant, or irrational.

good faith. That which is well-intended; honest.

good sa·*mar*·i·tan *doc*·trine. The legal principle that one who risks his or her own life, or serious injury, cannot commit a TORT in attempting to rescue one who is in peril, provided the attempt is not rashly or recklessly made. Courts following this doctrine usually say that the negligence of one volunteering to rescue another must seriously worsen the position of the individual in distress before liability can be charged to the rescuer.

goods. See MERCHANDISE.

grace. A reprieve or EXEMPTION from some legal obligation, usually the payment of a debt or insurance premium.

grand *ju*·ry. A board (group) of inquiry, selected and assembled by law, to receive accusations and complaints in criminal matters, to hear the evidence presented by the state (PROSECUTION), and to return an INDICTMENT in each case where they are satisfied a trial ought to be held. At COMMON LAW a *grand jury* varied in makeup from 12 to 23 men. In courts in the United States the number is frequently less, by statute. Some jurisdictions require a *grand jury indictment* before an individual can be prosecuted for a FELONY. This is the provision in the U.S. Constitution for the prosecution of any Federal felony, and is also required for all felonies in some states. In those jurisdictions, a *grand jury indictment* serves as a safeguard against prosecutions that might be brought by the prosecutor, even though they have no real merit. At the other extreme, a grand jury indictment forces the prosecution in cases where the prosecutor refuses to bring charges because of political bias or downright dishonesty.

grand *lar·ce·ny*. LARCENY or theft of money or property over a certain amount, which is usually set by statute. Laws in many states set up grades of theft, with *grand larceny* being a theft in excess of a set amount, such as $50, or $200, and *petty larceny* being a theft of less than this amount in value. These statutes typically have more serious penalties for thefts of larger amounts. (It is to be noted that *larceny,* theft and stealing are used synonymously.)

grand theft. See GRAND LARCENY.

***grand·fa·ther* clause.** An exception to a statutory prohibition that allows individuals who were doing something by a certain date to continue doing it, even if otherwise prohibited by a new restriction. For example, in some states an individual in possession of a valid driver's license in 1940 may continue to hold the license, without being required to pass a driving examination for competency before a state examiner.

grant. A transfer by deed of real property. To make a conveyance, or pass title to property. (Title passes from the grantor to the grantee.) See CONVEYANCE.

gran·*tee*. The individual to whom a GRANT or CONVEYANCE of property is made.

gran·*tor*. The individual who makes a GRANT or CONVEYANCE of real property.

gra·*tu·i·*tous li·cen·*see*. Generally used synonymously with *licensee.* Any visitor allowed on the property, or invited on the property, other than one invited to come on the premises for business purposes. See LICENSEE.

gra·*va·*men. The significant part of a complaint or grievance.

***griev·*ance pro·*ce·*dure.** A systematic, orderly procedure for hearing and settling problems between workers and employers.

ground lease. A LEASE agreement for the use of land only. A retired farmer, for example, might agree to a *ground lease* covering farm lands, while retaining use of the farmhouse for himself.

ground rent. Rent paid to the property owner for land when the tenant has erected the building or buildings on it.

grounds. A foundation or basis, for belief, action, or argument.

grub•stake. A contract used in mining law, in which one party provides supplies, provisions, tools, and equipment, and the other party is obligated to prospect, file a claim, and acquire mining property for the benefit of both parties.

guar•an•*tee.* Same meaning as GUARANTY.

guar•an•tor. A COSIGNOR, ENDORSER, or SURETY. One who makes a GUARANTY. See GUARANTY.

guar•an•ty. An undertaking to be legally responsible for the payment of a debt of another or for the performance of another's act that is required as a legal obligation. A *guaranty* differs from a SURETY obligation, in that a surety has primary liability along with the PRINCIPAL. A guarantor (one who furnishes a guaranty) is secondarily liable, and in some instances may be released from liability if there is a failure to make demand on the principal debtor, or to pursue available remedies against the debtor.

guar•di•an. A person appointed by a court, with the power and duty to look after another person and manage the property and rights of one who is legally incompetent. A *guardian* may be appointed for a minor, one who lacks mental or physical control, an insane person, or anyone incapable of conducting business and personal affairs.

guar•di•an ad *li*•tem. A guardian appointed only for the duration of a lawsuit. See GUARDIAN.

guest *stat*•ute. A statute in force in some states, providing that an individual who rides as a guest in another person's car is not permitted to sue the owner for damages in case of an accident, unless more than ordinary negligence was involved.

guil•ty. (1) One who is convicted of a crime, or enters a plea admitting responsibility for a criminal act. (2) The status of being found civilly responsible for a tort.

H

ha•be•as cor•pus. (Latin–*hay*•bee•us *kor*•pus) *You have the body.* The right embodied in the U.S. Constitution proper (not the Bill of Rights) as a protection against any illegal imprisonment or detention.

Habeas corpus dates from the time of the signing of the Magna Charta (Carta) by the British King John in 1215, and is one of the most fundamental rights known to the English-speaking world. Filing of a writ of *habeas corpus* is the procedure generally used to free a suspect from police custody, when the police really do not have evidence on which to file a criminal charge, and the suspect is held for an extended period of time.

ha·ben·dum. A clause in a deed that specifies the type of estate, or property interest, that the buyer is to receive. For example, the buyer may receive only a LIFE ESTATE, or only the mineral rights.

hab·it·a·*bil*·i·ty. The legal requirement that rented property must be suitable for human occupation. This means the landlord has a legal responsibility to make sure the property is vermin-proof, that it will heat properly, that stairs and elevators are safe, etc. Some courts hold that the tenant can withhold rent until such time as the premises are *habitable.*

ha·*bit*·u·al *crim*·i·nal. Under statutory law in some states an individual convicted of any crime, after one or two prior FELONY convictions. Such an individual is called a *habitual criminal,* and is automatically subject to increased penalties for the latest violation. *Habitual criminal* laws vary from state to state as to the number and type of prior convictions required. Five prior MISDEMEANOR convictions may suffice in some states.

ha·*bit*·u·al in·tox·i·*ca*·tion (or habitual drunkenness or habitual intemperance). The constant or habitual use of intoxicating drinks. It does not necessarily imply continual drunkenness, or a fixed daily habit. The legal test is whether the habit is so persistent that it seriously interferes with work or business habits.

har·bor. The crime of clandestinely concealing, providing food, shelter, clothing, a place to live, or the means of getting away for someone wanted for crime. State statutes prohibiting *harboring* vary somewhat.

har·bor·ing. See HARBOR.

harm·less *er*·ror. See ERROR.

hear·ing. (1) An administrative or quasi-judicial hearing conducted under the powers granted to an administrative agency. (2) Any court proceeding in which the parties whose rights are involved have a right to be heard. (3) Any proceedings in a criminal case before a committing magistrate, magistrate setting bail, or making any determination that affects the rights of the accused. **(4)** A public forum conducted by a governmental or monopolistic agency, such as a public utility, where testimony is heard as the rate changes, or new procedures. *Hearings* of this type are usually open to the public, for comment, criticism, or approval.

hear·ing *of*·**fi**·**cer** (or hearing examiner). A quasi-judicial official in a governmental administrative agency that is empowered to hold HEARINGS for that agency on administrative matters. For example, an official of the U.S. Immigration Service may be empowered to hear certain matters that relate to deportation of aliens.

hear·**say**. EVIDENCE that is not within the personal knowledge of the witness in a trial. The basic rule of evidence law is that a witness cannot testify to hearsay. This is because the courts know that the facts are frequently changed or shaded in repetition, and besides, the parties involved should have a basic right to question and confront those who actually furnish information. There are, of course, a number of exceptions to the so-called *hearsay rule*. Hearsay evidence is second-hand evidence.

heart balm act. The popular name given to state statutes that have eliminated or considerably restricted lawsuits based on BREACH OF PROMISE to marry.

heat of *pas*·**sion.** That uncontrollable flare-up of violent temper, resulting from provocation, that causes some individuals to commit crime while in that rage. In CRIMINAL law, this kind of activity reduces the crime of MURDER to the grade of MANSLAUGHTER. This reduction will not be allowed, however, if the accused has time to reflect and to meditate before acting. The *heat of passion doctrine* requires that the accused's act be an almost spontaneous thing. The most common situation where the rule is invoked is the case in which a husband unexpectedly finds his wife in bed with another man, going into a rage and killing the paramour. If the husband knows that this situation has been going on, and the husband lies in wait and kills, the crime is premeditated murder.

heir. An individual who inherits property. One who succeeds to the estate of another, whether the deceased dies without a will, or under the terms of a will. If there is no will, state statutes specify which kin will receive or share in an estate.

he·**re**·*dit*·**a**·**ments.** Anything capable of being inherited.

her·me·*neu*·tics. That systematic body of rules used by judges and legal scholars used to examine the construction and interpretation of legal instruments, or documents.

high crimes and mis·de·*mean*·ors. There has never been any adjudication as to what is meant by this phrase, and there is considerable conjecture among constitutional lawyers. Article II, Section 4 of the U.S. Constitution provides for removal of the President through IMPEACHMENT for, and conviction of, treason, bribery, or other "high crimes and misdemeanors."

hold. (1) To take possession lawfully, or by right of title. (2) The action of a court, in deciding or adjudicating a matter in dispute before the court. (3) To bind, or to obligate, as to *hold* someone to a contract. (4) To take an estate, as a tenant, on condition of paying rent. (5) To have earned, or been awarded, such as a law degree. (6) To keep control or authority over, or to keep in legal custody, such as to *hold* the prisoner. (7) To administer, such as to *hold* an election, or to *hold* court. (8) To retain or keep an object.

hold *harm*·less. A type of surety agreement, to pay any monetary costs that may arise out of a particular transaction. For example, a manufacturer of parts for a mechanical toy may sign an agreement with the principal manufacturer of the toy to stand good for any lawsuits resulting from malfunctions or injuries to the public that may be directly traceable to the first manufacturer's part. This would be a *hold harmless* agreement.

hold·**er.** One who has legally come into possession of a NEGOTIABLE INSTRUMENT, such as a check, or bill or exchange, and may therefore be legally entitled to payment on the instrument.

hold·**er in due course.** One who has legal possession of a NEGOTIABLE INSTRUMENT, having obtained it in good faith and without any knowledge of fraud or dishonesty involving the instrument. It must be obtained for value, and without notice that it is overdue, or that payment has been refused, or that the maker has a defense against it.

hold·**ing.** (1) The basic ruling in a judge's decision. Subsequent judges and subsequent courts are, of course, bound by precedent, and will usually follow the *holding* of a prior judge in the same situation. (2) A tract of land held under a lease or rental agreement for agricultural or grazing purposes.

hold·**ing *com*·pa·ny.** A company that owns so much stock in one or more other companies that the parent company (*holding company*) has dominance or control over the other companies.

hol·o·graph. Any document or instrument prepared wholly in the handwriting (not hand printing) of the individual making the document, and whose signature it bears.

hol·o·*graph*·ic will. A WILL prepared wholly in the handwriting of the person making the will. Wills of this type are not always accepted as valid wills under some state statutes, and are completely unacceptable in some states.

***home*·stead ex·*emp*·tion.** Statutory enactments in many states permitting the head of a family to designate a house and land as the family *homestead*, and exempting this property from execution for the general debts of the family head. Most states limit the value of the house and the amount of acreage in the homestead designation. Usually, the head of the household is required to file a form with the county or state recorder, putting the homestead right on notice for creditors. In most states the location of the homestead may be changed from one piece of property to another if the family moves, and the family must actually live in the house that is claimed as the *homestead exemption*.

hom·i·cide. The killing of one human being by another. *Homicide* is a necessary part of the crime of murder or manslaughter, but not all *homicides* are necessarily criminal. *Homicide* in self defense by a police officer who is being fired upon by a bank robber is not criminal. The wrongful killing of a human being, however, is either murder or manslaughter under statutory provisions or under the common law.

hon·or. (1) A customary title of respect given to judges, especially those of the higher courts. (2) To accept and pay a bill of exchange when due, and according to its terms. This includes items such as bank checks and promissory notes.

***horn*·book.** A basic treatise on a legal subject that sets out principles and rules of law dealing with various aspects of the subject. Most law schools use the so-called CASE METHOD in teaching, rather than a *hornbook*. *Hornbooks* are frequently used by law students, along with course outlines, to supplement the case study method. See CASE METHOD.

***hos*·tage.** (1) One held for ransom. (2) One held by a criminal to guarantee the safety or to permit the escape of the criminal. (3) A person held as SECURITY in time of war, to stand as performance for a contract with or promise to a belligerent power.

hos·**tile** *wit*·**ness.** A witness subpoenaed to testify by one side that unexpectedly exhibits prejudice or hostility against the side that called the witness. When this happens, the courts allow the *hostile witness* to be cross-examined in detail, as though he or she had been called to testify by the other side.

house·**break**·**ing.** The breaking and entering into a dwelling with the intent to commit a felony therein. Sometimes the term is used synonymously with BURGLARY. By statute in some states *housebreaking* is a crime, with housebreaking between the hours of sunset and sunrise being called burglary. Under some statutes *housebreaking* is classified as a type of burglary. Some laws prohibit breaking out of a house after gaining access by stealth or without breaking.

house·**hold.** Those in a family who dwell under the same roof. A *household* also usually includes any servants who live with the family. The individuals living together will legally constitute a *household,* although the breadwinner may be temporarily working in another state.

hung *ju*·**ry.** A JURY that cannot arrive at a VERDICT, after deliberation and vote. When this happens, the case may be tried a second time. When there is obvious disagreement, the trial judge may sometimes point out to the assembled jury that the group has a responsibility to arrive at a just verdict, overlooking personal foibles and arriving at substantial justice.

hy·*poth*·**e**·**cate.** To give or pledge a thing as security, without the necessity of giving up possession of it. For example, the owner of a ship may *hypothecate* a ship and its cargo to raise money to pay the sailors to make a voyage. See also BOTTOMRY.

hy·**po**·*thet*·**i**·**cal** *ques*·**tion (or hypothetical legal question).**

I

ibid. See IBIDEM.

i·**bi**·**dem.** (Latin) In the same place. Generally used to mean on the same page.

i·**dem.** (Latin–*eye*·dem, *ee*·dem) The aforesaid; the same; something previously mentioned.

i·*den*·ti·ty. That sameness of personal characteristics, individuality, qualities, appearance, etc., of a person or thing before the court, with the person charged, or the sameness of the thing claimed or represented to be. Fingerprints are among the most obvious ways of establishing personal *identity,* since no two individuals have ever been found to have prints that match completely.

ig·no·mi·ny. Dishonorable or disgraceful conduct, especially on the part of a public official.

ig·no·ran·tia le·gis nem·in·em ex·cu·sat. (Latin-igg·noe·*ran*·she·uh *leh*·jis *neh*·min·um ecks·*kyoo*·zott) Ignorance of the law excuses no one.

il·*le*·gal. Contrary to, or forbidden by law.

il·le·*git*·i·mate. (1) Contrary to law. (2) Born out of wedlock.

il·*lic*·it. Prohibited by law; unlawful.

im·ma·*te*·ri·al. Not pertinent to the issue at hand; not essential or of serious consequence. Not decisive.

im·*me*·di·ate cause. In TORT law, the most recent in a chain or series of causes that results in injury or damage. See PROXIMATE CAUSE.

im·*me*·di·ate *is*·sue. Children. *Immediate issue* is sometimes distinguished from immediate descent, although at times they may mean the same thing. In the event a grandfather leaves property to a grandchild, since the father is dead, it is said that property goes by *immediate descent,* but not to immediate issue.

im·mi·nent *dan*·ger. That kind of danger which must be instantly met to avoid serious consequences. To justify killing in self defense under the laws pertaining to justifiable homicide, the *imminent danger* must be of a serious kind and such an immediate threat that it could not be prevented by sending for the protection of the law.

im·*mu*·ni·ty. (1) A freedom from a legal burden, such as a charitable organization or church that has immunity from property taxes. (2) An exemption from criminal prosecution, granted to one who agrees to testify against other criminal associates or conspirators.

im·*pan*·el. To assemble and select qualified persons to sit as a jury in a civil or criminal trial, or as a grand jury. See EMPANEL.

im·*peach*. (1) In evidence law, to call in question and to discredit the testimony of a witness by calling other witnesses who testify in contradiction. (2) To bring an accusation against a public official, as the first phase of removal from public office for crime or misfeasance.

Through custom, the general public has come to use the term *impeachment* to refer to the quasi criminal trial proceeding itself.

im·*ped·i·ment*. A bar, hindrance, disability, or obstruction to the making of a valid contract. For example, an existing marriage is an *impediment* to a valid contract of marriage. Commitment for insanity would be an *impediment* to a contract to purchase an automobile.

im·*plead*. To bring in additional parties after a lawsuit has been filed.

im·*plied*. Understood without being directly expressed; understood by indirection or as an inference, from attendant words and circumstances, rather than that which is expressly stated. Gathered by deduction from the conduct of the parties, by the general tenor of language, and by the surrounding circumstances. If a student gave another student a ticket for the cafeteria line, saying, "Here, it is yours," it could fairly be *implied* that the student receiving the ticket had permission to use it.

im·*plied a·*gen·cy. An AGENCY relationship recognized by the courts, in which a third party is led to believe an actual agent-principal relationship exists, based on reasonable inferences or conclusions from the relationships and activities of the other parties. See AGENCY.

im·*plied no·*tice. See IMPUTED KNOWLEDGE.

im·*plied rem·*e·dy. A right to sue (a legal REMEDY) that is inherent in rights recognized by the courts as provided by the U.S. Constitution or statutes. For example, the Constitution sets out no provisions for filing a private lawsuit if not permitted to attend a church service. The courts say the right to sue is inherent in the enjoyment of the Constitutional right to freedom of religion.

im·*plied war·*ran·ty. A WARRANTY that automatically comes into existence when a merchant sells goods, guaranteeing that items sold are fit for the purpose for which such goods would ordinarily be used. This guarantee applies even though it is never expressed verbally or in writing. For example, a store that sells a boat has given an *implied warranty* that it will float when placed on the water. If built in such a way that it consistently capsizes in calm water, then obviously the merchandise does not meet the standards for which a boat would ordinarily be used.

im·pos·si·*bil·i·ty*. That which is not capable of being done. When it turns out that a contract is impossible of performance, it is considered as legally void. Sometimes this impossibility is physical in nature, or is caused by some supervening event which renders performance either physically or legally impossible. A trapeze artist signed a contract to perform personally at each public appearance of a circus. To cut expenses, the circus subsequently scheduled performances in two nearby towns at the same time, with half of the acts being performed at each of the locations. Since the trapeze artist could not perform in two places at once, the appearance at each place became an *impossibility*.

im·post. A tax, usually a duty on imported goods.

im·*pound*. (1) To take and hold a document, evidence, etc., in the custody of a court, pending a determination as to whether it is genuine. (2) To hold an improperly controlled, improperly registered or stray animal in detention. (3) To gather and enclose water for irrigation, under laws pertaining to RIPARIAN RIGHTS.

im·*pris*·on·ment. (1) Confinement of an individual in jail, prison, or other place of confinement, by legal authorities or under due process of law. (2) Confinement that prevents the free exercise of an individual's power to move about. This may result, not from the actual use of locks, bars, etc., but from a display of force that takes away personal liberty. If this deprivation occurs without lawful authority, it is termed *false imprisonment*.

im·*pute*. To credit to, attribute, or charge; to lay blame or responsibility to someone, falsely or not.

im·*put*·ed *knowl*·edge. Sometimes used interchangeably with IMPLIED NOTICE. Knowledge that an individual is charged with possessing, since the facts in question were easily available, and the person charged had a duty to keep himself or herself advised. For example, the owner of a machine shop has *imputed knowledge* of unsafe working conditions in the establishment, since a state statute requires the owner and management to stay abreast of such conditions at all times.

im·*put*·ed *neg*·li·gence. Those damages or injuries that are chargeable to an individual owner, or other owners of a commercial venture, owing to the negligence or injuries (TORTS) caused by employees or agents of the owner (principal). By statute in some jurisdictions, negligence is imputed to the owner of the family car, when driven by any family member.

im·*put*·ed *no*·tice. That kind of knowledge which is charged or ascribed to an individual, even though there is no showing that this individual has actual knowledge. It is that which the individual is obligated or bound to know, from a legal standpoint. For example, a grocer may inform the agent of a canning company that a shipment of canned peaches was spoiled on arrival, and not acceptable. This notice to the agent, who is the representative of the cannery, is *imputed notice* to the owners or managers of the cannery.

in·ad·*mis*·si·ble. Cannot be allowed, accepted or used. For example, if evidence is improperly obtained through an illegal search, the evidence from the search will be *inadmissible* if the matter comes to trial.

in·*al*·ien·able. (1) Cannot be taken away, sold, or transferred. For example, we are all born with certain *inalienable* rights, according to the United States Constitution. (2) Certain objects, such as public roadways, navigable rivers, waters in the bay, etc., are not subject to private ownership or control, and are legally said to be *inalienable*.

in blank. The type of indorsement on a NEGOTIABLE INSTRUMENT (check promissory note, etc.) which makes it payable to anyone who is a legal holder (an indorsee), without restrictions. A mere signature of the indorser on the back is such an indorsement *in blank*.

in *cam*·er·a. In chambers, or in the judge's chambers. A hearing *in camera* is either a hearing in the judge's private chambers, or a hearing in the courtroom when all spectators have been excluded.

in·ca·*pac*·i·ty. Lack of legal ability to act. An insane person is legally *incapacitated* to sign business contracts. In some instances minors may make voidable contracts that can be either ratified or voided when legal *incapacity* is removed by reaching the age of majority.

in·car·cer·*a*·tion. Imprisonment; confinement in a house of detention, jail, or prison, by competent public authority or due legal process. Mere confinement alone may constitute false IMPRISONMENT, KIDNAPPING, or some other criminal violation.

in·cest. Sexual relations or COHABITATION between individuals too closely related to be legally married. *Incest* is a crime in most jurisdictions. Statutes in these jurisdictions set out degrees of family relationship wherein marriage is prohibited. Intercourse between individuals within these relationships constitutes *incest*. For example, a relationship between an aunt and a nephew is the kind that may be prohibited, or father and daughter.

in·*cho*·ate. That which is begun but not completed. An *inchoate crime* may be an attempted crime that was frustrated short of completion. It may not be possible to sustain a prosecution for the substantive crime, because some of the essential elements of the crime are lacking. For example, an assailant may be successfully prosecuted for some variation of the *inchoate crime*—aggravated assault, assault with a deadly weapon, or attempted rape, since a prosecution for rape would not hold up in court.

in·*cite*. To provoke; to urge to action; to instigate; to stir up; to induce another to commit a crime. In some usages the word is synonymous with the term ABET.

in *com*·mon. The use, enjoyment, benefits, or title in property that is held jointly for equal advantage of all owners, without division into individual shares of ownership.

in·*com*·pe·ten·cy. Lack of legal qualifications or physical fitness to handle one's own legal problems. *Incompetency* may include mental disabilities such as insanity, chronic drunkenness that robs of reason, or physical illness that debilitates. The law will usually appoint a guardian to look after the interests of *incompetents.*

in·cor·po·*ra*·tion. The process whereby a stock company or CORPORATION is created. *Incorporation* is usually regulated and controlled by statutes administered by the state Secretary of State.

in·cor·*po*·re·al her·e·*dit*·a·ments. Any kind of property that can be inherited, but which is not tangible property, such as a share of stock.

in·cre·ment. That which is added, increased, or gained. The process of augmenting or growing.

in·*crim*·i·nate. (1) To involve oneself or another individual in criminal activity. **(2)** To accuse or charge another with a crime.

in·*croach*. See ENCROACH.

in·*cul*·pate. To accuse of a crime; to impute guilt or criminal responsibility.

in·*cum*·bent. (1) One who is already the holder of an office, usually used in connection with an elected public official. **(2)** Dependent upon.

in·*cum*·ber. To make real property subject to a MORTGAGE, LIEN, or other legal claim that will be a burden on the TITLE.

in·*cum*·brance. A charge or LIEN against land. *Incumbrances* include MORTGAGES, judgments against the owner, LIENS, writs of execution, or any other binding liability against the property.

in·de·*feas*·i·ble. Not capable of being voided, annulled, or undone. For example, a lawyer may say that an estate in FEE SIMPLE is indefeasible

—there are no conditions or restrictions that keep the owner from absolute enjoyment of the estate.

in·*dem*·ni·ty. **(1)** A collateral contract for the reimbursement of losses sustained by the results of one's actions, or by the actions of the third party. Insurance is a contract of *indemnity.* **(2)** Reimbursement for a wrong already sustained, as where the National Art Gallery would give *indemnity* to the owner of a picture loaned for display to the art gallery. **(3)** A statutory enactment, exempting a class of persons from prosecution for failure to do their duty. For example, a legislative enactment (rather than a Presidential pardon) excusing draft evaders would be an *indemnity.*

in·*den*·ture. Any written legal agreement, such as a contract or a deed.

in·de·*ter*·mi·nate. Inexact; indefinite; uncertain. A limited number of states use an *indeterminate sentencing* procedure, in which the sentencing judge sets a minimum and a maximum sentence. Special boards thereafter decide the exact time to be served within the limits set by the judge, based on the prisoner's apparent progress toward rehabilitation.

in·*dict*·ment. A formal accusation of crime, which suffices to begin a criminal prosecution based on the accusation. The *indictment* is voted by a GRAND JURY on the basis of evidence furnished to that body. The *indictment* is then returned to the court by which the grand jury was impaneled. See *presentment.*

in·di·gent. One who is without any substantial amount of money; one who is needy and poor; one who does not have the means for subsistence. An *indigent* charged with a serious crime is entitled to a lawyer at government or state expense, as a matter of right.

in·di·*rect* at·*tack*. See COLLATERAL ATTACK.

in·*dorse*·ment. One who writes his or her name upon the back of a NEGOTIABLE INSTRUMENT (check, promissory note, etc.) otherwise than as maker or acceptor, and delivers it with the new signature thereon to another person. Each INDORSEMENT is a new and substantive contract by which TITLE to the instrument is passed, and by which the indorser becomes a party to the instrument and is liable for its payment under most conditions. For example, a grocer may endorse a check which has been received from a customer. If the grocer gives the check to a wholesaler, and the check is worthless when de-

112

posited by the wholesaler, the bank goes back on the last indorser (wholesaler), who goes back on the next to last indorser (grocer and so on. By adding some words, along with his or her signature, the indorser can make a RESTRICTIVE ENDORSEMENT, QUALIFIED INDORSEMENT, CONDITIONAL INDORSEMENT, etc., changing the legal relationship with subsequent holders. See those terms.

in·*duce*·ment. (1) In contract law, the monetary benefit or other advantage which the promissor is to receive on that side of the bargain as motive or incentive for the agreement. (2) In criminal law, that motive which led the criminal to commit the violation. (3) In legal pleadings, the explanatory introduction and background preparatory to the main allegations or claims for relief.

in *es*·se. (Latin) *In existence.* That which actually exists, as distinguished from that which will come into being. Before birth, a child is *in posse;* after birth the child is *in esse.*

in *ev*·i·dence. (1) Testimony or facts that have already been submitted before the court as evidence. (2) Those facts that are accepted as already having proved, based on the evidence previously submitted.

in ex·*ten*·so. (Latin) At full length. Leaving out nothing.

in ex·*tre*·mis. (Latin) At the last gasp. In the final stage of life.

in·fa·mous crime. A crime punishable by imprisonment in the state prison or penitentiary, with or without hard labor. (This is the definition under Federal law and most states, but there are variations in some states.) At COMMON LAW, one who committed an infamous crime was not considered competent to serve as a witness in court. This was on the idea that a person would not commit so heinous a crime unless that individual was so depraved as to be unworthy of belief under oath. This idea is still followed in some jurisdictions.

in·fa·my. Public disgrace; a total lack of character in public esteem. See INFAMOUS CRIME.

in·fan·cy. The legal state of one who has not yet reached majority (age 21 under the common law, but varying from jurisdiction to jurisdiction).

in·*fe*·ri·or court. Any court of lesser rank than the court of LAST RESORT, or highest ranking tribunal. The court of last resort, or last appeal, is the Supreme Court in the Federal court system and in most states. However, this is not true in all states, such as New York State.

in·*fir*·mi·ty. (1) Any legal defect, or lack. (2) In insurance law, any injury or illness that affects health to a substantial degree.

in *for*·ma *pau*·pe·ris. (Latin–in *for*·muh paw·*pair*·iss) *In the manner of a pauper.* The procedure whereby a court may allow a pauper to file a lawsuit, even though the pauper may not have the money needed to pay filing fees and court costs. The courts look to the substantial injustice that could be created by withholding the right to sue, due to lack of money.

in·for·*ma*·tion. An accusation charging an individual with the commission of a crime. It differs from an INDICTMENT only in that it is filed by the prosecutor or other designated public official, rather than being a presentment by vote of a GRAND JURY. It is usually a simpler way to proceed in a criminal prosecution. In some states and in the Federal system only misdemeanors are prosecuted by information, and any person accused of a FELONY must be INDICTED. In those jurisdictions the accused can, of course, waive indictment and proceed to trial. In a few jurisdictions, an information must be filed as a preliminary to seeking an indictment.

in·fra. (Latin) Under. Below; underneath; beneath; sometimes meaning within.

in·*frac*·tion. A violation of law; a breach of a contract; an infringement or violation of a right.

in·*fringe*·ment. An interference with legal rights of another; especially used to designate an infraction or violation of copyright, trademark, or patent laws.

in fu·*tu*·ro. (Latin–in few·*too*·roe) *In the future.* At a future time.

in·*her*·ent *pow*·er. A power or authority within the thing itself. For example, a policeman has an *inherent power,* arising out of his position, to make arrests for violations of the law.

in·*her*·ent·ly *dan*·ger·ous. That instrumentality or condition that is dangerous within itself, by the very character or nature of its properties. A stick of dynamite is *inherently dangerous,* while a cord of firewood would not be.

in·*her*·i·tance. That property, real or personal, which is received from a deceased person, either under the terms of a will or by laws of descent from an ancestor.

114

in·*her*·i·tance tax. A tax on the transfer or passage of property by legacy, devise, or INTESTATE SUCCESSION. In other words, it is a tax on the transfer of property from the dead to the living. It is not a tax on the property itself, but on the legal right to acquire it.

in·*i*·ti·a·tive. A procedure whereby voters propose new laws and enact or reject these proposals at the polls, regardless of the fact that the legislature has the authority to enact new laws. The *initiative* procedure is used in instances where the legislature ignores the legislative needs and desires of the people.

in·*junc*·tion. An order or writ issued by a judge requiring the individual to whom it is directed to take some specific action or to refrain from doing a particular thing. In a typical case, an *injunction* would order an individual to cease a wrongful kind of conduct that is harmful to another, restraining the wrongdoer from the continuance of this conduct. If the wrongdoer persists after issuance of the *injunction,* the judge will order the arrest of the wrongdoer for contempt. An *injunction* may be issued in cases where substantial justice could not be done by waiting for the wrongdoer to go ahead and commit a threatened wrong that may not be adequately compensated for in a lawsuit.

*in·*jure. **(1)** To do damage or harm. **(2)** To violate the legal rights of others.

*in·*ju·ry. Damage or wrong done to another, either to person, property, or reputation. Injury is used interchangeably with DAMAGE or LOSS.

in·*jus*·tice. Unfairness. The denial of justice. In legal context, this term is usually used to imply fault, omission, or error on the part of a court, as distinguished from the mistake of an individual.

in lo·co pa·ren·tis. (Latin–in *loe*·koe puh·*ren*·tis, *instead of a parent*) A substitute parent in the eyes of the law. Juvenile courts act *in loco parentis* for juvenile wards or orphans under the jurisdiction of the court. In legal terms, one who adopts a child must act *in loco parentis.*

in med·i·as res. (Latin–in *may*·dee·as race, *Into the heart of the subject*) Getting directly into the matter.

*in·*no·cent. Lacking in guilt; not guilty. One who acts in good faith.

in·nu·*en*·do. (1) In legal pleading, an explanatory phrase or parenthetical explanation introduced into the text of a legal document. (2) An indirect accusation or aspersion.

in·*op*·er·a·tive. Not functioning, or not in effect. A contract may have *inoperative* provisions that do not go into effect except in the event of a breach by one of the parties.

in pa·ri de·lic·to. (Latin–in *pah*·ree duh·*lick* toe, at equal fault) In many legal situations where both parties are equally at fault, the law will leave the case as it finds it, *in pari delicto.*

in per·*so*·nam. (Latin–in per·*soe*·num, against the person) A legal suit brought to enforce rights against, or with reference to, a particular person. This is distinguished from a lawsuit *in rem,* or an enforcement of rights against the whole world. A lawsuit for injuries caused by another individual who wilfully struck the plaintiff with an ax would be *in personam,* since it would be a judgment against an individual. A lawsuit to settle title to a tract of land would be an action *in rem,* since it has for its object the settlement of ownership of property, without reference to the title of individual claimants, and the judgment is binding against the whole world.

in·quest. An inquiry conducted by a group of individuals, called together by law, to inquire into any situation that needs judicial examination. Historically, a grand jury was sometimes termed the *grand inquest.* In modern law, an *inquest* usually means an inquiry held by a jury before a coroner to ascertain the cause of any death under suspicious circumstances.

in·quis·i·*to*·ri·al *sys*·tem. The court system, or trial system, used in most European countries, excluding England. The *inquisitorial system* differs from the so-called adversary system used in England, the United States, Canada, and other nations with a COMMON LAW or British law background. In the *inquisitorial system,* the judge is not a completely impartial official, representing justice, but not obligated to either side. The judge may act as a combination presiding judge and prosecutor, and may also take the initiative in digging out facts that prove the guilt of an accused criminal. Both systems strive for justice, by taking different approaches. See ADVERSARY SYSTEM.

in re. (Latin–in ray, *in the matter of*) Used in writing the caption, entitling a judicial proceeding in which there are no adversary parties, but the matter must nevertheless be adjudicated. For example, *In re U.S. Highway 91.* A child neglect case might be entitled, *In re Irene Smith.*

in rem. See IN PERSONAM.

in·*san*·i·ty. Madness, mental derangement, or unsoundness of mind, not including certain types of transitory mental disorders such as *delirium, epilepsy, intoxication, hysteria, shock,* or *trance. Insanity* is sometimes described as a prolonged departure of the individual from his or her natural mental state. The English and American criminal law has long held to the principle that an individual would not be punished for criminal acts unless there was sufficient mental capacity and moral freedom to do or to abstain from doing the prohibited act. As said by the Supreme Court of the United States (U.S. v. Fielding, 251 F. 2d 878), "Our collective conscience does not allow punishment where it does not impose blame." Legal tests for insanity are not uniform throughout the state courts. Most courts hold that the accused is not insane unless the accused is mentally unable to distinguish right from wrong. Some other courts use the so-called *irresistable impulse* test, while others say that the jury must simply decide from the entirety of all the facts, taken together.

in·*sol*·ven·cy. Inability to pay one's debts. If assets and liabilities were all immediately available, the former would not be sufficient to pay off the latter.

in·*sol*·vent. (1) An individual or firm that is unable to pay bills or debts as they come due in the regular course of business. Some court cases have qualified this term, however, stating that an individual or firm that has sufficient property subject to legal process to satisfy all legal demands is not an insolvent. **(2)** Being unable to pay bills.

in spec·ie. (Latin–in *speece·*ee, *in kind*) In the same or like form or kind. If a riding horse is loaned and is to be returned *in specie,* then the same animal is to be returned. If a farmer places wheat in a grain elevator, *to be returned in the same grade, but not in specie,* then the identical wheat need not be returned so long as it is of the same grade.

in·*stall*·ments. One of the parts into which a debt is divided when payment is made at successive intervals. Each of the parts may be referred to as an *installment,* or an *installment payment.* Partial payments on a debt at specified payment intervals.

in•sti•**gate.** To incite, or stir on to some action, such as a crime. To cause by fomenting or inciting. See ABET.

in•*struc*•**tions.** The guidance that is given by a judge to a jury, informing the jurors how they should go about their duties. The judge may list the facts to be decided by the jury, and make a statement concerning the law that applies to the case at hand, and which phases of law the jury is bound to accept and apply in this matter. In the *instructions* the judge may also point out the problems of proof, the weight to be given to testimony, and which party has the legal burden to prove the case.

in•*stru*•**ment.** A writing made for a legal purpose, such as a deed, a contract, a will, or a check. An *instrument* may record a legal right, transfer money or property, or serve as written evidence of a transaction.

in•**suf**•*fi*•**cien**•**cy.** In legal pleading, the inadequacy of an answer which does not specifically and adequately respond to the charges, allegations, or interrogatories set forth in the pleadings of the other party.

in•*sur*•**a**•**ble** *in*•**ter**•**est.** Any interest in property, or liability in respect thereto, of such a kind that a loss or peril might directly cause financial loss, is an *insurable interest*. For example, if you own a home you would be caused serious loss if it burned to the ground. You therefore have such an interest in the home that it is insurable. Somewhat similarly, if you have a reasonable expectation of financial benefit from the continued life of an individual, then you have an *insurable interest* on which life insurance can be based. Usually, this relationship arises from marriage or family relationships. But business partners can likewise insure the lives of the partners to compensate for financial losses that would probably arise if one should die.

in•*sur*•**ance.** A contract agreement between two parties (the insurer and the insured) that in consideration of a payment or series of payments made by the insured (premiums), the insurer agrees to compensate the other against loss, damage, or liability on a specified event happening during a given time in the future. An agreement to reimburse for specified types of loss, should they occur.

in•*sured.* An individual whose property or life is insured. See INSURANCE.

in·*sur*·er. An insurance company or underwriter; one that insures. See INSURANCE.

in·*tan*·gi·ble. That property which has no real marketable or intrinsic value, but which is evidence of value or worth. A bond, stock certificate, promissory note, or franchise is each an example of an *intangible.*

in·te·grat·ed bar. An association of all those lawyers in a state who have a right to practice law in that state. Most states by statute have conferred authority on the state's highest court to integrate and supervise the bar. Each member of the *integrated bar* is expected to perform public services when called upon in turn, such as defending indigents in the criminal courts when there is no available public defender. When we say that "John Smith is a member of the bar," we mean the *integrated bar,* rather than a voluntary association. And by *passing the bar,* we mean passing the examinations given for membership of the integrated bar, carrying the right to practice law in that area.

in·*teg*·ri·ty. **(1)** Incorruptibility; honesty; of unquestioned moral uprightness. **(2)** That which is sound, or unimpaired.

in·*tent*. The purpose, design, or resolve with which a person acts. In TORT law, the general principle is that a wrongdoer is personally responsible for deliberate or wilful acts, regardless of good intent. In criminal law, the MENS REA or criminal state of mind is a specific requirement or element of crime. *Intent and motive do not have the same meaning in criminal law. Generally, in a criminal prosecution the courts say that the offender must have the intent* to do the forbidden (criminal) act—the criminal *intent* requirement is satisfied if the accused actually meant to do what he or she did, regardless of *motive.* Mental *intent* is rarely susceptible to direct proof, but must usually be inferred from all the attendant circumstances.

in·ter a·li·a. (Latin–*in*·ter *ay*·lee·uh) *Among other things.*

in·*ter*·est. **(1)** The ownership of any kind of right in real property of chattels. **(2)** The monetary return that is payable for the use of money, with the rate of such payment expressed as a percentage.

in·ter·*loc*·u·to·ry. Temporary; provisional; not final. An *interlocutory decree* or order is provisional until a legal disagreement is settled.

in·ter·*plead*·er. A legal proceeding that enables a person holding money or property to compel other parties claiming the money or property to litigate the matter between themselves. The administrator of an estate, for example, may hold a large sum of money left by an individual who died. The deceased had one child, who disappeared. After the reported death, two men appear on the scene, both claiming to be entitled to the money as the long lost son. Laying no claim to the money himself, the *administrator* may file a bill of INTER-PLEADER with the court handling this matter, forcing the two claimants to settle the matter in a binding lawsuit. The administrator can then turn the money over to the litigant who is legally determined to be the missing son, without fear of a lawsuit from the other claimant.

in·ter·*rog*·a·to·ries. (1) A series of written questions used in the judicial examination of a witness or a party to a lawsuit. They are usually prepared by the counsel for one side, and must be answered in writing, under oath, by the adversary or the adversary's witnesses. The questions are answered before an examiner or commissioner, who is a court functionary. Usually these questions are a part of the formal portion of a lawsuit, and are answered before trial. (2) Sometimes *interrogatories* are written questions that are directed to any witness, rather than an adverse witness or party to the lawsuit.

***in*·ter·state.** That which is between places in two states. An *interstate violation* involves the crossing of the boundary from one state to another.

***in*·ter·state *com*·pact.** A treaty or agreement between states, passed into law by the Congress of the United States. For example, both Arizona and California lay claim to the irrigation water from the Colorado River, which separates the states. The rights to the water may be settled by approval of the two state legislatures, followed by statutory approval by Congress, in an *interstate compact.*

in·ter·*ven*·ing cause. In TORT law, the act that intervenes, or comes between the eventual act and the original act that set circumstances in motion to cause injury or damage. It is an act initiated by an independent agency which destroys the causal connection between the negligence and the injury. The independent (second) act becomes the immediate cause, and damages are not recoverable from the wrongdoer who acted originally, since the original wrongful act is not the proximate cause. See PROXIMATE CAUSE.

in·ter·*ven*·or. One who voluntarily interposes in a lawsuit or other legal proceeding, with the permission of the court.

in·ter vi·vos. (Latin–*in*·ter *vee*·voce, *among the living*) Between individuals who are alive at the time of the transaction. An *inter vivos* trust is generally called a LIVING TRUST, which see.

in·*tes*·ta·cy. The condition of dying without leaving a valid will. If only part of an individual's property is disposed of by will, that individual is said to have died *intestate* as to that portion of the property.

in·*tes*·tate. (1) Dying without leaving a valid will. (2) The legal term for one who dies without leaving a valid will.

in·*tes*·tate suc·*ces*·sion. The passing on of property to heirs if a valid will is not left by the deceased.

in tes·ti·mo·ni·um. (Latin–in tes·ti·*moe*·nee·yum, *in witness*) A legal phrase that states the writing of that particular document authenticates itself, and that the writing can be trusted to verify its authenticity.

in *to*·to. Completely, or wholly. If a court holds that an award of damages is void *in toto,* then no award is allowed.

in·tra·*state*. Within the same state.

in·*trin*·sic *ev*·i·dence. The bare evidence learned from a document itself, without any testimony to explain the document or the circumstances under which it was prepared or used.

in·*ure*. To accrue to the benefit of; to result, or take effect.

in·*val*·id. Without any legal effect or force. Completely lacking in authority.

in·*vi*·tee. An individual invited to come on the premises to conduct business for the benefit of the property holder. For example, a customer invited into a retail store to look at merchandise is an *invitee,* whether or not the customer makes a purchase. In TORT law, the courts say that more care is required from the property holder to protect *invitees* from personal injury than others permitted on the property. The courts usually say there are three standards of care, with the minimum protection owed to a TRESPASSER, next to a so-called LICENSEE, and the greatest duty owed to an *invitee.* The standard of care required of the property holder is greater to the extent that the presence of individuals on the property is helpful or profitable to the property holder. See LICENSEE.

in·*vol*·un·ta·ry. Without the power of free will or choice.

in·*vol*·un·ta·ry *man* slaugh·ter. The killing of a human being while committing an unlawful act not amounting to a felony, or while committing an act without due circumspection and caution. For example, a hunter failed to obtain a hunting license, and had committed a MISDEMEANOR by hunting without this permission. While so involved, the hunter mistook a second hunter for a deer, shooting and killing the latter. Since there was no premeditated intent to kill, and since the hunter was acting illegally, this killing would be *involuntary manslaughter* in some jurisdictions. In another example, an individual made a practice of shooting at a target behind his back. The target was located along a pathway that was sometimes used by neighbors going to the village store. The shooter never looked when he shot, and he killed a neighborhood child. This was also *involuntary manslaughter,* since the shooter did not use the kind of circumspection or caution that any reasonable person would use.

ip·so *fact*·o. (Latin) By the fact itself. As a consequence of the fact that; because of the fact that.

ir·*rel*·e·vant. Not relating to the matter in question; not to the point; not pertinent. Evidence is not allowed in a trial when it is irrelevant, that is, when it neither tends to prove nor disprove the matters in issue.

ir·*rep*·a·ra·ble *in*·ju·ry. The kind of harm that will not be recompensed by a money award alone, and that is so serious that a court may issue an injunction against the individual who appears about to commit the injury.

ir·re·*sist*·i·ble *im*·pulse. A term used in criminal law to mean an inner urging or impulse to commit a criminal act, which cannot be resisted by the actor because mental disease or insanity has destroyed freedom of will or power to control actions.

ir·rev·*o*·ca·ble. That which cannot be revoked, recalled, or withdrawn.

is·sue. (1) Descendants; offspring; progeny. (2) To send out, or promulgate, such as a search warrant, writ, etc. (3) A legal point of dispute between two or more parties. (4) A block of stock or bonds placed on sale.

J

jail. A building used for the confinement of individuals awaiting trial, or who have been convicted of minor offenses. The term PRISON is sometimes used interchangeably with *jail,* but PRISON is usually the place where only those with long-term sentences are confined. *Jail* is distinguishable from a *lockup,* which is a temporary holding cage used to confine those who have just been arrested.

J. D. Abbreviation for *Juris Doctor*–a law degree, that has replaced the degree of L.L.B., used in some schools. Law degrees offered by some schools include L.L.M.; L.L.D.; B.L.; J.C.D.; D.C.L., and Doctor of Jurisprudence.

jeop•**ard**•**y.** (1) That hazard or risk under which a prisoner is put when regularly charged with a criminal offense before a competent court. (2) Any danger, peril, hazard, or risk.

join•**der.** The uniting or coupling together of two or more defendants or plaintiffs in some legal process, such as a criminal trial. Defendants frequently ask to be tried separately so the confession of one may not prejudice the jury against the other. Thorny legal problems may arise when the courts decide whether the accused has a right to be tried separately.

joint ad•*ven*•**ture.** An association of persons with intent, by way of CONTRACT, either express or implied, to carry out a single business venture for joint profit. Without creating a partnership or corporation, either in the legal or technical meaning, they agree that there shall be a community of interest. Each coadventurer stands in the relation of PRINCIPAL, as well as AGENT, to each of the others, with an equal right of control of the means employed to carry out their common purpose. The coadventurers combine their efforts, property, money, skill, and knowledge, to some extent.

joint and *sev*•**er**•**al.** A debt or liability is described as being *joint and several* when the creditor has the legal right to sue any one of the separate parties, or to proceed against all jointly, at the creditor's option.

joint *ten·an·cy.* A form of co-ownership of real property. *Joint tenancy* is regarded as a single estate, held by two or more persons jointly. Legally, such *joint tenants* hold as though they collectively constituted but one person, a fictitious entity. The main characteristic of *joint tenancy* is the right of survivorship. When a *joint tenant* dies, that individual's interest in the land is terminated, and the ownership continues in the survivor or survivors. When there is but one survivor, the estate becomes an *estate in severalty* (it is completely owned by the survivor). In some legal documents a joint tenancy is referred to as a *joint tenancy with right of survivor.* See TENANCY IN COMMON, from which *joint tenancy* is distinguished.

joint *ven·ture.* See JOINT ADVENTURE.

J. P. Abbreviation for JUSTICE OF THE PEACE.

judge. (1) A public officer who presides over a court and administers justice. The terms *judge* and *court* are often interchangeable or synonymous. (2) The term is sometimes used to designate all officers appointed to decide administrative or litigated questions, but this is not the meaning of the word in ordinary legal use. (3) To adjudicate, or decide a legal matter.

judge *ad·vo·cate.* A legal officer for military courts, who swears in other members of the court and serves as PROSECUTOR. At the same time the *judge advocate* has some responsibilities to the accused, from a legal standpoint. In some respects the *judge advocate* functions as both judge and lawyer.

judg·ment. The official decision, or adjudication, of a court in a civil lawsuit. A *judgment* may be based on a jury's verdict, or in the absence of a jury, on the law and facts as found by a trial judge. When the rights of the parties have been determined, the *judgment* awarded by the court may consist of monetary damages, and/or an INJUNCTION forbidding the defendant from continuing a wrongful course of conduct. If the defendant fails to appear or fails to contest the lawsuit, the judge may enter a *default judgment,* or *judgment by default.* (Both terms are used.) (See DEFAULT JUDGMENT.) A judgment is sometimes ordered entered by the judge *on the pleadings,* in a situation where the defendant's written answer or pleadings are completely frivolous or fail to put up a defense that is recognized by the courts. See CONSENT JUDGMENT; CONFESSION OF JUDGMENT; CONDITIONAL JUDGMENT. When someone speaks of winning a *judg-*

ment, this is generally known as a monetary judgment, or simply as a judgment. In most states a monetary judgment acts as a judgment lien against all the land owned by the loser in the lawsuit. See JUDGMENT LIEN.

judg‧**ment by de‧***fault.*   Same as DEFAULT JUDGMENT.

judg‧**ment** *cred*‧**i**‧**tor.**   One who has obtained a court judgment against a debtor. The judgment can be used to force execution, that is, sale of the debtor's property to satisfy the amount of the judgment and usually some statutory costs.

judg‧**ment lien.**   A LIEN on all the land of a debtor against whom a court JUDGMENT has been obtained. Purchasers of property and mortgages must undertake a search of judgment records to learn whether there are any *judgment liens* against property about to be purchased or mortgaged. Otherwise, the purchaser buys subject to the lien, and the person loaning money on a mortgage may have only a secondary security interest in the land.

judg‧**ment note.**   A note containing authorization to the clerk of court, to an attorney, or simply to the holder, instructing the individual in possession of the writing to confess a judgment against the maker of the note. In short, it is written permission for a CONFESSION OF JUDGMENT.

judg‧**ment proof.**   An individual who will not be financially harmed by a JUDGMENT against that person. Those without property or assets, or those sheltered by wage protection laws, are sometimes described as *judgment proof.*

ju‧**di**‧**care.**   (Latin) **(1)** To decide or determine judicially. **(2)** A system for providing public financing for those in need of an attorney.

ju‧**di**‧**ca**‧**ture.**   **(1)** That which pertains to the administration of justice. **(2)** That which pertains to the courts or the act of judgment.

ju‧*di*‧**cial.**   **(1)** Pertaining to a court. **(2)** Matters having to do with a judge; of judges and their functions. **(3)** One of the three branches of government—the EXECUTIVE, LEGISLATIVE, and *judicial.*

ju‧*di*‧**cial** *no*‧**tice.**   The court's action in conducting a trial, or in framing a decision, to recognize the existence of certain facts without requiring evidence to prove those facts. This is done on the court's own motion. For example, the court would take *judicial notice* of the fact that the state of Hawaii is not within the continental limits of the United States, or that Valentine's Day fell on Tuesday, February 14,

1978. This can be determined by a glance at a calendar, without bothering to make one side present evidence. In a criminal prosecution or in a lawsuit, the prosecution or the plaintiff may have the burden to prove all the material facts of the case. While the limits of *judicial notice* cannot always be prescribed with exactness, the judge will usually take cognizance of certain facts to save time, since the judge and jurors already know those facts.

ju·*di*·cial re·*view*. The constitutional doctrine that authorizes a court system to review and annul any legislative or executive acts that are unconstitutional, or to interpret laws passed by the legislature.

ju·*di*·ci·ar·y. The branch of government invested with the judicial power; the court system; sometimes the judges in that court system.

ju·rat. A certificate added to an affidavit stating when, before whom, and where it was made. The form of the *jurat* varies slightly from state to state.

ju·*rid*·i·cal. Concerned with the administration of justice or with the functions and duties of the courts and judges.

ju·ris·*dic*·tion. The right, power, or authority to administer justice by hearing and determining legal controversies and trying cases. The legal capacity or authority of a court.

    In order to handle a criminal case, the court must have *jurisdiction* over the subject matter, over the person on trial, and over the class of cases to which that particular trial belongs.

ju·ris·*dic*·tion·al. That which has to do with jurisdiction. See JURISDICTION.

ju·ris·*dic*·tion·al a·*mount*. The amount of monetary claim made in a case, which places the case within the class of litigation handled by a specific court. For example, a particular small claims court may have a *jurisdictional limit* of $500.00. Cases involving claims for a higher amount could not be brought in the small claims court. A Federal court might have authority to handle lawsuits between residents of different states where the claim is more than $5,000.

ju·ris·*pru*·dence. The principles, philosophy, and study of law. The science of law, as it pertains to principles on which legal rules are based, and the way in which new or doubtful cases should be brought into the courts and decided.

ju·rist. (1) A judge. (2) One skilled in international law. (3) Those who have distinguished themselves by writing on legal subjects.

ju·ror. One who serves on a JURY.

ju•ry.   See PETTY (petit jury), GRAND jury, CORONER'S jury, SPECIAL jury.

ju•ry **box.**   An enclosed place in a courtroom in which jurors are seated throughout the course of a trial. It is generally in an elevated area, where the jury can easily observe and hear while remaining segregated from others in the courtroom.

ju•ry **com•***mis***•sion•er.**   An official charged with responsibility for selecting the names to be put into a JURY WHEEL or of drawing a panel of jurors for a particular term of court.

ju•ry **list.**   A written list of persons called to attend court from which a jury will be selected. Sometimes used interchangeably with *jury panel.*

*ju•ry pan•*el.   See JURY LIST.

*ju•ry tri•*al.   Trial by jurors. The right to a *jury trial* in either a criminal or civil case means not merely a trial by a specified number of people, but by qualified and impartial individuals selected by law, with a fair judge who passes on the legal questions involved, and has supervision over the trial. The term *impartial* means that the jurors cannot be related to, nor dependents of, the parties involved. The judge instructs the jurors concerning how the law applies to this particular case, and advises them on the facts. Except on an acquittal on a criminal charge, the judge has power to set aside the findings of the jury if completely contrary to the law or the evidence.

ju•ry **wheel.**   A machine, or lottery wheel arrangement, containing names of persons qualified to serve on juries. Individuals are selected for JURY LISTS by the spin of the wheel.

*ju•ry•***man.**   A juror; one who is called to serve on a jury.

*ju•ry•wo•***man.**   A female juror.

jus.   (Latin) *Law.* **(1)** The entire body of law, as distinguished from a specific statute. **(2)** A specific area of the law, as *jus civile* (civil law). **(3)** A specific right, as *jus accrescendi* (the right of survivorship).

jus bel•li.   (Latin) The law of war; international law as applied to war, defining in particular the rights and duties of combatants and neutral nations.

jus gen•ti•um.   (Latin) International law.

jus ha•ben•di.   (Latin) The right to the property. Usually used to mean the right to be put in actual possession of property.

jus nat•u•ra•le.   (Latin) *Natural law.* See NATURAL LAW.

jus ter·ti·i. (Latin) *The right of a third party.* The right of a party that is not involved in a lawsuit to property that is in dispute between the litigants. For example, a salesman who is being sued for the return of sample merchandise from the supplier, may defend on the basis that the supplier is not the real owner, and that the owner does not want the merchandise returned to the supplier, as the owner has information to the effect that the supplier intends to flee to another state with the items in dispute.

***jus·*tice.** (1) The constant and perpetual intent to render every man his due; impartiality and fairness to all. (2) A title given to judges of the King's Bench and the common pleas in England, and later to judges of the Supreme Court of the United States and of high ranking courts of many of the states.

***jus·*tice of the peace.** (Sometimes abbreviated as J.P.) In most states, a magistrate with jurisdiction over a small district or part of a county. Generally, this official has authority to try minor cases, such as traffic violations; to commit those who have been arrested on a criminal charge, binding such persons over to trial in a higher court; to perform marriage ceremonies, and other administrative duties.

***jus·ti·ci·a·*ble.** That which may be properly settled in the courts. A fit subject or dispute to be handled by trial.

***jus·ti·fi·a·*ble.** That which is right; sanctioned by law; defensible.

***ju·*ven·ile court.** Courts that handle juveniles in two distinct situations: (a) those who have violated the criminal laws, and (b) those who have been abandoned or neglected. The latter class of children may not have committed any violation whatever, but need someone to stand in the stead of their natural parents.

K

kan·ga·*roo* court. The slang name for a mock court that has no authority or power. For example, the existence of *kangaroo courts* was frequently ignored by authorities operating poorly supervised jails in bygone years. After a new prisoner was booked, the prisoner was assessed half the money he/she had brought into jail by a *kangaroo court* set up by other inmates. Those who did not go along with the fine might be shoved or beaten, or forced to clean jail latrines by members of the *kangaroo court.* Revenues obtained by the court were used to buy such items as cigarettes, candy bars, or comic books for all the inmates.

kid·nap·ping. The seizing and holding of an individual against his or her will. There must be a carrying or forcing away, for some unlawful purpose. The intent may be to hold for ransom, to use as a hostage, or to rape. Most states classify the offense as *kidnapping* if the victim's automobile is entered and the victim is forced to drive to some other location.

Some states provide different penalties, depending on whether or not the victim was harmed.

kin. (1) A relation by blood. (2) Sometimes loosely used to mean either relationship by blood or marriage, but this is not the usual legal meaning.

kit·ing. A chain-type scheme for building up a bank account temporarily by depositing insufficient-funds checks drawn on one or more other banks, which in turn are covered by depositing insufficient-funds checks drawn on other banks, sometimes including the first bank involved. Check *kiting* is, of course, criminal in that it may involve the issuance of a number of insufficient-funds checks. State laws and penalties vary widely on the writing of bad checks.

know·ing·ly. Intentionally; wilfully, consciously. If an individual is required to have knowledge of particular facts in order to be convicted of a crime, the prosecution must prove that the accused had actual knowledge; mere constructive knowledge will not suffice. The prohibited act must be done *knowingly,* if required for a conviction.

L

lach·es. Undue delay by someone seeking to enforce a legal right, which delay has worked to the harm of the other party. When a procrastination or unwarranted delay prejudices the other party, the courts may say that the legal right may not be enforced.

land grant. (sometimes called land patent). A devise or grant of land from the government, usually for roads, railroads, or agricultural colleges. Some such grants were given to the states and others to firms such as private railroads. The term *land grant college* comes from this origin.

land•**mark case.** See LEADING CASE.

land•**mark de**•*ci*•**sion.** See LEADING CASE.

lapse. (1) The termination of a legal right, that was not exercised within a required time limit or because of neglect. (2) In insurance law, the termination of coverage in a policy, due to non-payment of premiums or compliance with other conditions. (3) The passage of time. (4) The failure of a gift left by will to take effect, because of impossibility or other technical reasons.

lar•**ce**•**ny.** (Used synonymously with theft or stealing). An unlawful taking and carrying away of a thing, without claim of right, and with the intent of converting it to one's own use. It is the taking and carrying away of goods or money of another, with intent to convert it to the taker's use. *Larceny* is distinguished from EMBEZZLEMENT, in that the embezzler has lawful possession from the owner, and thereafter decides to make off with the property.

las•*civ*•*i*•**ous.** Lewd, lustful, wanton. Tending to excite immoral and lewd emotions.

last clear chance. The principle in TORT law that the party who has the last clear opportunity to avoid injury or damage to another is held to liability. Stated in other terms, the negligence of the party having the *last clear chance* of avoiding the accident is the sole PROXIMATE CAUSE of the injury. This legal doctrine places a duty upon all parties to exercise ordinary care in avoiding injury to another who has negligently placed himself or herself in a situation of danger. According to the reasoning of some courts that apply this doctrine, the theory is that the negligence of the injured party had ceased. See PROXIMATE CAUSE.

last re•*sort,* **court of.** The highest ranking court in a court system. In the Federal court system, and in most states, the court of last appeal, or last resort, is called the SUPREME COURT.

lat•**er**•**al sup**•*port.* A landowner's right to have support from adjacent property. Digging a gravel pit on adjoining property could cause a collapse, with serious property damage, as well as a threat to harm individuals. Destruction of *lateral support* gives rise to a cause of action for DAMAGES.

law. Those customs, practices, or rules which must be followed by the inhabitants of a country, subject to legal consequences or sanctions. Those rules of human relationship and custom that govern the conduct of society and human institutions.

law day. The due date for a mortgage or bond, after which the debt is in default and may be foreclosed.

law *mer•*chant (or laws *mer•*chant). The old rules of commercial law that came into general use between European merchants during the Middle Ages. The rules of *law merchant* were gradually absorbed into the English COMMON LAW, as well as into the laws of other modern European countries. The *law merchant* still serves as the basic commercial law in the United States, through adoption of common law principles. Trade would be extremely difficult without some general uniformity among the rules of commercial law between nations.

law of the land. Generally used synonymously with the term DUE PROCESS OF LAW.

***law•*ful.** That which is authorized or established by law. Sanctioned, and neither contrary to nor forbidden by law.

***law•*suit.** (Used interchangeably with *suit, legal action,* or *cause*) A civil action as distinguished from a criminal prosecution. A legal contest in the courts, instituted by one party to compel another party to do him or her justice.

***law•*yer.** (1) An individual educated in the legal profession. (2) An individual licensed to practice law. In the United States, the terms *lawyer, attorney, counsel, legal advisor,* and *legal counsel* are used to mean the same thing.

lay. Not of a particular profession. To a lawyer, any nonlawyer is a *lay person.* A *lay judge* is a judge who is not trained in the law. In a few jurisdictions a JUSTICE OF THE PEACE or judge over some minor matters is not required to be a graduate of an accredited law school.

lay *ad•*vo•cate. A non-lawyer who makes a specialty of representing individuals at administrative hearings before specialized governmental or trade boards.

***lead•*ing case.** A case that demanded unusual attention from judges and lawyers, looked on as having settled the law on a troublesome problem and as a precedent or guide for subsequent decisions on the same issue. From the importance thus acquired, such a decision is called a *leading case, landmark decision,* or *landmark case.* Cases of this kind are usually found in decisions of the U.S. Supreme Court, or in the decisions of state courts of LAST RESORT.

lead•ing *ques*•tion. A question asked of a witness on the witness stand, phrased in such a way that it suggests the answer that is wanted. A question that puts words into the witness' mouth that are to be echoed back.

lease. A written agreement under which possession and use of property is granted, for a specified time, for a specified payment. The landlord (lessor or leasor) and tenant (lessee or leasee) relationship. The terms lessor and lessee are more commonly used.

lease-*back*. An arrangement by which one party sells a property and simultaneously obtains a long-term lease from the buyer for continued use of the property.

leas•*ee*. See LEASE.

lease•hold es•*tate*. The property interest, or estate, of the occupier (lessee) under a lease is called a *leasehold* or *leasehold estate*. Leases for a definite period of time are considered to be personal property. Most oil and gas leases for an indefinite period (a specified term + so long as production shall last), are regarded by the law as REAL PROP-ERTY. This could be important, since there may be some basic dif-ferences in laws concerning personal property and laws pertaining to real property.

leas•er. See LEASE.

leas•or. See LEASE.

least fault di•*vorce*. See COMPARATIVE RECTITUDE THEORY OF DIVORCE.

leave. (1) To bequeath or devise by will. (2) An authorization to do some-thing, as to obtain leave of the court to enter a plea of NOLO CON-TENDERE. (3) To let stay, or to continue.

leg•a•cy. Any disposition of personal property left by will.

le•gal. (1) In accordance with, or conforming to law. (2) Deriving author-ity from or founded on law. (3) Of, or relating to law. (4) Relating to the profession of law. (5) Pertaining to a court of law, as distinguished from a court of EQUITY.

le•gal age. The age of legal responsibility; that age at which an individual becomes old enough to transact business and handle legal matters, such as the capacity to make contracts or transfer property. *Legal age* varies from 18 to 21, depending on individual state law. For some specific purposes, such as the right to obtain a driver's license, the age may be set below that for handling of business responsibilities.

le·gal **aid.** A bureau or agency that furnishes free legal assistance to those who are unable to pay, or who can afford very little.

le·gal **as·*sis*·tant.** Usually termed a paralegal. See PARALEGAL.

le·gal **cap.** A type of white writing paper for legal use, generally ruled and 8½ inches wide by 13 or 14 inches long, with a wide left-hand margin.

le·gal **cause.** See PROXIMATE CAUSE.

le·gal *det*·**ri**·**ment.** The legal position in which an individual or company is placed when making a contract by taking on duties or liabilities that can be enforced against that contracting individual or company in a court of law. Some kind of *legal detriment* (obligation) is taken on by any party to a contract that promises performance in the future.

le·gal *eth*·**ics.** **(1)** Those customs and moral obligations owed by members of the legal profession to the courts, to clients, to the public, and to one another. **(2)** The name of a short course of study sometimes required of all students in law schools, sometimes combined with *legal bibliography.*

le·gal **pro·*ceed*·ings.** Any action sanctioned or authorized by law, and filed or brought in a court of justice for the enforcement of a legal remedy or right, or to secure justice for a client.

le·gal *res*·**i**·**dence.** The place where one actually lives and intends to stay, at least for the foreseeable future.

le·gal **rights.** Claims that are enforceable in court, or by legal procedures against individuals or against the community; claims and rights recognized and enforced by the law.

le·gal *ten*·**der.** Money that would be legally acceptable for the payment of debt. It is that kind of money or coins which the law compels a creditor to accept in payment for debt, when the right amount is offered. For example, in some jurisdictions payment of more than $10 in pennies would not be acceptable. It would be absurd to require an individual owed $1,000 to wait while a debtor counted out 100,000 pennies in satisfaction.

leg·a·*tee*. Someone to whom a LEGACY, or gift of property, is left by will. The term is generally used without distinction as to whether personal property or realty is included in the gift. A *residuary legatee* receives the property that is left after bills are paid and such other legacies as may have been included in the will have been disposed of.

leg·**is**·**late.** To make or enact laws. To orginate, bring into being, and secure passage of statutes by committee action and vote of a legislative body.

leg·**is**·**la**·**tive** **in**·*tent* *doc*·**trine.** The principle followed by the courts in interpreting statutes passed by the legislature, whereby the court may examine testimony of witnesses who have appeared before legislative committees to determine what the law makers actually intended. The courts may also examine hearing report records of the committee that approved the legislation. See LEGISLATIVE PURPOSE DOCTRINE, which is a different approach.

leg·**is**·**la**·**tive** *pur*·**pose** *doc*·**trine.** The principle followed by the courts in interpreting laws whereby the court looks at the problem the legislature was trying to change, or prior legislation that was replaced by the law under interpretation. Where possible the court follows an interpretation that assumes the law was intended to correct the stated problem. It is to be noted that this approach is not the same as that of the LEGISLATIVE INTENT DOCTRINE, although the results may be the same in many instances.

leg·**is**·**la**·**tor.** (or legislative officer) A member of a Federal, state, or municipal lawmaking body. These officials are usually restricted in the governmental duties to the making of laws. In cases of IMPEACHMENT, however, one house of the legislative body may bring charges, while the other house acts as a court in trying such impeachment. In the Federal system, the lawmaking bodies are the Senate and the House of Representatives. Most states have similar two-house systems, with a Senate and House of Representatives. Municipal governments usually have a one-chamber legislative body.

le·*git*·**i**·**mate.** (1) That which is legal, and in accordance with the law. (2) That which is not false or spurious. (3) Born in wedlock. Frequently, laws specify that the issue is *legitimate* if the parents are subsequently married.

less·*ee.* See LEASE.

less·**er** **of**·*fense.* (sometimes termed *lesser included offense,* or *less serious offense*) A principle sometimes included in criminal statutes providing that an accused charged with one of the offenses enumerated in a criminal accusation cannot be convicted or sentenced for one of the *less serious offenses* that were necessarily included in the criminal activity. For example, an individual may be charged with murder. If the accused committed the murder, then he also necessarily committed an assault which merged in with the major charge (murder). A statute of this kind precludes a jury from evading their responsibility by finding the accused guilty of assault only, since jurors do not like to feel responsible for serious punishment. If the jury simply will not convict for murder in accordance with their duty, then the responsibility will rest on the jurors' shoulders.

less·**or, less·***or.* See LEASE.

let·**ter of at·***tor*·**ney.** A term that means the same as a POWER OF ATTORNEY. See ATTORNEY IN FACT.

let·**ter of** *cred*·**it.** A letter addressed by a bank to a correspondent bank certifying that an individual named therein is entitled to draw on the original bank, up to a specified sum. This, of course, is of considerable help to merchants doing business in faraway places.

let·**ters of ad·min·is·***tra*·**tion.** Letters of authority from the appropriate court empowering an administrator to settle the estate of a deceased person.

let·**ters** *ro*·**ga·to·ry.** A formal, written request from a court in which a lawsuit or action is pending to a court or judge in a foreign country, requesting the examination or interrogation of a witness in the latter country concerning knowledge of a matter before a court in the first country. The witness' AFFIDAVIT or testimony is forwarded by authorities taking this testimony, for use in the pending action.

let·**ters tes·ta·***men*·**ta·ry.** The papers of authority given to an EXECUTOR, by the appropriate court, authorizing the executor to handle the duties connected with the will and settlement of the estate of the deceased who selected the executor.

lev·**y.** **(1)** To seize property or money, in order to satisfy a judgment or execution. The most frequent example would be in a sheriff's sale.

lewd. Obscene; immoral; lascivious; evil; sexually unchaste.

lex. (Latin) *Law.* **(1)** A collection of laws. **(2)** Sometimes used to mean a collection of laws that have been neither systematized or codified.

lex lo·ci. (Latin-leks *loe*·see, leks *loe*·sigh) The law of the place where a contract was made. As a general legal principle, contracts concerning matters other than real estate are made with reference to the law in that jurisdiction. Courts presume that the contract is to be performed where the contract was made. Therefore, the *lex loci* (law of the place) determines questions relating to its validity, and to the rights, duties and obligations of the parties under the contract. If one party is discharged from performance under the law of the place where made, this fact will operate as a discharge everywhere.

li·a·*bil*·i·ty. (1) A general legal term, describing any monetary responsibility, indebtedness, or debt. (2) Every type of legal responsibility or hazard, whether absolute, contingent, or likely. (3) Something that works as a drawback or disadvantage.

***li*·a·ble.** Obligated or bound by principles of law or equity. Answerable to give satisfaction. Having an obligation that could be enforced in a court of law by another person.

***li*·bel.** (1) Any written, printed or pictorial statement that damages a person's character, or exposes to ridicule or contempt; written defamation; that written or printed matter that holds a person up to ridicule, contempt, shame, or disgrace, or that degrades in the estimation of the community. (2) To publish or make a libel against. (3) The written claims presented by a plaintiff (pleadings) in an action at admiralty law.

***li*·bel·ant, *li*·bel·lant.** One who institutes a suit in maritime law, by filing a *libel*. See PARTIES.

li·bel·*ee*. A defendant in a suit in maritime law.

***li*·bel·er or *li*·bel·ler.** A person who commits LIBEL.

***li*·bel·ous, *li*·bel·lous.** Of the nature of LIBEL.

***lib*·er·ty.** Freedom from any restraints, except those justly imposed by law. The power to do as one pleases. Exemption from arbitrary and despotic control.

***li*·cense.** (1) Permission to act. (2) Specific permission granted by competent authority to engage in an occupation, business, or activity that would be otherwise unlawful. (3) The document itself, which shows permission to engage in an activity requiring a *license*. (4) To *take license* is to act in disregard of the law, or without legal restraint.

li·cens·*ee*. (1) An individual who enters another's property with the owner's toleration or permission, but without an invitation. Those who come into a retail store to get out of the rain, persons taking shortcuts across a vacant lot, those making a tour of a manufacturing plant for their own enjoyment, travelling salesmen, and social guests are all classified by most courts as *licensees*. These are in a different class from INVITEES, those invited into a retail store to do business, for example. Under TORT law, the courts say that the property holder has a maximum duty to protect *invitees,* but less responsibility to the *licensee.* Most courts say the standard of care required of the property holder is greater to the extent that the presence of people on the property is helpful or profitable to the property holder. **(2)** A person to whom a license is granted.

li•cen•tious. **(1)** Seriously lacking in moral restraints and sexual principles; lascivious. **(2)** Having almost total disregard of the rights of others. Doing what one pleases, without consideration of ethics or respect of the general public.

lien. The right to take and hold or sell the property of a debtor as security for the debt. A *lien* is a right established by law, rather than by an agreement or contract between the parties involved. Examples are a landlord's *lien,* to hold property of a tenant for unpaid rent. Another example is a mechanic's *lien,* giving an auto mechanic the right to hold an automobile until repairs are paid for. The holder of the *lien* is usually required to give notice of his claim by recording it in the office of the public recorder or some other designated public office. In most states, a MORTGAGE on real estate acts as a *lien,* and takes precedence over a mechanic's *lien.* See RECORDING: see JUDGMENT LIEN.

life es•*tate.* An interest in property, real or personal, that lasts only for the duration of the owner's life. A *life estate* may also be for the duration of another's life, or may end with the happening of a certain contingency. For example, a man may leave a *life estate* in a cattle ranch to his wife, with the provision that the estate terminates in the event of her remarriage. Ordinarily, the owner of the *life estate* cannot sell off, consume, or deliberately ruin any of the property which makes up the *life estate,* but may enjoy the use and benefits of the property. The legal interest left after the termination of a life estate is a REMAINDER. In a typical life estate situation, a grandfather with a daughter and a son deeded his property to grandchildren who are the offspring of both children. Realizing that his daughter had not done well financially, the grandfather includes his home in the property deeded to the grandchildren, but left his financially troubled daughter a *life estate* in the home. The grandchildren are the owners of the home, but it remains subject to the daughter's *life estate.* The grandchildren do not receive a FEE SIMPLE title to the home.

life ten•ant. A person who holds an ESTATE in lands for the period of his or her own life, or that of another certain person. The *life tenant* enjoys all the privileges and benefits of ownership during the term of the LIFE ESTATE.

lim·i·*ta*·tion. (1) A statute setting a time after which prosecution cannot be brought in a criminal case. For example, by statute, a robbery prosecution may not be brought in some jurisdictions after a lapse of three years. See STATUTE OF LIMITATIONS. There are, of course, some exceptions. Murder and treason charges can be brought at any time because of the extremely serious nature of the crimes. (2) Any restraint or restriction of power or authority.

lim·it·ed. Confined within bounds or limits; restricted in scope, extent, duration, or a combination of any of these.

lin·e·al de·*scent*. Descent in a direct line, or by issue; persons directly related to each other as ascendants or descendants. Legally, the term generally includes an adopted child.

liq·ui·da·ted *dam*·a·ges. Damages, specified in amount, that are to be recovered by one party to a contract or to a bond in the event of failure to perform or of default by the other party. Sometimes called liquidated damages and penalties. See DAMAGES.

liq·ui·*da*·tion. The act of winding up financial affairs; clearing away; the act of discharging.

liq·*ui*·di·ty. The speed and ease with which assets can be converted into cash at market value.

lis. (Latin–liss) A dispute. A lawsuit or legal controversy.

lis pen·dens. (Latin–liss *pen*·denz, a pending suit) (1) Pending litigation. (2) The control which a court acquires over property in a suit pending final judgment.

lit·i·gant. One who is involved in a lawsuit.

lit·i·gate. To file or carry on a lawsuit.

lit·i·*ga*·tion. A legal contest carried on by judicial process; a lawsuit.

li·*ti*·gious. Contested in a lawsuit; being subject to litigation.

lit·to·ral. (1) Pertaining to the shore. (2) Referring to the shore zone between water marks of high and low tide.

liv·ing trust. The type of trust that becomes effective while the individual setting it up is still living. This is distinguished from a gift given at death, as a result of provisions in a will. The former is sometimes known as an INTER VIVOS TRUST, while the latter is called a *gift mortis causa.*

lob·by·ing. Making personal contacts or conducting activities designed to influence members of a legislative body on pending or proposed legislation.

lo·cal *ac*·tion. A legal action (lawsuit) that can be filed in only one location.

lo·cus. (Latin–·kuss) *A place.* The location where something transpired. *Locus in quo* means the place in which; *locus sigili,* the place where the seal is located on a formal legal document.

lo·cus cri·min·is. (Latin–·*lo*·cus *kri*·min·tee) The location of the crime. The place where the crime occurred.

lo·cus de·lic·ti. (Latin–*lo*·cus duh·*lick*·tee). The place of the offense. The where the violation was committed.

lo·cus in quo. (Latin–*lo*·cus inn kwoe) *The place in which.* The place of occurrences that are the subject of a lawsuit.

lo·cus si·gil·li. (Latin–*lo*·cus sig·*eel*·ee) The place where the seal is located on a formal legal document.

loss. See INJURY.

l. s. See SEAL.

lu·na·cy. Any type of mental unsoundness. Sometimes used to describe an insane individual who has periods of lucid intervals. Legally, it is the equivalent of INSANITY.

M

mag·is·trate. A judicial officer with summary jurisdiction in quasi-criminal and minor criminal offenses. A magistrate may have authority to issue search warrants, issue arrest warrants, hold preliminary hearings, and set bail, as well as conduct arraignments. Authority of a magistrate varies considerably from state to state, and is usually less than that of a judge.

maim·ing. See MAYHEM.

main·te·nance. An improper or unlawful intermeddling in a lawsuit by assisting either party with money or other means to carry it on. This is in a situation where the individual meddling is not a party to the suit. *Separate maintenance* is a grant allowed to a wife or dependent husband for the support of that spouse and children while living apart.

ma·*jor*·i·ty. **(1)** The age, set by law, at which an individual is entitled to handle his or her own affairs and to the enjoyment of civic rights, such as voting. *Majority* means the opposite of minority. Under the common law, an individual had reached *majority* upon becoming 21 years of age; however, this age has been lowered in some jurisdictions in the United States. **(2)** Under election laws, a *majority* is any number of votes greater than half the total.

ma·**la.** (Latin) Bad.

ma·**la** *fi*·**de.** (Latin) Bad faith. Anything done in bad faith.

ma·**la in se.** (Latin) Wrongs in themselves. Violations or acts that are against conscience. For example, an act such as murder is not only prohibited by the criminal law, but is also *mala in se.* Speeding in an automobile may also be classed as a criminal type violation (misdemeanor); it is not *mala in se* if the driver exceeded the limit without realizing.

mal·*fea*·sance. (French) Wrongdoing. Evil conduct; the commission of any act which is definitely wrongful.

mal·**ice.** The deliberate and intentional doing of a wrongful act without just cause or excuse, under such facts that the law will imply an evil intent. A conscious condition of mind, showing a will deliberately set on mischief or lack of concern.

ma·*li*·cious pros·e·*cu*·tion. A prosecution begun because of personal spite or hate, without real justification.

mal·*prac*·tice. The lack of reasonable and ordinary skill and diligence resulting in injury to a patient or client on the part of a physician, surgeon, dentist, lawyer, or other professional who offers services for a fee. A physician undertakes to give reasonable skill, diligence, and care, and if injury results to the patient for want of reasonable care, diligence, or skill, the physician is liable for DAMAGES. The medical man is not required to be infallible in diagnosis. It is a defense to show that the treatment was in accordance with the ordinary and usual treatment by competent physicians in such cases. The physician is not responsible for an honest error in judgment, either as to the ailment or the treatment that would be most successful.

man·*da*·mus. (Latin) *We command you.* A writ, or order, that is issued by a court of superior jurisdiction. The order commands a lower court board, corporation, or individual to do an act, or not to do an act, the performance or omission of which the law enjoins as a duty. If discretion is left to the lower court, the *mandamus* only compels it to act, and cannot control such discretion.

***man*·slaugh·ter.** The unlawful killing of a human being without premeditation or without express or implied MALICE. The difference between MURDER and *manslaughter* is that premeditation or malice is lacking. Manslaughter is usually of two grades: voluntary and involuntary. In both murder and manslaughter the accused may intend to kill the victim. Malice aforethought makes use of the reasoning process of the accused in a deliberate and planned decision to kill. In the intentional killing called *voluntary manslaughter,* the illegal act takes place immediately after the defendant is so provoked that reason is clouded by passion. If the defendant does not kill until after regaining control of his or her reasoning process, the crime is murder. In short, then, voluntary manslaughter is a killing in a blind mental rage that has blotted out the thinking of the defendant. In *involuntary manslaughter,* the accused does not intend to kill at all. It is the killing during the commission of an unlawful or inherently dangerous act, such as killing a pedestrian while driving drunk.

***mar*·i·time law.** Law that pertains to marine affairs generally, including harbors, ships, navigation, cargo, and the transportation of persons on the high seas. Practically all nations have adopted rules that are universally applicable to all ships, in all waters.

***mar*·ket·a·ble *ti*·tle.** A TITLE to real estate that is clear of incumbrances such as would be accepted as a valid title by a reasonable, prudent buyer.

***mar*·shal.** An administrative official of the court system, whose duties are usually similar to those of a sheriff, or, in some instances, to those of a constable. The *marshal* may take prisoners between the courts and the jails, may deliver legal orders, or execute processes of the courts.

***mar*·tial law.** The system of law administered by military authorities under the direction of the President or the governor of a state when regularly constituted law enforcement agencies are unable to maintain law, order, and safety. It overrides and suppresses all civilian law, and is normally used only in time of actual war or uncontrollable riot.

141

ma·*te*·ri·al·man. An artisan or individual who supplies construction materials for a vessel, building, or structure. In some instances that person may have a LIEN for these materials.

ma·tu·ri·ty. The date on which a legal obligation such as a promissory note or bill of exchange falls due. It may also be the date when a legal right becomes enforceable.

***may*·hem.** (sometimes called maim·ing) A CRIMINAL offense under the COMMON LAW, and a FELONY violation in almost all jurisdictions. The definition of *mayhem* varies from state to state. Usually it is a violation to: unlawfully and maliciously disable, disfigure, render a facial feature useless, cut or disable the tongue, put out an eye, slit the nose or lip, or deprive a human of a member of the body. The law has usually been changed somewhat to punish someone who wanted to "cut his mark" on someone else.

me·*chan*·ic's lien. A legal claim, usually created by statute, securing priority of payment of the value of work performed and the value of materials furnished in constructing or repairing a building or other structure, or on a vehicle. This right of priority of payment attaches to land, as well as to buildings and improvements thereon. A vehicle mechanic has the right to hold an automobile until vehicle repairs are paid for.

mem·o·*ran*·dum de·*ci*·sion. A decision of a court that is a bare statement of opinion only, with no elaboration of why or how the opinion was reached.

mens rea. (Latin–mens ray) The guilty intent or guilty state of mind that must exist before an individual can be convicted of most crimes. The general rule of criminal law is that "a crime has not been committed when the mind of the person doing the act in question is innocent." Unknown to the accused, a co-worker inserted a company tool into the accused's lunch box. When the tool was found in a search at the plant gate, criminal charges were filed. The necessary guilty intent, or *mens rea,* was lacking, and a crime had not been committed by the accused.

To be complete, most crimes require the *mens rea,* coupled with a positive act committed by the accused in furtherance of the forbidden activity.

men·sa et tho·ro. (Latin–*men*·zuh et *thuh*·roe) *From bed and board.* A type of separation in which the parties no longer live or cohabit together, although other aspects of the marriage are unchanged. It is sometimes called a type of divorce; however, this may be a misnomer since other legal rights growing out of the marriage relationship are unchanged. For example, one of the parties could not marry again without committing BIGAMY.

men·tal *cru*·el·ty. A pattern of conduct by one spouse toward the other, which may be so injurious to the mental or physical health of the other that the marriage becomes intolerable.

mer·can·tile law. Another name for LAW MERCHANT, which see.

mer·chan·dise. All wares, goods, commodities, or articles sold in trade and commerce. The word is never understood to include real estate.

metes and bounds. The boundary lines of a parcel of land, with terminal points and angles, as used in legal descriptions.

mi·*nor*·i·ty. (1) An individual under legal age (this may vary from place to place, but is usually 21 years of age). (2) A group within the population, differing from others in some characteristics, and that could be subjected to different treatment. (3) A group having less than the number of votes necessary for control.

mis·ad·*ven*·ture. A casualty resulting from accident or mischance. When an individual performing a lawful act, without any intent to harm, unfortunately kills another, it is called homicide by *misadventure.* While regrettable, it is legally excused.

mis·de·*mean*·or. A class of crime that is less serious than a FELONY, usually punishable by fine or imprisonment other than in a penitentiary. Under Federal law it is a crime punishable by imprisonment of one year or less.

mis·*pri*·sion. (1) Neglect or wrongful performance of a governmental duty. (2) Concealment of knowledge of TREASON or any FELONY by one not actively involved in that treason or felony. This type of *misprision* is a felony in itself, in most states and under Federal laws, in some form or another.

mis·tri·al. A trial which is held invalid and of no effect, because of some material defect in procedure. This could involve an improper procedure: selection of the jury, allowing the jury to hear prejudicial material that is not evidence, or other procedural error. After a *mistrial,* the court proceeds as though no trial had ever previously been held. A *mistrial,* in itself, does not constitute double jeopardy, so as to excuse the accused from additional prosecution in a criminal matter.

mit·i·*ga*·tion. Lessening of responsibility for wrongful acts, offered not to excuse from blame, but to reduce or lessen moral responsibility and reduce the criminal penalty or civil damages that may be imposed.

mit·i·*ga*·tion of *dam*·a·ges. Facts that tend to show that the plaintiff's legal action does not justify an award of the amount being claimed as due by the plaintiff.

mit·ti·mus. (1) A warrant of committment to prison. (2) A court order transferring records.

mod·el acts. Acts proposed for adoption into law, backed by the National Conference of Commissioners on Uniform State Laws.

mod·i·fi·*ca*·tion. A change in a contract or legal agreement, by mutual consent of the parties involved. A *modification* of a written contract must usually be in writing.

mo·*nop*·o·ly. An exclusive right given to one or more companies or individuals, to carry on a particular trade or business, or to be the exclusive supplier of a particular commodity. Any public utility, such as the gas company or telephone company, is normally a *monopoly,* since it has no competition and rates are set or regulated by the state.

mon·u·ment. A position or boundary marker left by survey crews to fix property lines for real property.

moot. (1) Unsettled, debatable. (2) A *moot point* is one that seeks to obtain a court judgment or ruling on an alleged right even before it has been asserted in the court. It is to be pointed out that courts do not make rulings of this kind, and they would not be binding in any event.

mor·al *tur*·pi·tude. An act of depravity or baseness, usually involving a criminal violation. Personal conduct that is completely improper, from the standards of morality, honesty, and decency.

mort·gage. (1) The transfer or *pledge of* property passing conditionally as security for debt. (2) The DEED or DEED OF TRUST by which this pledge is made. (3) The claim of the MORTGAGEE on the property.

mort·ga·*gee*. One who loans money, obtaining a MORTGAGE as security.

mort·ga·gor. One who gives a MORTGAGE as security for a loan on his or her property.

mor·tis cau·sa. (Latin–*mor*·tiss *kos*·uh) *By reason of death,* or *in contemplation of death.*

mo·tion. A request or application to a judge for a ruling or order in favor of the requesting party, or directing that something be done for the benefit of the requesting party. A *motion to suppress evidence,* for example, would be a request for a ruling that a specific piece of evidence could not be used in a trial.

mo·tion to ad·*vance.* A request for an immediate trial, without delay.

***mu*·ni·ments.** (1) Documents of TITLE. (2) The instruments of writing and other written evidences by which the owner of land, possessions, or legal rights is able to defend the TITLE to his property.

***mur*·der.** The killing of another, deliberately, with forethought, and illegally. The crime committed when one kills any human creature in being (not unborn), illegally and with malice aforethought. A soldier, killing in war, is not guilty of any crime. Neither is an electrocutioner hired by the state to carry out a sentence of execution.

mu·tu·*al*·i·ty. A common, or mutual understanding, where all parties intend the same thing.

N

na·tion·*al*·i·ty. (1) The relationship between an individual and a nation, with the individual owing allegiance and the nation owing protection of the rights of that country's citizens. (2) The ethnic group to which one belongs by reason of birth or citizenship.

***nat*·u·ral law.** Those rules and principles of human conduct that are common to all peoples in many nations. For example, premeditated murder, rape, robbery, and theft have been recognized as criminal acts from the experiences of decent individuals from all countries and in all stations in life. The early-day English courts, in developing the COMMON LAW, drew from common experience traditions and from folk law traditions as to what should be criminal. Certain activities, contrary to *natural law,* have been regarded as wrong from time immemorial, both by the average person on the street and the judge on the bench. Roman jurists, using the term *jus naturale,* were the first to write about *natural law.*

nat·u·ral·i·*za*·tion. The process by which one becomes a citizen, acquiring political rights and assuming the obligations of citizenship.

nav•i•ga•ble. An arm of the sea, a river, or other waters which provide a channel for useful commerce. The definition of a navigable stream under the law in some states goes farther, declaring that if a stream or body of water may be put to public use it is *navigable,* whether it can be used for commercial transportation or not.

ne•*glect*. (1) To fail to do that which is required. (2) A lack of legal care in performing some act. *Wilful neglect* of a husband is a deliberate failure to provide the necessities of life to his wife, even though financially able. *Culpable neglect* usually implies criminality.

neg•li•gence. That want or failure to exercise the degree of care that would be used by a reasonable, prudent individual under the same circumstances. The standards that must be used are those which a reasonable man would ordinarily use to regulate human affairs.

ne•*go*•ti•a•ble. A type of transferable INSTRUMENT calling for the payment of money. It is a SECURITY or instrument which not only transfers or carries with it the legal title by delivery and endorsement, but also those legal rights created by the document (such as the right to sue). TITLE to some securities passes without ENDORSEMENT.

ne•*go*•ti•a•ble *in*•stru•ment. A bank check, PROMISSORY NOTE, bill of exchange, or any other written SECURITY document that can be transferred by ENDORSEMENT and DELIVERY, or in some cases by delivery only. The effect of this transfer is to VEST legal ownership, giving the new owner the right to demand payment of the face amount of the INSTRUMENT, along with any interest that may be due. A bearer bond, for example, may be negotiable by delivery only, without an endorsement of the former owner.

ne•*go*•ti•ate. (1) To arrange, discuss, or conduct a business transaction, contract, or sale. (2) To transfer a negotiable instrument.

ne•mo. (Latin–*nee•*moe) *No person,* or *no one.*

net. (1) An entrapping situation. (2) That which remains after the deduction of all charges, or costs. Clear of all charges, expenses, discounts, deductions, commissions, taxes, etc.

net worth. The sum of money that would remain after all assets were sold off and all debts paid. In short, *net worth* is the market value of assets, less liabilities.

next of kin. (1) In the law of descent and distribution, those individuals who are the closest relatives of a deceased who did not leave a will. The order of inheritance is usually specified by state statute, and there are minor differences from state to state. (**2**) Individuals who are most closely related to a deceased, in ascertaining who has the legal right to a body for burial.

ni·hil. (Latin–*nie*·hill) Nothing. Often contracted to *nil.* Nil debt, or nihil debit, means nothing is owed.

nil. See NIHIL.

ni·si. (Latin–*nie*·sie) *Unless.* A provisional or conditional decree or writ, by which the judge holds that unless the party affected by the writ can come in and show some other more appropriate way to handle the matter in question, the judge's holding will be final. A judge's *decree nisi* is one which will definitely conclude the defendant's rights in that court, unless within the specified time the defendant comes in and convinces the judge that some alternative solution would be more just. If the defendant fails to show, the judge's *rule nisi* automatically becomes final. The terms *decree nisi* and *rule nisi* are generally used interchangeably.

ni·si pri·us. (Latin–*nie*·sie *pri*·us) *Unless before.* In American JURIS-PRUDENCE this phrase is used to denote the trial court that handled a matter, rather than an APPELLATE COURT that handled an appeal.

no fault in·*sur*·ance. An insurance system that seeks to have auto victims compensated for their losses without regard to their degree of negligence or fault in an accident. The *no fault system* also seeks to minimize the number of lawsuits by limiting recovery to actual economic losses such as medical expenses, wages and salary, and other real costs, eliminating payments for pain and suffering. Insurance laws vary widely from state to state; states with *no fault insurance* systems have different stipulations on rights to sue on bodily injury claims.

nol·le pros·e·qui. (Latin–*noll*·ee *pross*·eh·kwee) A binding agreement entered into the court record to the effect that a lawsuit or prosecutive action will not be further pursued. In a civil case, the entry into the court record is made by the plaintiff. In a criminal case, the prosecuting attorney specifies in the record that he will not further prosecute a specific count, or a specified individual among several defendants. Sometimes abbreviated as *nolle pros,* or as *nol. pros.*

no·lo con·ten·de·re. (Latin–*noe*·low kun·*ten*·duh·ree) "I will not contest it." A type of plea such as GUILTY or NOT GUILTY, that can be made by a defendant in some criminal courts. In some jurisdictions the accused cannot plead *nolo contendere* but must plead either *guilty* or *not guilty. Nolo contendere* is a pleading which does not admit guilt, but subjects the accused to criminal punishment as though he had pleaded guilty. In most courts the difference between a *nolo contendere* and a plea of *guilty* is that the former cannot be carried over into a civil damage suit that is an outgrowth of the same wrongful act. When a criminal pleads *guilty* in criminal court, the criminal court record will be accepted in a civil court as PRIMA FACIE proof of negligence or wrongdoing.

nom·i·nal. (1) Something that is in name or form only; of token or insubstantial value. (2) That which may be connected in a legal proceeding *in name only,* and not of real interest.

nom·i·nal *dam·a·ges.* A trifling sum of money (often one dollar), awarded to a plaintiff in a lawsuit where there was no substantial loss or injury, but where the law recognizes a wrong was done, however technical.

non. (Latin) Not. *Non culpabilis* means not guilty; *non obstante* means notwithstanding.

non·con·*form·*ing use. An exception allowing in the property zoning laws for a particular area.

non·*fea·*sance. Failure to do what ought to be done; failure to perform a legal duty or obligation.

non ob·stan·te. (Latin–non obb·*stan·*tee) *Notwithstanding.* Generally used to mean notwithstanding. In old English law it was said that the king had power *non obstante,* meaning the crown (or the government) had power to do things which no other person would be allowed to do. This feature of English law was done away with by the Bill of Rights in the U.S. Constitution.

non pros·e·quit·ur. (Latin–non proe·*sek·*wit·uhr) *He does not follow up.* Sometimes called a *motion to dismiss.* A judgment for the defendant because the plaintiff has neglected to fulfill some of the requirements necessary in pursuing the plaintiff's case.

non seq. Abbreviation for NON SEQUITUR.

non seq·ui·tur. (Latin–non *sek·*wit·uhr) *It does not follow.* An inference that does not follow from what went before.

non·*suit.* The termination of a legal action which was not based on an adjudication of the merits. A judgment given against the plaintiff if the case should be abandoned prior to trial, or by failure of the

PLAINTIFF to offer any valid evidence in substantiation of allegations.

non·sup·*port*. Deliberate neglect or failure to provide financially for a spouse or children. In some jurisdictions this is a criminal offense that is sometimes called *failure to provide*.

non vult con·ten·de·re. (Latin–non vult kun·*ten*·duh·ree) A variation of NOLO CONTENDERE.

***no*·ta·ry *pub*·lic.** A public official who attests or certifies certain classes of documents to give them authenticity in foreign jurisdictions, who takes acknowledgments of deeds and other conveyances, and who takes AFFIDAVITS, DEPOSITIONS, and protests for non-payment of negotiable instruments.

no·*ta*·tion *vot*·ing. Voting by an authorized group or board, such as by directors of a CORPORATION, at a time and place other than a regular meeting of the group. In many instances this kind of procedure allows certain individuals to control an organization or group, without permitting opposition to be voiced or voted. Consequently, this type of voting is often prohibited by organizational bylaws, or may be actually illegal in a vote by a legislative body.

note. A written promise to pay a specified sum owing to the holder of the *note*.

***no*·tice.** Knowledge or information about the existence of some fact. Legally, there are two types of notice: ACTUAL NOTICE and CONSTRUCTIVE NOTICE. ACTUAL NOTICE is information that can be proved to have been communicated to an individual directly. *Constructive notice* is knowledge of a fact, or information, imputed by law to an individual, although the individual may not actually have it. This is the type of situation where the individual involved would have discovered the fact by proper diligence, and that individual had a duty of inquiring into it. For example, a divorced husband may place a notice in the legal notice section of the neighborhood newspaper stating that he will no longer be responsible for the debts of his wife. (This is the procedure required by law in some jurisdictions.) Thereafter, a merchant who sells to the wife cannot look to the husband for payment since the merchant had *constructive notice*.

***no*·tice of ap·*pear*·ance.** A formal notice by the defendant who has been served with a summons for a lawsuit, advising that the defendant will appear in court to contest the plaintiff's claim.

no·**tice of lis pen**·**dens** (*pen*·**denz**). A notice to warn all persons that title to property is in LITIGATION. This serves as a warning that anyone purchasing the TITLE may not acquire a clear claim to the property.

no·**tice of** *pro*·**test.** A formal statement made by a NOTARY PUBLIC under seal, at the request of the holder of a bill or note which has been dishonored on presentation for payment. This notice is usually one of the steps preliminary to charging an endorser with responsibility for payment of the bill or note.

no·**tice to pro**·*duce.* A formal document by which one party to a lawsuit requests the opposite party to produce the original of specified papers or documents needed at the trial, or to accept the presentation of secondary copies for trial use, under the best evidence rule.

no·**tice to quit.** Written notice given by a landlord to a tenant, that the tenant must vacate. If the tenant has a LEASE, and the landlord gives *notice to quit,* the property must be vacated at the end of the lease.

no·*va*·**tion.** In contract law, the substitution of a new contract by mutual agreement. It may be similar to the old contract, but with one or more provisions definitely changed. A *novation* assumes a previously valid obligation.

nu·**dum pac**·**tum.** (Latin–*nyoo*·dum *pak*·tum) A naked pact. A bare agreement or promise to do something, without any requirement for performance, or consideration on the other side. It is an agreement merely, short of an enforceable contract.

nui·**sance.** A condition or situation that causes annoyance or danger to either the general public or a limited number of individuals, especially those in possession of property. That which disturbs the use and enjoyment of property, or that creates a hazard to safety, health or public morals.

nul·**la bo**·**na.** (Latin–*null*·uh *boe*·nuh) No goods. The notation made by the sheriff or sheriff's deputy after serving a writ of execution and finding no chattels or property on which to levy.

nul·**li**·**ty.** Anything that is null, or of no legal effect or force.

nun·**cu**·**pa**·**tive will** (nung·*kyoo*·**pate**·**ive** or nung·*kyoo*·**puh**·**tive**). An oral will dictated before witnesses by a person facing impending death. When subsequently reduced to writing, the written version may be PROBATED as a will. Because of the likelihood that fraud could occur, this kind of will is allowed in only a few states.

oath. To solemnly swear in a formal manner. An attestation. A pledge by which one renounces mercy and asks for the vengeance of heaven if he or she does not tell the truth.

ob·i·ter dic·tum. (Latin) See DICTUM.

ob·*jec*·tion. (1) An expression of disapproval or opposition. (2) The technique used by a lawyer in a trial to assert the error of some ruling or procedure, and to place this matter in the record for possible use in an appeal.

ob·li·*ga*·tion. Any duty imposed by law. That which an individual is legally bound to do, or forbear from doing.

ob·li·*gee*. One to whom another is obligated for payment of money or other legal duty.

ob·li·*gor*. One who assumes a debt or legal obligation.

ob·*scene*. Definitions have varied from time to time, according to court decisions and pronouncements. In general, it is that which is calculated to corrupt, debauch or harm the morals of the people; lustful; licentious; sexually depraved. The test is usually that of an average person applying community standards (varying from community to community), with the dominant theme of the material as a whole appealing to immoral interests, and if it is utterly without redeeming social importance.

ob·*struc*·tion of *jus*·tice. Any act of hindrance designed to block or prevent the execution of lawful process. It may consist of interfering with a police officer who is trying to make an arrest, of hindering a witness from appearing, or wrongfully influencing or tampering with jurors, witnesses, or judges. *Refusing to aid an officer* is a separate offense.

oc·cu·pan·cy. The physical possession and/or use of any real estate, land, or property, whether or not the possessor has TITLE or right to be on the premises.

of *coun*·sel. Used to describe an attorney hired to help the attorney of record in the preparation or trial of a case. See ATTORNEY OF RECORD.

of·*fense*. (1) Any violation of the laws, whether a MISDEMEANOR or a FELONY. (2) Sometimes the term also includes those criminal violations of law that are punishable only by a suit to recover a penalty.

of·fer. (1) To express willingness or intent to do something. (2) To present for approval or acceptance. (3) In contract law, to make a proposal, supported by adequate consideration, the complete acceptance of which constitutes a contract.

of·fice. A position of authority and trust in government. An office is not a contract with the government, and any officeholder can be removed for misconduct.

of·fi·cer. Any individual duly elected or appointed to a position of authority in a business, government, institution, or organization, especially for the purpose of directing or managing.

off-set. See SET-OFF.

of *rec*·ord. Has been entered on the appropriate record.

om·buds·man. An official in an agency or bureau who has authority to investigate any grievance or complaint from a citizen alleging misconduct or improper treatment. In some instances the *ombudsman* has authority to right the wrong or press criminal charges if the wrongdoer committed a crime. The *ombudsman* concept was apparently first used in the Swedish government.

om·ni·bus. (Latin) For all. Providing for a number of things at once. *Omnibus legislation* may group a number of matters that are not completely related.

on de·*mand*. When due. A negotiable instrument payable *on demand* is payable immediately.

on·us pro·ban·di. (Latin–*oe*·nus proe·*ban*·dee) *Burden of proof.*

open end *mort*·gage. A MORTGAGE which secures additional advances of money that may be advanced to the borrower (mortgagor) after the mortgage has already gone into operation.

o·pen·ing *state*·ment (of *coun*·sel). The oral outline given to the jury at the beginning of a trial, concerning the facts involved and the law that applies to the case. The *opening statement* usually shows what will be proved and the significance of testimony; also, how the evidence will piece together to give a complete picture of counsel's case.

op·er·*a*·tion of law. Those legal rights and responsibilities that may automatically devolve upon an individual without any deliberate effort on the part of that person. For example, when a man marries and has children, there is a legal responsibility to provide for the support of those children by *operation of law.*

o·pin·ion. (1) A document prepared by a lawyer for the client, stating the lawyer's understanding or opinion of the law as it applies to the client's case. (2) A statement by a judge or by an appellate court, setting forth the decision reached in a legal cause of action or in a matter appealed before them, giving the law as it applies to this particular case, along with the legal reasoning and precedents on which the decision was based.

o·pin·ion *ev·i·*dence. The opinion of an EXPERT WITNESS, concerning what the witness believes, thinks, or deduces from information that is in issue. Ordinarily, *opinion evidence* is not admissible in courtroom testimony; the witness must confine himself or herself to matters that were observed, heard, smelled, etc. But expert witnesses are in a different category. Expert witnesses are used because they have experience, education, or unusual background that makes their opinions valued. They are called in for this opinion, and it is highly unusual for one of these experts to have been present when some critical activity in the case took place.

op·tion. (1) A continuing contract or offer by which the owner of real estate gives a prospective purchaser the right to buy the property at a fixed price within a specified period of time. If the potential buyer does not purchase the property under the terms of the *option,* the money paid for the *option* is forfeited. If the purchase is made, however, the money paid for the *option* is sometimes credited toward the purchase price. (2) An *option* may also be given to buy merchandise or securities from another at an agreed price and within a specified time. An *option* may also involve the right to sell property, merchandise, or SECURITIES at a set price and time.

O.R. Abbreviation for *own recognizance.*

o·ral *con·*tract. A CONTRACT that is completely or partly spoken. If the contract is only partly in writing, it must necessarily depend on the *oral* part of the understanding.

o·ral *ev·i·*dence. Testimony of a witness; evidence given in court by word of mouth.

or·*dain.* To establish or to institute; as to enact a law or constitution.

or·der. (1) A written instruction or direction given by a judge; a mandate. (2) A regulation or ruling by an administrative body, as by the Federal Aviation Authority. (3) A check or other negotiable instrument may

be made *payable to the order of* a specific individual; a blank EN-
DORSEMENT then makes it negotiable.

or·der to show cause. A direction of a court obtained on a motion by
one party directing the second party to show any good cause why an
INJUNCTION should not be issued, and forbidding the second party
from committing wrongful acts that may be harmful to the first
party.

or·di·nance. (1) A law passed, or enacted, by the legislative body (city
council, town council, etc.) of a city government. (2) Sometimes used
to mean any law or statute, as *The Northwest Ordinance,* but this is
not the most commonly used legal term.

or·di·nar·y *cred·i·tor.* A CREDITOR who has no special preference or
pecuniary assurance for payment of a debt. *Ordinary creditors*
generally are paid after secured creditors. See SECURED CREDITORS.

or·gan·ic. Fundamental, or basic, especially as the word relates to law.

o·rig·i·nal ju·ris·dic·tion. JURISDICTION of a case in the first instance.
This involves the authority to try the case, as distinguished from
jurisdiction to hear a case on appeal.

or·phans' court. The name used in some states for the probate court of
another state.

os·ten·si·ble *a·gen·cy.* An AGENCY relationship recognized by the courts,
when the principal intentionally, or by want of proper care, causes a
third party to believe that someone is actually an agent of the principal.
See AGENCY.

o·ver·draft. The act of writing a check for more than one has on deposit
in a bank account or other depository.

o·ver·head. The continuous expenses of a business. Those business expenses not chargeable to a specific part of the work or production.

o·ver·rule. (1) To annul by subsequent court decision or ruling. A later
decision, handed down by the same court or by an APPELLATE COURT
in the same system, giving a judgment on the same question of law,
directly opposite to that which was previously given. This has the
effect of completely nullifying the first judgment. (2) To decline to
sustain, or to reject an OBJECTION made by an attorney during the
course of a trial.

o·vert. That which is open to view; manifest.

o·vert act. An open, manifest act from which criminality may be implied.
An act done to carry out the intention of crime.

o•**yez.** An old word used by a court crier to gain attention, especially at the start of a court session.

P

pan•**der.** (1) To solicit business for a prostitute. (2) To exploit, or cater to, the weakness of others.

pan•**el.** The list of names returned to the court by the sheriff, identifying those persons who have been summoned for JURY duty at court.

pa•**per.** (1) Any written or printed document, book, or account book, INSTRUMENT or written evidence that may be pertinent to a case in a law court. (2) Sometimes used to mean any negotiable paper, or NEGOTIABLE INSTRUMENT. (3) That which is of value in name only. For example, a *paper owner* of mining stock may possess nothing of real worth.

par. (Latin) equal; equality.

par *val*•**ue.** At equal value, or at nominal value. If a stock sells *below par,* it is below the value at which originally issued.

pa•ra•*le*•**gal.** A non-lawschool graduate who assists a lawyer, judge, or judicial body in a professional capacity. Most *paralegals* today have special training to prepare for their responsibilities. A *paralegal* is not licensed to practice law, but can perform many of the functions handled by attorneys.

par•**a•mount** *ti*•**tle.** A TITLE that is superior to another, and will prevail over the latter in a court of law. Generally used to refer to titles to real property, it may also be used in referring to CHATTELS. For example, the purchaser of a used bicycle has a title that is good against all the world, unless it turns out that the bicycle is stolen, in which case the original owner has *paramount title.*

par•**cel.** (1) A portion of land. (2) Sometimes used to mean a small package.

par•**don.** The act of forgiveness, release, or exemption from punishment for a criminal offense by the executive authority (President of the United States in Federal cases and governor of the state in state cases). A *pardon* releases the offender from all punishment and blots out the violation as though it had never occurred in the first place. The *pardon,* however, must be accepted by the offender. A *pardon* is distinguished from a PAROLE or commutation of sentence, since in the eyes of the law neither of the latter two wipe out what went on in the past.

par•ens pat•ri•ae. (Latin–*pay•*renz *pay•*tri•ee, *pah•*renz *pat•*ree•ie) Literally means parents or father of the country, or the king. In the United States it refers to the government or sovereign power, especially as a substitute father or guardian over insane persons, incompetents, and minors.

par•i ma•*ter•i•a.* (Latin) *Of the same matter.* On the same subject.

pa•*rol.* By word of mouth; oral.

pa•*rol ev•i•*dence. The principle of law that oral testimony will not be permitted to add to, subtract from, vary, or contradict written contracts, written documents transferring ownership of real estate, or judicial and official records, and which are valid, complete, unambiguous, and not drawn up through fraud. This legal principle protects against PERJURY, FRAUD, weakness of memory, or death of witnesses. The principle here is that previous oral agreements merge into the contract as written, and the contract cannot be altered on *parol evidence* (oral testimony) that contradicts the written contract. It prevents someone who signs a contract from having a change of heart and later testifying in court that the written contract did not represent the agreement of the parties at all. But the rule does not forbid the use of oral testimony to explain an ambiguous contract, if the oral testimony is not inconsistent with the matters stated in writing.

pa•*rol ev•i•*dence rule. The rule in evidence law that all verbal agreements or understandings about a matter merge into any written contract on the same subject matter. In the absence of fraud or mistake in the preparation of the written version, the writing cannot be modified or changed by verbal evidence. The reason for this rule is to eliminate FRAUD. Otherwise, one of the parties could later present a new verbal version any time it developed that the contract was not as favorable as expected.

pa•*rol* gift. A voluntary transfer of property, without compensation or payment. A *parol gift* may be either personal property, money, or land. It is unusual for TITLE to land to pass without the delivery of a deed. In some states, however, the owner can declare that he or she is giving a specifically described tract of land. If the DONEE then enters on to the land and makes substantial improvements, title will pass by operation of a *parol gift*. This is on the theory that it would be unjust to allow the donee to spend money or labor for improvements, and to thereafter deprive the donee of the property. A *parol gift*, however, cannot take effect against the rights of CREDITORS of the owner (donor), since those rights were already in existence at the time the gift was made.

pa·*role*. (1) A conditional release of a convict in criminal law. If the prisoner makes good, an absolute discharge will be given from the balance of the sentence. A released individual who does not abide by conditions of the *parole* will be returned to serve the unexpired time. (2) A pledge or promise given by a prisoner of war to return to custody at the time and place required, unless discharged. A *parole* is sometimes a pledge by a prisoner of war being set at liberty to never again take up arms against the government by whose forces the prisoner was captured.

par·**ties.** Persons or groups of persons taking one side in a legal dispute or contest. In a civil suit, the parties are called the *plaintiff* and the *defendant;* in criminal prosecutions the parties are the *prosecution* (the government, or state) and the *defendant.* (Sometimes the defendant may be called the *accused.*) In admiralty law, the plaintiff may be termed the *libelant,* with the defendant termed the *respondent.* When a case reaches the appellate courts (higher courts), the side making the appeal may be called the *appellant,* with the other party called the *respondent.* At other times, the appellant may be called the *plaintiff in error,* with the respondent called the *appellee* or the *defendant in error.* In the appeal of some criminal cases, the parties may be called the *prosecutor* and the *prisoner.*

par·*ti*·tion. The dividing of land owned by joint tenants, tenants in common, or co-heirs, so each may own a specific portion. A partition may be voluntary, each owner giving a conveyance or release to the others. If the parties cannot agree to a division, a petition may be made to the state court having jurisdiction, and the property divided according to procedures authorized by statutes. Under some circumstances, one of the parties may buy the whole tract, with cash payments made to other owners.

part·ner·ship. An association of two or more individuals to carry on any business or business venture by mutual effort participation in profits or losses. It is, in legal effect, a contract of mutual agency, with each partner acting as a principal in his or her own behalf, and as agent for the other partners. There is a tendency for some individuals to prefer participation in a corporate venture, rather than a *partnership,* since all partners may be liable for the debts incurred by another partner. In *limited partnerships,* however, this liability may be limited.

par·ty **wall.** A wall built for the benefit of joining and consenting property owners, with half of the construction on the land of each owner. State statutes usually specify that owners shall share construction costs. One owner does not have the right to cut windows in the wall without the consent of the other, but either owner can put roof joists in the wall, as well as floor supports. Sometimes a *party wall* is built for the immediate use of one owner, while the second owner consents but does not desire to make any immediate use. In a situation of this type, state statutes usually require the first owner to pay for the entire cost of the wall, with the second owner repaying half of this cost when use is made of it.

pat·ent. **(1)** A grant by the Federal government to an individual, giving the exclusive right to use, manufacture, or sell an invention. This right may be sold or assigned. Infringement makes the violator automatically liable for damages. **(2)** In real estate law, the INSTRUMENT by which the government grants title to land in the public domain that is sold to private interests, or to an individual who has proved up a homestead of public lands. **(3)** Any grant of privilege, property, or authority made by the government to private interests or to an individual. **(4)** That which is evident, apparent, or obvious.

pa·*ter·ni·ty* suit. A court action to determine parentage of a child, and to compel the payment of support money for the child. Technically, these are procedures of a criminal nature, with the prosecutor usually trying to compel support, rather than to confine a breadwinner who should be contributing. A criminal penalty is usually asked only when it is obvious that the father will not respond to other sanctions.

pas·sim. (Latin) *Everywhere.*

pau·per. **(1)** Any person who is unusually poor. **(2)** One who lives on charity.

pay·a·**ble.** Describes a sum of money that is due when someone is under obligation to pay it. When not qualified, the term *payable* means payable at once, rather than at a future time.

pay·*ee.* The individual to whom a NEGOTIABLE INSTRUMENT (promissory note, check, or bill of exchange) is made out. It is the party in whose favor the instrument is made or drawn.

pay·**ment** *in*·**to court.** Money paid into the court registry (to the clerk of the court) on instructions or with permission of the judge. Such a payment is discretionary with the judge, but ordinarily the court will accept money upon application of the party holding it if **(a)** whereabouts of the individual entitled to the money is unknown, **(b)** several parties claim the money, **(c)** the individual entitled to the money will not accept it, or **(d)** where there may be no one qualified to receive it. When payment of this kind is made into the court registry, the person making the payment is relieved for further responsibility for the money.

peace bond. A bond put up by someone threatening to harm someone or someone's property, on instructions of a competent judge. Rather than send the person making threats to jail, the judge orders the bond. The bond, of course, is to be forfeited if the peace is violated by the individual covered. Sometimes this procedure is more effective than an actual jail sentence, and it allows the individual under bond to continue at his or her job.

pec·u·*la*·tion. The criminal misappropriation of money or property that has been entrusted. Used synonymously with EMBEZZLEMENT. The property must be in the custody of the person who misappropriates it, otherwise the crime is LARCENY or theft.

pe·*cu*·ni·ar·y. Of, or involving, money.

ped·**er·as·ty.** A criminal offense, the definition of which may vary somewhat from state to state. It is generally defined as unnatural sexual relations between males, and is sometimes specified as oral copulation, anal copulation, or any other abnormal relations. Under statutory definitions in some jurisdictions, *pederasty* is identical with SODOMY.

pe·**nal.** Punishable or relating to punishment, especially from a criminal standpoint. Specifying or requiring punishment.

pen·**al·ty.** **(1)** A punishment fixed by law for a criminal offense. **(2)** The fixed sum of money which a party is obliged to pay for failing to carry out the terms of a bond or contract. (3) Any unfortunate result or consequence of an act or condition.

pen·dent jur·is·*dic*·tion. The principle of law under which a Federal court handles all questions involved in a case, if the Federal court originally got JURISDICTION under a substantial Federal question. This means that after the Federal court begins to handle the matter, the state issues involved in the situation will be adjudicated in the one action by the Federal court.

pen·den·te lite. (Latin–pen·*den*·tuh lite) During the lawsuit; pending litigation.

pe·*nol*·o·gy. An area of criminology that deals with prison management and the treatment and handling of inmates.

per *cur*·i·am o·*pin*·ion. (Latin–per *kyoor*·ee·am) An opinion of the whole court, as distinguished from an opinion written by an individual judge. At times, a *per curiam* opinion may be one written by the presiding judge or chief justice.

per·*emp*·to·ry *chal*·lenge. A challenge to a JUROR by an attorney for either side who can reject a prospective juror as a matter of right. After hearing the questioning of a prospective juror, an attorney may feel that the client's case would not best be served by having this particular individual on the jury.

per·*form*·ance. See SPECIFIC PERFORMANCE.

per·*form*·ance in *spe*·cie. In CONTRACT law, a requirement that performance must be in exact accord with the specifications or conditions set out in the contract.

pe·ri·*od*·ic *ten*·an·cy. An occupancy agreement by which the landlord and tenant agree that the tenant shall continue to hold the property for successive periods of the same length, unless terminated sooner by notice. An example would be a tenancy from year to year, or from season to season. A tenancy of this type is regarded as continuing at the end of each of the specified periods, unless terminated by notice.

per·ju·ry. Willfully making a false statement concerning a material matter by a witness under oath in a judicial proceeding. The crime occurs any time the witness is put under oath, whether at a trial, a GRAND JURY inquest, or any other judicial proceeding.

perk. Colloquial form of PERQUISITE.

per·*pet*·u·al es·*tate*. Another name for an estate in fee simple. See FEE SIMPLE; see ESTATE.

per·*pet*·u·at·ing *tes*·ti·mo·ny. Any technique used for the preservation of testimony for future use from witnesses who are so old, disabled, or diseased that they are likely to die before a matter can come to trial, or are known to be moving from the country or state. Usually, testimony is gotten on the record by the taking of DEPOSITIONS with the prior approval of the court.

per·pe·*tu*·i·ty. (Sometimes called the *rule against perpetuities*). A principle of old English law that forbids tying up estates and preventing them from being sold for any great length of time. Many of the old English lords and estate owners wanted to make sure their holdings would pass on to their family line forever. Consequently, wills left by these landowners granted LIFE ESTATES to their heirs, indefinitely. To prevent the *dead hand* from controlling the efforts of the living, English courts ruled that an estate may not be tied up for a period longer than the lifetime of a person or persons living when the will was made (sometimes legally termed "persons in being"), plus an additional 21 years and a few months thereafter to allow for a gestation period for unborn offspring. After that period of time, title to the land must pass absolutely. Variations of this old principle are part of the statutory law in all jurisdictions in the United States. If property could be tied up indefinitely, a few land-owing families could eventually control all real estate.

per·qui·site. Any gain, profit, or privilege due to or received by an employee, other than salary or wages from the job.

per se. (Latin–per see, per say) *Of, or in itself.* In itself, or taken alone.

per·son. Any individual or *artificial person* created by law, including a CORPORATION. From a legal standpoint, people and corporations are all protected by the law. For example, the Constitution of the United States provides that "The rights of the people to be secure in their persons, houses, papers, and effects, against unreasonable searches and seizures..." also applies to corporations. In like manner, *artificial persons* (corporations) are given "equal protection of the laws," and property may not be taken from them without "due process of law."

per·son·al·ty. Any item of personal property, CHATTELS, automobiles, etc. Any property except real property.

per stir·pes. (Latin–per *stir*·peez) By stock. Describes a procedure for settling inheritance of an estate by giving equal shares to family groups, rather than an equal percentage to each descendant. Under *per stirpes* distribution, each child (son or daughter) would get an equal part of a father's estate. If a child was deceased at the time of the father's death, then the children descended from the deceased child (grandchildren of the donor) would receive the child's inheritance, divided equally among those grandchildren.

pet·**it** *ju*·**ry.** See PETTY JURY.

pe·*ti*·**tion.** A written application or request, addressed to a court or official body, asking for the exercise of authority in correcting some wrong. It is a written request for relief or REMEDY.

pe·*ti*·**tion in** *bank*·**rupt**·**cy.** The request filed with a BANKRUPTCY court requesting that a debtor be adjudged a bankrupt and be allowed the privileges of the bankruptcy laws. A *petition in, bankruptcy* is usually filed by the debtor in a *voluntary bankruptcy,* but may be filed by creditors in an *involuntary bankruptcy.*

pe·*ti*·**tion**·**er.** One who presents a cause of action, or legal petition to a court, asking for a legal relief or compensation. The *petitioner* is, therefore, identical to the PLAINTIFF in a lawsuit. The party to the lawsuit against whom the action is filed is called the *respondent,* or more commonly *defendant.*

pet·**i**·**to**·**ry** *ac*·**tion.** A court action brought to establish the TITLE to real estate. It is distinguished from a mere action to gain possession of property, as to evict a renter occupying land. In a petitory action the plaintiff must recover on the strength and proof of his or her own title, and not by proving that there are defects in the title of the party occupying the property.

pet·**ty** *ju*·**ry.** A jury for the trial of a civil or criminal case. Historically, a *petty jury* was called a *petit jury* or *small jury,* from the Norman French terms sometimes used in early England. Traditionally made up of 12 jurors, it was called a *petit jury* to distinguish it from the larger early day grand jury, which has a different function. Under statutes in a number of states in the U.S., a *petty jury* may be composed of fewer than 12 jurors. See GRAND JURY.

plain·**tiff.** The party who commences a court action; the one who begins a lawsuit.

plain·**tiff in** *er*·**ror.** See PARTIES.

plea. (1) The answer made by a defendant when faced with a criminal charge. If the defendant *stands mute,* that is, refuses to enter a plea, then the judge will automatically enter a *plea* of not guilty. The pleas

162

accepted by all courts are *guilty,* or *not guilty,* with some courts accepting a plea of *nolo contendere.* (2) A method of putting forward a defense in a civil case. (3) A descriptive term for several old types of civil motions that have largely been replaced. For example, a *plea in bar* may today be called a motion for dismissal.

plead•ing. The formal allegations by the parties to a civil lawsuit of the claims and defenses of each side. The case begins with a written statement by the plaintiff, followed by a statement by the defendant concerning any legal defense or COUNTER CLAIM that may be asserted, followed by the plaintiff's response, until the court has a clear picture of the entire dispute.

pledge. The depositing of personal property by a debtor with a creditor as security for payment of the debt. A BAILMENT of a chattel (generally personal property) as security for debt without effecting a transfer of title. See CHATTEL.

pledg•*ee.* One to whom pledged property is given. See PLEDGE.

pledg•or. One who puts up property in pledge as security for a debt. See PLEDGE.

ple•na•ry. Complete in every respect; full. A *plenary confession* would be full and complete.

plot•tage. A term used in appraising several parcels of land joined under one ownership, making possible greater value and utilization than could be obtained for the individual parcels. The term is frequently used in EMINENT DOMAIN to designate additional value given to lots that are contiguous.

plur•ies *sum*•mons. See ALIAS SUMMONS.

points of law. (1) Those distinct propositions of law, or arguments, on which each side relies in a lawsuit. (2) Those distinct propositions of law, or legal principals, on which a court relies in handing down an opinion.

po•*lice pow*•er. The inherent powers of a government to exercise reasonable controls over matters that affect the security, health, safety, morals, and welfare of the general public, except where specifically prohibited by constitutional or legislative regulations.

po•*lit*•i•cal rights. Those rights that pertain to participation in the governmental process, such as the right to hold government office, to vote, to be issued a passport.

poll. A head; an individual.

poll tax. A tax levied on individuals as a prerequisite for voting.

poll•ing a *ju*•ry. The act of asking each member of a jury to individually declare his or her verdict. This polling may be done after the FOREMAN has reported the verdict, which allegedly is the unanimous decision of all individual jurors. With some rare exceptions *polling a jury* is authorized by statute where a unanimous verdict is not legally required.

pol•y•an•dry. See POLYGAMY.

po•*lyg*•a•my. A criminal offense, consisting of having more than one wife or husband at the same time. This is also a valid definition\of BIG-AMY. When used in a legal sense, BIGAMY usually means a second marriage while not divorced from a living spouse. *Polygamy* usually implies more than two plural marriages, while BIGAMY usually means only two. In common usage *polygamy* means having multiple wives, while *polyandry* means having multiple husbands.

pos•i•tive *ev*•i•dence. See DIRECT EVIDENCE.

pos•se com•i•ta•tus. (Latin-*poss*•ee com•i•*tat*•us) *Power of the County.* The manpower of the county that may be drawn up by deputizing individual males to assist law enforcement officers. Unless changed by statute, this includes every male over 15 years of age. Whether equal rights legislation has changed this authority to include women has not been settled.

pos•*ses*•sion. (1) Legal control of real estate or personal property. The holding for one's use and enjoyment, either as owner or under authority from the owner. If property is held without lawful authority it is said to be *unlawful possession.* (2) Under some criminal statutes, merely having something on one's person or in one's car is *possession.* An example would be having a smuggled diamond hidden inside one's stocking while going through customs.

post *dat*•ed. To date an INSTRUMENT or document later than the date on which it was really made. Checks and other instruments of this kind may be invalid, depending on the circumstances and individual state laws.

pos•*ter*•i•ty. (1) Future generations. (2) All descendants of an individual in a direct line.

post•hu•mous. (1) Arising or continuing after one's death. (2) Published after the death of the author. (3) Born after the death of its father, or after the death of the mother where birth was made possible by Caesarean section.

pow·er of at·*tor*·ney. A formal document by which one individual gives power to another to perform a specific act or to transact general business for the former. It is in effect, a contract of AGENCY. The person designated to act for the PRINCIPAL may be any legally and mentally competent adult, and is not necessarily a lawyer or attorney at law. See ATTORNEY IN FACT. The person who holds a *power of attorney* for another is sometimes called a "private attorney," as distinguished from a "public attorney" or "attorney at law."

pow·er of sale. A provision sometimes included in a MORTGAGE, permitting the holder of a mortgage to sell the property if payments are not made. This provision is not as widely used as it once was. A provision of this kind may also be inserted in a DEED OF TRUST.

prac·tice. (1) Customary usage of any kind. (2) The method of proceeding in the court system for the enforcement of rights. This is in contrast with SUBSTANTIVE LAW, which sets out a legal right or denounces a legal wrong, without instituting action to correct it. (3) The giving of legal advice to clients, or presenting and arguing a case for the client in court. These are the basic activities in the *practice of law.*

prae·ci·pe. (Latin–*press*·uh·pee, *prees*·uh·pee) *In practice.* A written order, directed to the clerk, requesting the clerk to issue a WRIT or take some action that does not need to be presented to the judge personally, or in open court.

pray·er. A request set forth in legal PLEADINGS, asking for relief such as damages or an injunction.

prec·a·to·ry. Words of request or entreaty. Words that are advisory only, and not legally binding. For example, *precatory* words in a will may express the testator's desires, but are binding only from a moral standpoint when they are not included in words of command or imperative terms.

prec·e·dent. A previously decided case on the same set of facts is usually regarded by the courts as binding, or as a *precedent.* It is a previously decided authority or example for a case that comes after.

pre·cept. (1) A command or principle, intended to be followed as a general rule of action. (2) A command or order by a legally constituted authority to a subordinate.

pre·*clude*. To prevent, to ban, to bar. For example, an injunction by the court may *preclude* a builder from building an office building on a foundation that is not as substantial as those required under the building code.

pre·cog·*ni*·tion. Questioning or examination of a witness prior to trial.

pre·*emp*·tion. The right to buy something before it can be sold to anyone else. *Preemptive rights* are rights that must be honored before other rights are exercised.

***pref*·er·ence.** (Or creditor's preference) **(1)** An insolvent debtor's payment to one or more GENERAL CREDITORS to the exclusion of others. Under the Federal Bankruptcy Act, if creditors are given preference on payments made within four months prior to bankruptcy, the court may order these payments to be distributed to all general creditors on a PRO RATA basis. It should be noted, however, that so-called PREFERRED CREDITORS have the first right to be paid off, and first claim on the debtor's assets. Claims of these preferred creditors may arise from a lien, mortgage, or other security arrangement. A general creditor is on notice (at least CONSTRUCTIVE NOTICE) of the existence of the rights of preferred creditors, since these are usually recorded at the county clerk's office (or other required location) when credit is extended by the general creditor.

pre·*ferred* stock. See STOCK.

***prej*·u·dice.** A preconceived bias; a prejudgment, without attention to the facts involved.

prej·u·*di*·cial *er*·ror. An error that substantially affects the legal rights and obligations of a party to a lawsuit. It is the type of error that may be sufficient to order a new trial when the matter comes up on APPEAL.

pre·med·i·*ta*·tion. Plotting, contriving, planning, or deliberating in advance to commit a criminal act. MANSLAUGHTER is usually distinguished from MURDER by the absence of malice aforethought, or *premeditation*.

***pre*·mi·um.** **(1)** The amount paid in one sum, or periodically, for coverage under an insurance policy. **(2)** Any bonus or reward for an act done. **(3)** Stock of a corporation is described as *at a premium* when the selling price is above nominal or face value.

pre·*pay*·ment *pen*·al·ty. A charge sometimes made for paying off a loan prior to the due date. The charge is usually a percentage of the balance, such as one percent. A *prepayment penalty* is sometimes called an ACQUISITION CHARGE.

pre·*pon*·der·ance of *ev·i·*dence. That balance of evidence which seems most consistent with reason and probability under the facts; the greater weight of evidence from the standpoint of credibility and that which is convincing to the mind. The *preponderance of evidence* does not necessarily mean the largest volume or quantity of evidence, or the greatest number of witnesses who take the witness stand.

pre·*rog*·a·tive writs. A group of legal WRITS, including HABEAS CORPUS, QUO WARRANTO, MANDAMUS, PROHIBITION, and procendendo. The issuance of these writs by the courts is now generally regulated by statute. These writs were used by early English courts in only exceptional cases, and were regarded as the prerogative of the crown, hence the name *prerogative writs.*

pre·*scrip*·tion. The acquisition of the title or right to something through its long continued possession and claim of ownership. The length of time needed varies from state to state. For example, a stray dog may eventually be owned by possession and claim of ownership for the prescribed number of years. A claim of this kind must be open and public at all times, however. If neighbors have used a path across land for many years, they may have acquired an easement by *prescription,* but the use must have been open, notorious, and under claim of right for the specified number of years determined by state statute. There is a distinction between title to real property by *prescription* and by LIMITATION, in that the title by prescription is based on a claimed or presumed grant or deed to the property.

pre·*sent*·ment. (1) A form of INDICTMENT returned by a GRAND JURY from information originating from knowledge or initiative of jury members. It differs from the usual form of indictment which involves the presentation of evidence already developed from outside sources and presented for grand jury consideration by the prosecuting attorney. (2) The exhibition of a NEGOTIABLE INSTRUMENT on which payment is due, and an accompanying request for payment. For example, when a PROMISSORY NOTE falls due, the holder may make a *presentment,* which is in effect a demand for payment. The note must be exhibited at the time of the demand, for the *presentment* to be valid as the basis for a lawsuit for the sum due.

pre·*sump*·tive *dam*·a·ges. Sometimes used to mean EXEMPLARY DAMAGES.

pre·ter·*mit*·ted heir. A child or other descendant that is not included in a will. This may result from deliberate intent, oversight, or because of the fact that the child was born after the will was made. If this is deliberate, the will is usually drafted to cut off the heir with a nominal inheritance. Unless deliberately cut off, statutes in a number of states provide that such unmentioned child shall share in the estate in proportion to the other heirs.

pri·ma fac·ie. (Latin–*pry·*muh *fay·*shee, "at first sight," or "on its face") Describes material or EVIDENCE that is legally sufficient to establish a fact or a case, unless disproved.

pri·ma·ry ev·i·dence. Original, or first hand EVIDENCE; that which affords the greatest likelihood of certainty. The original of a document is *primary evidence,* since the document speaks for itself and its contents. A stenographic or xerographic copy would be secondary evidence, rather than *primary evidence.*

pri·mo·gen·i·ture. (1) The right of the eldest son to inherit the property or TITLE of a parent, to the exclusion of all other children. (2) The state of being the first-born child among several children of the same parents.

prin·ci·pal. (1) In civil law, one who hires another to act for him in business dealings, subject to control and instruction of the *principal.* The person hired to act for the *principal* is called an AGENT. As a general rule of law, the *principal* is legally responsible for the acts or contracts of the agent, so long as the agent acted within the scope of authority given by the *principal.* (2) In criminal law, the chief or another actual participant in the crime.

pris·on. A penitentiary; a location for holding those serving long-term sentences for crime. It is distinguished from a JAIL, which is used for those serving short-term sentences and those awaiting trial.

pris·on·er. An individual held to await trial, or following conviction for crime. The *prisoner* may be confined to a JAIL or PRISON.

pri·vate at·tor·ney. See PUBLIC ATTORNEY, from which a *private attorney* or holder of a POWER OF ATTORNEY letter is distinguished.

pri·vate law. (1) Law that relates to the relationships between individuals, rather than law that pertains to the general public (public law). (2) A statute passed to give some right to one individual only. For example, a postal worker may have been fired and prosecuted since he was mistakenly identified as an armed robber. As a result, the worker lost pension rights. These could be restored by a *private law bill* introduced by a sympathetic Congressman.

priv·i·lege from ar·rest. A privilege extended to certain classes of individuals who are free from arrest on CIVIL process and in some cases on CRIMINAL charges. Under the customs of international law, ambassadors and other high diplomatic officials are exempt from arrest. Members of Congress, attorneys while conducting court business, clergymen going to church, and some witnesses and parties to lawsuits, may all be exempt from arrests in civil cases and some kinds of criminal violations. This privilege is statutory, and varies from state to state, except in the case of diplomatic officials who may be exempt by international law.

priv·i·leged **com·mu·ni·*ca*·tion.** Discussions, revelations, or conversations that one cannot be legally compelled to disclose. Included are communications between lawyer and client, priest and penitent, doctor and patient.

*priv·i·*ty. **(1)** A mutual or successive relationship to the same property rights. An heir is in *privity* with his ancestor. **(2)** The relationship of mutual interest existing between parties to a contract. **(3)** Private or secret knowledge shared with another or others and usually implying consent or concurrence by those who share it.

prize. Ships, cargo, or other property captured at sea during wartime.

pro *bo·*no. Describes legal work done for the benefit of the public interest, or for charity.

pro *bo·*no *pu·*bli·co. (Latin) *For the public good.*

pro *for·*ma. (Latin) *As a matter of form.* To facilitate proceedings, or as a matter of form.

*pro·*bate. **(1)** The broad legal meaning is *to prove.* **(2)** As more commonly used, to prove the authenticity of a will. **(3)** All matters within the jurisdiction or under supervision of a PROBATE COURT.

pro·*ba*·tion. The suspension of a jail or prison term for one convicted but not imprisoned, on condition of continued good behavior and reporting to a supervising probation officer.

pro·*ba*·tion·er. One convicted of crime but allowed to stay out of jail or prison under supervised PROBATION.

*pro·*ba·tive. Offers proof of evidence.

pro·*ce*·dur·al law. That part of the law which applies and handles the substantive law; the legal machinery by which rights and duties of a legal nature are enforced. This is distinguished from SUBSTANTIVE LAW, which deals with the rights and duties of persons to each other and to society in general. See ADJECTIVE LAW.

pro·*ce*·dure. Techniques, processes, or machinery used for enforcing a legal right. The methods and rules for using the law. SUBSTANTIVE LAW gives or defines a legal right. PROCEDURAL LAW encompasses those steps used to secure or preserve that right.

pro·*ceed*·ing. The method of conducting judicial business before a court or judge. Any legal action.

***pro*·cess.** (1) Any WRIT or order issued at the start or during the progress of a legal proceeding; especially, a writ issued to bring a defendant into court. (2) The whole course of proceedings in a case, civil or criminal, from beginning to end. (3) In patent law, a method of effecting a useful result other than by a machine or mechanical device.

***proc*·tor.** An individual appointed or employed to manage the affairs of another; an AGENT or an ATTORNEY with authority to handle affairs of another person.

pro·*duce*. (1) To deliver up or bring forward. To *produce* on a subpoena ordering a witness to bring a record implies the handing of the record to the judge and the reading aloud in court if desired. A *motion to produce* is a request of the court that you or your attorney be allowed to examine documents in the possession of the opposing party in a legal controversy. (2) Agricultural production and products, as well as the offspring of domesticated animals that are subject to ownership and property rights.

pro·*gres*·sive tax. A tax that levies assessments increasingly in proportion to ability to pay. An income tax is an example.

pro·hi·*bi*·tion. The name of a writ issued by a court, directed to the judge and parties to a suit in a lower (inferior) court, ordering the discontinuance of a lawsuit because the original cause of action (or some matter arising out of it) is properly within the JURISDICTION of another court. A writ from a higher court that prevents a lower court from exceeding its jurisdiction.

***prom*·is·so·ry es·*top*·pel.** The legal principle that someone who makes a promise and expects another to do something in reliance on that promise cannot later renege on the promise and expect that it will not be binding as a contract. For example, a businessman requested a management consultant to fly to Guatemala City to look over a factory in company with the businessman. The consultant flew to Guatemala City at the time scheduled, but the businessman had a change of mind and decided he was no longer interested in the factory, or having consulting work done there. Under the *promissory estoppel* principle the businessman would be liable to the consultant for costs and reasonable fees for the time expended. See ESTOPPEL.

prom·is·so·ry **note.** A written promise by one person to pay, unconditionally, to another person named therein, to order, or to the bearer, a certain sum of money at a specified time or on demand.

proof. Anything that serves to convince the mind of the truth or falsity of a fact or proposition, including evidence for or against it.

prop·er·ty. **(1)** The legal right to the possession, use, enjoyment, and disposal of a thing; an unrestricted and exclusive right or interest in or to a thing. **(2)** Anything that may be owned or possessed.

pro·*po*·nent. **(1)** One who proposes or argues in favor of something; one who makes a proposal or proposition. **(2)** The individual who offers a will for PROBATE.

pro·*pri*·e·tar·y rights. Those rights that accrue to the owner of property by virtue of the ownership itself.

pro ra·ta. (Latin–pro *ray*·tuh or *rah*·tuh) Proportionately. According to a fixed share, rate, or percentage.

pro·*rate*, *pro*·rate. To share or distribute proportionately; to make a pro rata distribution.

pro·ro·*ga*·tion. A contract agreement to have any disputes concerning the contract handled in the courts of a specified state, and to abide by laws and court decisions of that state.

pros·e·cute. **(1)** To pursue or follow up a civil right. **(2)** To initiate criminal charges and to bring to trial.

pros·e·cu·tor. The attorney who initiates proceedings and tries individuals accused of crime, representing the state or Federal government. See PARTIES.

pros·ti·*tu*·tion. The practice of indulging in promiscuous sexual acts for money or other things of value. It is a criminal act in most states, and in some the law pertains to men who sell their sexual favors as well as to women.

pro·test. **(1)** A formal notification, usually by a NOTARY PUBLIC, for the holder of a bill or note stating that the instrument was duly presented for payment at the proper time and place, and that payment was refused. This is usually a necessary procedure that must be performed to recover from those secondarily liable (the drawer and endorser).

(2) The term *protest* is sometimes loosely applied to the process of presenting an instrument for payment, demanding payment, and giving notice to the drawer or endorser that they may be held responsible for payment. (3) A written declaration by the master of a ship, stating that damages to cargo were occasioned by storm or other unavoidable causes, and rejecting liability on the part of the crew. (4) Any document stating that the writer objects to a payment demanded, is paying under protest, and reserves the legal right to pursue the matter.

pro·*thon*·o·tar·y. The principal or chief clerk of certain courts in some states.

pro·*vi*·sion·al *rem*·e·dy. A class of legal REMEDY adopted for the immediate occasion or for present need. An injunction of a temporary nature, or the appointment of a receiver, are examples of provisional remedies.

prov·o·*ca*·tion. Action or behavior by one person toward another that incites the latter to do a particular deed.

prox·i·mate. Next in order; nearest; closest in causal connection; next in relation to cause and effect.

prox·i·mate cause. In TORT law, the cause that necessarily sets in operation the events that result in injury or damage. That without which an injury would not have resulted. The real cause, or producing cause which results in a tort. Stated in other words: that which, in a natural and continuous sequence, unbroken by any efficient intervening cause, produces the injury, and without which the result would not have occurred. One of the basic problems in tort law is the connection between the act or omission of the DEFENDANT and the damage which the PLAINTIFF has suffered. A principle of tort law is that the defendant is not responsible for damages unless the defendant's action was the *proximate cause,* or *legal cause* of the injury or damage to the plaintiff. But the *proximate cause* may be distinguishable from the *immediate cause* of harm. For example, without thinking or looking, "A" allowed an inflated automobile tire and wheel to roll down the hill. Half way down the incline, the rolling wheel struck a wandering horse. In turn, the horse bolted in surprise and ran into a pregnant woman on the sidewalk. The woman was knocked down, sustained broken bones, and had an immediate miscarriage. From past court decisions it is likely that the court would hold "A" responsible for the unthinking, negligent act in letting the wheel run free. In assessing responsibility, we could say that the horse was the *immediate cause* of the injury, and that the uncontrolled wheel was the *proximate cause.* There is a great diversity of court decisions in this field, and if the owner of the stray horse was negligent in allowing the animal to get out, then the horse's owner might also be liable. The problem is in evaluating which causes are so closely connected with the result and of such significance that the law is justified in imposing liability. *Proximate cause* is an extensive, complicated study in tort law, and some authorities point out that *proximate cause* is an indefinite term–merely a limitation which the courts have placed on a wrongdoer's responsibility for the consequences of conduct.

*prox.*y. **(1)** An authorization to vote at a meeting in place of an absent stockholder. Although statutory provisions vary, the usual provisions are: **(a)** that the *proxy* shall be in writing, **(b)** that the individual giving it can revoke at any time, **(c)** that it will expire within a statutory number of months or years from date, unless otherwise specified. **(2)** The name given to the individual holding the authority to vote for another.

*pru.*dence. In a legal sense, good judgment, attentiveness, or precaution applied to conduct or business.

*pru.*dent *per.*son rule. The principle in TRUST law that a trustee must invest trust funds in conservative, comparatively safe investments, or run the risk of being personally liable if investments are lost through bad investments. The trustee is not held liable, however, for investing trust funds in a prudent manner.

*pub.*lic at.*tor.*ney. A term sometimes used to mean an attorney at law, as distinguished from a private attorney or attorney in fact. See ATTORNEY IN FACT.

*pub.*lic charge. See CHARGE.

*pub.*lic cor.po.*ra.*tion. A corporation created for the administration of civil government, such as a municipality.

*pub.*lic de.*fend.*er. An attorney, usually holding public office, whose duty is to defend individuals accused of criminal offenses and who are unable to pay for their own lawyer.

*pub.*lic do.*main.* **(1)** Publicly owned land. **(2)** The public ownership status of writings, documents, or publications that are not protected by copyrights, and may be reprinted or quoted by anyone.

pub·lic *int*·er·est law. Legal efforts expended by an attorney for some deprived group or for the public interest and welfare. Usually this is done without pay, or for nominal pay. See PRO BONO PUBLICO.

pub·lic law. The law that relates to the public as a whole, or to the government, rather than to specific persons. It is distinguished from PRIVATE LAW that pertains to the relationships between individuals as such.

pub·li·*ca*·tion. In the law of LIBEL and SLANDER, the making of a libelous or defamatory statement to a person or persons other than the one who is defamed.

pu·ni·tive. That which relates to punishment; inflicting or aiming at punishment.

pu·ni·tive *dam*·a·ges. See EXEMPLARY DAMAGES.

pu·ni·to·ry *dam*·a·ges. See EXEMPLARY DAMAGES.

pur·chase *mon*·ey *mort*·gage. A MORTGAGE given, concurrently with a sale of land, by the buyer to the seller, on the same land, to secure all or part of the purchase price.

purge. To free, or exonerate from a charge. For example, "The attorney complied with the judge's order to *purge* himself from contempt of court."

pur·*port*. The legal effect, or substantial meaning; the substance; the meaning.

pur·view. Within the scope, or intent. For example, murder falls within the purview of the criminal law of all civilized peoples.

pu·ta·tive. Supposed; reported; reputed.

Q

quae·re. (Latin–*kwir*·ee) Question. That which is open to doubt or question.

qual·i·fi·*ca*·tion. (1) A condition that must be complied with in order to obtain a specified privilege. (2) A limiting modification or restriction. (3) A requirement or personal attribute that is a legal prerequisite for holding public office. For example, one *qualification* to hold the office of President of the United States is to be a native-born citizen. (Article II, United States Constitution.)

qual•i•fied ac•*cep*•tance. A counteroffer, proposing new terms or conditions of some kind that are not in complete agreement with the terms proposed by someone offering to make a CONTRACT. If accepted by the party making the original offer, a contract will result. (A term sometimes used in contract law that is a misnomer, since a *qualified acceptance* is not an acceptance at all.)

quan•tum mer•u•it. (Latin–*kwon*•tum *mer*•oo•it) As much as merited. An old English type of PLEADING for the recovery of work and labor. It was a claim for reasonable value of the services rendered, rather than a contract claim.

quash. To nullify by judicial order or action; to abate; to make void. The term frequently refers to the action of a court in nullifying an indictment or a lower court order.

qua•si. (Latin–*kway*•sie, *kway*•zie, *kwaw*•see, *kwaw*•zee) As if. Having resemblance to; approximately as if; having some of the qualities of.

qua•si-ju•*di*•cial. Semi-judicial in character; having some of the qualities of the judicial system. Administrative bodies are often said to be *quasi-judicial,* since they have the right to hold hearings and make investigations into disputed claims and alleged infractions of regulations and rules, and to make decisions that are regarded as legally binding, after the manner of the courts.

que•ry. A word used for questioning some legal term or holding. Sometimes used interchangeably with QUAERE.

quid pro quo. (Latin–kwid proe kwoe) *What for what.* As used in the law of contracts, the term means *something for something.* In other words, it means *valuable consideration,* which consideration, or inducement, is a basic requirement for the validity of a contract. See CONSIDERATION.

qui•et *ti*•tle. Describes an action to quiet title, or remove a CLOUD ON THE TITLE to real estate.

qui tam. (Latin–quie tam) *Who as well.* A legal action initiated by an informer under a statute which provides that part of any penalty assessed will go to the state and the remainder, to the informer. It is an action for the state, as well as for the informer.

quit•claim deed. A deed that transfers to the buyer only such rights or property title as the seller (grantor) had at the time the deed was delivered. This means that a *quitclaim deed* may transfer title or ownership as effectively as a WARRANTY DEED. If there should be a defect or a CLOUD ON THE TITLE, as the lawyers phrase it, the new purchaser buys subject to that defect. In buying under a *quitclaim* deed, the burden is on the purchaser to find out whether there are claims or encumbrances against the property.

quo an·i·mo. (Latin–kwoe *an·i·*moe) *With what motive.*

quod. (Latin–kwod) *That which,* or *that.*

*quo·*rum. A majority of members or officers of an organization or body that, when duly assembled, is a requisite number to do business.

quo war·ran·to. (Latin–qwoe *wah·*ran·toe–"Through what authority?") A writ by which a court questions and makes a determination of a public official's right to hold a public office or to take a specific action while holding that office. In some instances a *quo warranto* proceeding may be used to question whether a CORPORATION has the right to continue to make use of its CHARTER or FRANCHISE. This is on the idea that a franchise is a trust vested in the corporation by the state, and if the trust is violated with respect to any of the conditions, there should be a forfeiture of the corporate franchise or charter.

R

range. A term used in a survey description of land to designate a row or tier of townships. Descriptions are usually given by section, township, and *range* in U.S. government land surveys.

rape. An act of sexual intercourse by a male with a female other than his wife in which the female resists and her resistance is overcome by force. Any sexual penetration, however slight, is sufficient to complete the crime. Generally, both resistance and FORCE are required. If the perpetrator uses a weapon or threatens great bodily harm without exerting force, the courts usually say the woman need not cry out or resist if it appears serious harm is imminent. *Rape* is distinguished from seduction in that the former requires force or a serious threat, while in seduction the female is induced to participate. If the female consents in the end, it is not *rape,* even though force may be used at the outset. When the female is unconscious, dragged, mentally ill, or so drunk that she does not know what she is doing, the courts say that she is incapable of giving consent, and the offense is *rape*. Most courts also say that *rape by fraud* has occurred if a male impersonates a woman's husband to have sexual relations. A variation of this crime is *statutory rape,* which is sexual intercourse without force by a male with a female who is under the age specified by state law. This age, called the AGE OF CONSENT, varies in different states from 10 to 18 years of age. Criminal prohibitions against *statutory rape* protect girls of tender years by placing responsibility on the male to determine the girl's age. The law presumes without exception that a girl under the statutory age does not have sufficient experience or knowledge of human relationships to understand or judge the social, moral and physical consequences of a sexual relationship.

rate. (1) A fixed ratio between two things. A standard or proportion by which value is set. (2) A basic charge for service, as for a public utility.

rate *fix*.ing. The process by which the rate of charge is set for the customer, as the rate fixing payment to be made for electricity by the kilowatt hour used.

rat.i.fi.*ca*.tion. (1) The confirmation of an act previously done. The affirmance of an act which was not binding until that time. (2) An adoption. For example, the principal later *ratified* the unauthorized action of his agent.

***rav*.ish.** To rape. See RAPE.

real es.*tate*. Real property; realty; landed property; all estates in land or interests in land that are in FEE SIMPLE or for life.

real *ev*.i.dence. Objects that are exhibited to a jury, rather than oral testimony. For example a gun used to perpetrate an armed robbery would be REAL EVIDENCE.

real *prop*.er.ty. Land, that which is affixed to land, and that which is incidental or appurtenant to land. Any property which is not *real property* is personal property. A permanent fixture or counter affixed to the floor of a building is a part of the *real property,* unless excepted by statute. A number of states, by statute, specify that store fixtures and appurtenances, intended for use by the merchant in the day to day operation of his business, may be torn loose and taken by the merchant on the expiration of a lease. The merchant, however, has a legal duty not to seriously harm the building in removing fixtures, counters, or appurtenances. A building erected on leased land becomes a part of the *real property,* and may not be removed on expiration of the lease, unless the lease agreement so provides. A building erected on the wrong lot becomes a part of that lot, for legal purposes.

re·al·ty. Used synonymously with REAL PROPERTY.

rea·son·a·ble doubt. That doubt which does not leave the conviction of a moral certainty; the kind of doubt that leaves an ordinary, prudent individual with a question about the truth.

re·bate. A return of part of a payment; a discount paid at the end of a transaction.

re·*but*. To contradict or oppose; to dispute by evidence or proof.

re·*but*·tal. **(1)** The act of refuting or disproving something. **(2)** In courtroom practice, the introduction of evidence that refutes evidence previously offered by the opposing party in a lawsuit.

re·*call*, re·call. The procedure by which an office holder may be removed from office by a vote of the electorate. A *recall* is usually initiated by a petition with a specified number of signatures from qualified voters.

re·*ceipt*. **(1)** Written acknowledgment that money or a thing of value has been turned over, without stating any affirmative obligation upon either party to it. As a mere acknowledgment of payment, a *receipt* is subject to oral testimony to show the circumstances under which it was given. **(2)** The act of getting or obtaining.

re·*ceiv*·er. **(1)** An independent, outside individual appointed by a court to manage business, property, or money during a lawsuit. **(2)** An individual who gets stolen property. Knowledge of the stolen character of the goods is necessary to convict of the crime of RECEIVING.

re·*ceiv*·er·ship. A procedure by which a court appoints a TRUSTEE, ministerial officer, or RECEIVER, to take over the management of property, money, or a business. This step is usually taken in a situation where the property is in litigation, or in corporate reorganization; sometimes the receivership winds up the affairs of a business that is being liquidated. The CREDITORS of a business may ask the court for a receiver when there is reason to believe fraud or mismanagement exists in the operation of the business. The object of the *receivership* is to protect assets for those who will ultimately be entitled to them.

re·*ceiv*·ing sto·len goods. The acceptance of property or goods, knowing that such items have been unlawfully or feloniously obtained, as a result of theft, EMBEZZLEMENT, EXTORTION, or some other criminal act. *Receiving stolen goods* is a crime in all jurisdictions.

re‧**cess.** (1) A short interval during which a court suspends business, usually for a matter of an hour or two. (2) A suspension of legislative business.

re‧*cid*‧**i**‧**vist.** A criminal repeater; a habitual criminal; one frequently in trouble with the law.

re‧*cip*‧**ro**‧**cal** *con*‧**tract.** A bilateral contract, the parties to which enter into mutual engagements.

re‧*cip*‧**ro**‧**cal wills.** Wills executed by two or more individuals, containing reciprocal testamentary provisions in favor of each other. This may be handled by separate documents or by a united will.

rec‧**i**‧*proc*‧**i**‧**ty.** A mutual exchange of privileges. Mutuality.

re‧*cit*‧**al.** The narration or formal declaration in a legal document that sets forth the reason for the document, or the transaction which it represents.

reck‧**less**‧**ness.** Conduct amounting to more than NEGLIGENCE; wanton disregard for the probability of injurious consequences to others; heedlessness.

re‧*cog*‧**ni**‧**zance.** A promise or obligation to do some act, which obligation is entered into the court record. It may be a promise to appear for trial before a criminal court on a specified date without having to post a bail bond; it may be a promise to keep the peace, to pay a debt, or to satisfy some other legal obligation.

rec‧**on**‧**cil**‧**i**‧*a*‧**tion.** (1) Used as synonymous with *condonation* in divorce law. See CONDONATION. (2) Forgiveness of injuries by one or both sides in a legal dispute.

re‧**con**‧*vey*‧**ance.** The transfer of TITLE of real estate from the owner to the preceding owner. This particular transfer is commonly used in those states when a debt is satisfied under a DEED OF TRUST. In this situation the trustee conveys the title he has held on condition back to the owner who created the trust (the owner who borrowed on the property by creating a trust deed). See TRUST DEED.

rec‧**ord, court of.** Any court that retains a permanent record of proceedings and actions. Part of the record consists of papers and documents filed with the clerk of the court, and part consists of transcripts and materials compiled by the court reporter. Usually, the lowest ranking courts, such as the JUSTICE OF THE PEACE Court, are not courts of record.

re‧*cord*‧**ing.** The process of filing certain real estate agreements and certain other legal documents with an official recorder, for the purpose of legally establishing the existence of those agreements or documents, and placing others on notice. For example, the recording of a deed for the sale of land places the whole world on notice that the seller has transferred the ownership in the land. If the seller subsequently gives a second deed to a new buyer, the latter would have no claim that could be established to the land, if the first deed had been recorded. The act of *recording* places the second buyer on CONSTRUCTIVE NOTICE of the first deed, and the law treats the second buyer as being on notice, even if the second buyer does not check the records in the recorder's office. Legal relationships may be different, however, if the first deed was not recorded. If the second buyer could show that he or she had no knowledge of the unrecorded first sale or deed, and is a purchaser in good faith, then the legal claim of the second purchaser would prevail over the first buyer's claim as owner. Of course, the buyer who was not awarded the property could maintain a lawsuit against the seller, but that would prove of little value if the seller's assets had been dissipated. Records in the recorder's office are, of course, available to the public. Regulations for filing deeds are generally set out by state statute. In most states, mortgages, conditional sales contracts involving land, and long term leases are recorded. State laws differ on the necessity to record short term leases. Recording of a lease, for example, serves notice to the world that the lessee holds possession of the premises if the lessor sells the property. In most states failure to record does not make a legal document invalid, but it does allow a subsequent buyer in good faith to establish a claim. See RECORDING OFFICE.

re•*cord*•ing *of*•**fice.** A public office where legal instruments are filed so that they may be officially available to the public. *Recording offices* are set up by state statute, generally at the county or town clerk's office where the property is located. An individual desiring to record a deed, for example, deposits the original instrument with the recording official. It is then copied, indexed, and returned to the owner, sealed and/or stamped and signed by the recording clerk. See RECORDING.

re•*coup*•ment. The withholding of something that is owed, because of a COUNTERCLAIM or other justifiable reason.

re·**course.** The right of the holder of a NEGOTIABLE INSTRUMENT, such as a check, to demand payment from the maker or ENDORSER of the instrument. When the endorser of a negotiable instrument marks the instrument "without recourse," this means that a subsequent holder cannot come back to such an endorser for payment—the holder must look to the maker or to prior endorsers.

re·*cov*·er·y. (1) A restoration of rights or money by judgment of a court, or a return of some right wrongfully taken and restored by the court. (2) The money award obtained by judgment in a successful lawsuit.

re·crim·i·*na*·tion. A counter-accusation or countercharge.

rec·u·*sa*·tion. The procedure by which a judge is disqualified from hearing a lawsuit because of personal interest or prejudice. *Recusation* includes any instance in which the judge disqualifies himself or herself on his or her own initiative.

re·*deem.* To regain possession of something by paying a price; to repurchase.

re·*demp*·tion. The buying back of one's real estate after it has been lost in a foreclosure.

re·*duc*·ti·o ad ab·*sur*·dum. (Latin) *Reduction to an absurdity.* The method in logic of disproving an opponent's contention by showing that it leads to an absurd conclusion.

re·*en*·try. The act of resuming possession of property, based on a right that was reserved at the time possession was originally given up.

ref·er·ee. An official of a court who takes testimony, hears the parties in a dispute, and reports on these matters to the court.

ref·er·ee in *bank*·rupt·cy. An official appointed by a court of BANK-RUPTCY, with administrative and quasijudicial functions, to relieve the judge of handling business details connected with the relief of creditors, distribution of assets, and conservation of property.

ref·er·*en*·dum. A procedure for submission of a proposed public law to a vote of the electorate for ratification or rejection after it has been passed upon by a legislative body.

ref·or·*ma*·tion. A remedy allowed by the court to permit the correction of legal documents which carry a legal obligation. *Reformation* is permitted, for example, to correct a deed that failed to include a complete description of a parcel of land, intended by the parties to have been transferred by the deed.

re·*fresh*·ing the *mem*·o·ry. The right of a witness to consult his or her own notes (made at the time), documents, memoranda, or book-keeping records to bring more distinctly to recollection those details which may be testified to. The defense attorney has the right to examine the notes or documents used.

reg·is·ter. (1) A book of public records or documents. (2) The act of placing pertinent information in public documents of registry. See REGISTRAR.

reg·is·trar. The official who has custody and maintains a register of public documents or records.

reg·is·try. (1) Sometimes used synonymously with REGISTER. (2) The place where a REGISTER is maintained.

reg·u·late. To bring under the control of authority or law; to adjust by orders or rules; to direct subject to method or legal principles.

re·ha·*bil*·i·tate. To restore to former capacity or repute.

re·ha·bil·i·*ta*·tion of *crim*·i·nal. (1) Reestablishment of a criminal as a decent, law-abiding individual. (2) Restoration of civil rights which were lost upon conviction of a crime.

re·ha·bil·i·*ta*·tion of *wit*·ness. Reestablishment of a witness's credibility by additional testimony or other evidence, after the opposing party has cast doubt as to the veracity or believability of the witness.

re·in·*state*. To place again in a former condition or position. *Reinstatement* of a lawsuit is to revive it.

re·in·*sur*·ance. To insure again by transferring some or all of the risk assumed to another insurance company.

re·*la*·tor. One who relates; the individual who furnishes information on which a criminal or civil case is based. In a criminal case the *relator* is more often called an informer; in a civil case the relator is the PLAINTIFF.

re·*lease*. (1) The surrender of a right, claim, or privilege by the individual holding it, or to whom it accrues. (2) A discharge or freedom from confinement or imprisonment.

re·*lease* clause. A provision that upon the payment of a specified sum to the holder of a TRUST deed or MORTGAGE, the LIEN on the instrument as to a specific described lot or area shall be removed from the blanket lien on the whole area covered by the trust deed or mortgage.

rel·e·van·cy. That which has a demonstrative and significant bearing upon the matter at hand; evidence that tends to prove the matter at issue; applicability to the question.

rel·e·vant. Having a demonstrable, or significant bearing on the matter at hand. Tending to prove or disprove the issue in a lawsuit or criminal prosecution. Unless testimony or other evidence is *relevant,* it should be objected to by counsel, and the judge will order the jury to disregard it as having no bearing on the trial.

re·*lief*. (1) Satisfaction granted by the courts for a past wrong. (2) Support or assistance, especially for indigents or those unable to support themselves. (3) Freedom or deliverance from injustice, wrong, or oppression.

re·*main*·der. The balance of an ESTATE in land, depending upon the particular prior estate created at the same time and in the same INSTRUMENT; an estate to take effect and be available for use and enjoyment after another estate is determined. For example, if a life estate in an apartment building is created, the *remainder* would be the title in FEE SIMPLE that vests after the termination of the life estate. See LIFE ESTATE.

re·*main*·der·man. An individual who is entitled to the REMAINDER of an estate, after a particular estate carved out of the property has expired. For example, a transaction could involve three generations of a family. The grandfather left a deed for a parcel of land to his grandson, subject to a prior LIFE ESTATE granted to his son. When the life estate expired with the death of the son, full TITLE to the property would pass to the grandson, who is termed the remainderman.

re·*mand*. To return, or send back. For example, a prisoner will be remanded to custody following a hearing, unless discharged; an APPELLATE COURT may remand a case to a lower court, with instructions for the lower court to take further action.

re·*me*·di·al law. Synonymous with ADJECTIVE LAW.

rem·e·dy. The method for enforcing a legal right or for redressing, compensating, or preventing a wrong. Typical *remedies* awarded by the courts include money damages, restitution, or specific performances.

re·*mis*·sion. (1) The cancellation or release of a debt. (2) Legal condonation or forgiveness of an injury or offense.

re·*mit*·ti·tur. The power of a trial judge to decrease the amount of an excessive award made by a jury verdict. In the *remittitur* procedure, the amount of damages is decreased with the consent of the plaintiff as a condition for the denial by the judge of the defendant's motion for a new trial, because of excessive damages. Antonym: ADDITUR.

re-*mov*-**al.** (1) The transfer of a civil lawsuit from one court to another. For example, a defendant who is a legal resident of Maryland may be able to have a California state court suit transferred to Federal court in Maryland for personal convenience. (2) The transfer of an arrested criminal to the location where trial is to take place. (This is not extradition.)

ren-**der.** (1) To pronounce a judgment or decision. (2) To yield or surrender. (3) To give service to another.

re-*new*-**al.** (1) To revive, or to establish anew. (2) A monetary obligation is said to be *renewed* when the same obligation is carried forward by the new contract or undertaking, and the time for payment is extended.

re-**nun**-**ci**-*a*-**tion.** The act of an individual or CORPORATION in giving up or abandoning a right without transferring the right to another.

re-**or**-**gan**-**i**-*za*-**tion.** The process for the financial reconstruction of an insolvent business, with a transfer of ownership to the creditors and/or new owners. It is a business plan for winding up affairs, usually accompanied by judicial sale of corporate or company property and franchises. In a *reorganization* of a CORPORATION, the assets that are left are usually turned over to the new corporation, with stockholders continuing to own stock in the same proportion to stock in the old corporation.

re-*peal.* The annullment or revocation of a law by the passage of a subsequent statute (law) that declares the former law to be abrogated or done away with.

re-*plev*-**in.** A suit at law to obtain the return of unlawfully removed goods to the person entitled to possession.

re-*plev*-**y.** The return of property demanded in a REPLEVIN suit.

re-*ply.* On trial or pleading of a lawsuit, the *reply* is the plaintiff's answer to the allegations put forward by the defense. In the usual development of the pleadings, the plaintiff files a complaint alleging a wrong; the defendant answers with a denial or a counterclaim of some kind; the plaintiff then responds with a *reply,* that will vary with the defendant's answer.

re-**pos**-*ses*-**sion.** To resume possession of an object, as in default of payments of installments due. Legally, the TITLE frequently still rests in the seller until an item is completely paid for, or there is a mortgage on the property in question.

rep·re·*sen*·ta·tive *ac*·tion. A class suit brought by one stockholder in a CORPORATION for the benefit of all stockholders who have been harmed by improper or illegal action of company directors or officials.

re·*prieve*. To delay punishment of a condemned prisoner by executive decree. It is a stay of execution of a sentence under criminal law, and can usually be granted only by the executive head of the government (the President in a Federal crime, and the governor in a state crime). A *reprive* cannot be granted until after sentence.

re·*pu*·di·ate. To renounce or disavow, as a right, privilege, or duty.

res. (Latin–race, reez) A thing. In modern legal usage, any object, subject matter, or thing upon which persons may claim a legal right.

res ad·ju·di·*ca*·ta. A commonly misspelled and misused version of RES JUDICATA.

res ges·tae. (Latin–reez *jess*·tee) *Things done.* The principle in EVIDENCE law that when an act is admissible as evidence, any spontaneous utterances made in connection with the act are also admissible. This is in spite of the fact that out-of-court utterances or conversations are normally not admitted because they are second hand and in violation of the so-called HEARSAY RULE. Put in other words: spontaneous statements, which because of their intimate relation to facts become a part of those facts, are therefore admitted as such. Under some circumstances, the rule may be extended to include not only declarations made by the parties directly involved, but also spontaneous utterances by bystanders and strangers.

res ip·sa loq·ui·tur. (Latin–reez ip·suh lock·wit·uhr) The thing speaks for itself. A theory in TORT law that presumes the defendant was negligent. The idea is that the instrumentality causing the injury was in the defendant's exclusive control, and the accident was the kind that would not happen in the absence of negligence. Accordingly, the burden of proving the case shifts from the plaintiff to the defendant, to prove that negligence was not involved, if the defendant can in fact do so.

res ju·di·ca·ta. (Latin–reez jew·dik·*ay*·tuh) A thing decided. A legal controversy or dispute which is regarded as having been authoritatively and finally settled by a binding court decision.

re·*scind*. To make void; abrogate; annul; cancel; especially, to void a contract from its beginning, restoring the parties to the positions they occupied.

re·*scis*·sion. The nullifying or cancellation of a contract, particularly by the act of one of the parties. *Rescission* is generally considered to mean not mere termination and release of the parties from obligation to each other, but to put an end to the contract as though it never were, with all parties in the position they would have occupied had there never been a contract.

res·er·*va*·tion. (1) Any withholding or holding back of a right or a thing. (2) A provision in an instrument of CONVEYANCE (usually a DEED) through which the grantor reserves some right to himself or herself, which right was newly created by the instrument of conveyance. (3) An area of land set aside for a particular use, such as the U.S. Naval Oil Reserve, or the Navajo Indian Reservation.

res·i·dence. One's place of abode at any given time, whether it is temporary or permanent.

re·*sid*·u·a·ry es·*tate*. That which is left after the payment of debts, expenses, and costs of administration of the estate of a deceased individual.

re·*sid*·u·a·ry leg·a·*tee*. See LEGATEE.

re·sid·u·um. (Latin) *Leftovers.* The balance of a decedent's estate after debts have been paid and legacies deducted.

res·o·*lu*·tion. A formal statement of will or opinion, adopted by vote of a formal body such as a legislature.

re·*spon*·de·at su·*pe*·ri·or. (Latin) *Let the master answer.* The legal rule that a principal is liable in damages for wrongful acts of the principal's agent. This is an extension of the old rule that the master is liable for the acts of the servant, which is still a valid rule of law. This means, for example, that the owner of a bakery company is liable in civil damages for an automobile wreck caused by the negligence of a bakery truck delivery driver. This doctrine applies, however, only when the *agent* or *servant* is acting within the legitimate scope of authority. For example, the owner of the bakery company would not be liable if the driver had come back after hours, gotten the truck without authority, and then caused the wreck.

re·*spon*·dent. See PARTIES.

res·ti·*tu*·tion. (1) Restoration or return of property to the party entitled to it after the reversal of a court decision on which the property was taken. (2) In CONTRACT law, restoration of those involved in a contract to the positions they occupied before making the contract.

re·*strain*·ing *or*·der. An order by a judge that is a type of INJUNCTION. A *restraining order* is usually a preliminary legal order issued to keep a situation unchanged until a decision can be reached on whether a permanent injunction should be issued.

re·*straint* of trade. Understandings between companies, which understandings are designed to stifle competition, fix prices or otherwise obstruct the natural course of commercial and business activity.

re·*stric*·tive *cov*·e·nant. A restriction or limitation put into a deed, forbidding future owners of the property from using the land for specific purposes. Subsequent owners have a right of enforcement of the restriction by injunction or by lawsuit for damages against any future owner. For example, the deed could carry a *restrictive covenant* to the effect that horses may not be kept on the land. But not all *restrictive covenants* will be upheld by the courts. A restriction is void if it calls for the commission of a crime or the use of the land for immoral purposes. The courts also say that a *restrictive covenant* is void if it seeks to limit the price of resale, or requires approval of a former owner on a resale. Also, a limitation forbidding transfer of the property to individuals of a specific race has been held illegal by the U.S. Supreme Court (Shelly v. Kramer, 334 U.S. 1).

re·*stric*·tive en·*dorse*·ment. See ENDORSEMENT.

re·*sult*·ing trust. A trust that arises by implication of law, rather than by an express declaration. A *resulting trust* may be created when a transfer of property is made under circumstances that create an inference that the transferee was not intended to have the beneficial interest in the property. For example, a father who was a widower bought a tract of land and placed title in the name of his eldest son. The father told all his five children that he was going to Saudi Arabia for a year, and that in his absence the property was to be leased and the income put into a bank. He further told them that if he died before the year was up, the property was to be sold and the proceeds of the sale and the interest was to be split among all five children equally. The eldest son was the TRUSTEE of a *resulting trust.*

re·*tain*·er. (1) The act of an individual or a firm in hiring a lawyer. (2) The fee which the client pays on the hiring or *retention* of a lawyer. (3) The hiring agreement between the lawyer and the client.

re·*tal*·i·a·to·ry e·*vic*·tion. An eviction by a landlord prompted by the complaints of a tenant about unsanitary or unsafe conditions. An eviction of this kind is usually grounds for a damage suit against the landlord, although state laws differ.

re·*tire*·ment. (1) To separate, withdraw, or remove. (2) To pay off the final installment of bonds or other securities.

re·*treat* to the wall. A defense theory under HOMICIDE law, requiring anyone killing another on a claim of SELF DEFENSE to first make use of any apparent and reasonable avenues of escape if the killing is to be regarded as legally justified and excusable. The person committing the homicide must first be pushed into a position of no escape.

ret·ro·*ac*·tive. That which existed or originated in the past.

ret·ro·*spec*·tive law. Any law which attempts to affect legal rights that vested (became fixed) prior to passage of the law. Under the ex post facto provisions of the United States Constitution, a statute is not valid if it takes away or impairs VESTED rights acquired under existing laws, attaches any new disability, or attaches a new obligation. See EX POST FACTO.

re·*turn*. (1) A tax form filed by a taxpayer with the government. (2) The profit or yield of a security or investment. (3) A report by an official serving a legal WRIT or a SUBPOENA, showing the manner in which service was made in the delivery of the writ or subpoena, either by personal service or by mail (where permitted).

re·*ver*·sal. The making void, or undoing, of the judgment of a court because of an irregularity or error committed in the court where the judgment was returned. The *reversal* is ordered by an APPELLATE court reviewing the matter on appeal.

re·*ver*·sion. (1) The return of an estate to the grantor or the grantor's heirs, after the expiration of the term of the grant. (2) The name of the estate so returned to the original owner.

re·*ver*·sion·a·ry *in*·ter·est. The interest which remains in land or other real property upon the termination of a preceding estate, such as a LIFE ESTATE.

re·*view*. The judicial reconsideration or re-examination of a cause by an APPELLATE COURT.

rev·o·*ca*·tion. Annulment; cancellation; repeal; reversal; rescission.

re·*voke*. To annul by calling back, rescinding, or wiping out.

rid·er. An addition or amendment, as to an insurance policy, contract or legislative bill.

right. (1) A claim upon, or lawful interest in property. (2) The liberty or ability, backed up by the law, of acting or abstaining from acting in a certain way; the power of legally compelling someone to do or to refrain from doing a particular thing. (3) The underlying principle of law and justice.

right of *ac*·tion. The right to maintain a legal action; right to bring a lawsuit.

ri·ot. An unlawful disturbance by two or more people against the public peace and order. Statutes in some states require three or more persons to participate. Stated in more detailed terms, whenever three or more persons, having assembled for any purpose, shall disturb the public peace by using force or violence against any other person or property, or shall threaten or attempt to commit such disturbance, or shall do an unlawful act by force or violence, accompanied with power of immediate execution of such threat or attempt, they shall be guilty of a *riot*.

ri·*par*·i·an rights. The rights of one owning land along the shore of a river, lake, or ocean. This would include rights to access along the shore and bed and rights to the water, as well as access and use of tidelands. *Riparian rights* are often of considerable legal significance in states where agriculture is dependent on irrigation.

rob·ber·y. The criminal act (a FELONY) of taking the property of another from the victim's person or in the victim's presence against his or her will and by use of fear or FORCE.

ro·ga·to·ry *let*·ters. A formal request from one judge to another (usually in another state), requesting the second judge to supervise the taking of a written deposition (INTERROGATORIES) from a witness who resides at the place where the second judge is located.

rout. Criminal acts that constitute an attempt to commit the crime of RIOT. Stated in other terms, a *rout* is an attempt or an advance by two or more persons, assembled and acting together, toward the commission of an act which would be a RIOT if actually committed.

roy·al·ty. Payment made to an author or composer for each copy of a work sold, or to an inventor for each item sold under a patent.

rule against per·pe·*tu*·i·ties. See PERPETUITY.

rule of law. A basic legal principle or doctrine. Sometimes it may be expressed in the form of a maxim or logical proposition. A *rule of law* is a guide or norm for the courts.

rule ni·si. See NISI.

rul·ing. A decision or regulation made by a court of justice or public office with reference to the conduct of business before that court of public office.

S

sab·o·tage. The malicious damage or destruction of property to halt production or seriously interfere with production. A deliberate slowdown for the same purpose is also sabotage. Legend has it that the first act of *sabotage* involved a French worker placing his *sabot* (wooden shoe) inside a weaving loom.

safe de·*pos*·it box. A lock box, rented from a bank or trust company, used for the storing of money, jewelry, legal papers, or other valuables. Unless there is a specific contract with the customer, the bank or firm renting the lock box will not be liable for losses by burglary or robbery, unless gross negligence can be shown. Securities or money in a safe deposit box may be attached if the attachment process is proper, and the bank or trust company will be relieved of legal responsibility in complying with a court order of attachment.

sale. A contract under which property is transferred from one person (called the seller or vendor) to another (called the buyer or purchaser) in return for the latter's payment or promise of payment of a fixed price of money or property.

Sal·ic law. The body of law introduced into France around the 5th century A.D., by the Salian Franks. Provisions of this law found their way into French and English law, the most famous being that women were excluded from the inheritance of landed estates and could not succeed to the crown. This law influenced and complicated inheritance and property rights in England for hundreds of years.

sanc•**tion.** (1) The penalty or punishment for violating a law; or a reward for obedience. In international law, action by one or more states toward another state to force it to comply with legal obligations. (3) The act of a recognized authority ratifying or confirming an action.

san•**i**•**ty.** Of sound mind.

sans re•**cours.** (French–sawn ree•*koor*) *Without recourse.* An endorsement, usually written as "without recourse," on the back of a NEGO-TIABLE INSTRUMENT (a check, promissory note, etc.) to mean that this endorser will not be held responsible if payment should be refused. An endorsement of this kind cannot, of course, be placed on the instrument by the original maker (signer) of the instrument, since this would be contrary of the maker's intent to issue a negotiable instrument.

sat•**is**•*fac*•**tion.** The discharge, exhaustion, payment, or performance of some kind of obligation. A judgment, for example, is satisfied by money payment of the amount of the judgment.

sav•**ings bank trust.** Synonymous with TOTTEN TRUST.

sci•**en**•**ter.** (Latin–*sie*•en•ter) Knowledge. (1) In criminal law, the term means action with guilty knowledge. (2) Sometimes used in TORT law to allege that the defendant in a lawsuit had previous knowledge of a state of facts which it was the defendant's legal duty to guard against.

scil•**i**•**cet.** (Latin–*sill*•i•set) That is to say. An introductory statement sometimes used in legal pleadings inferring that the real gist, or substance, or the instrument will follow in detail.

scin•**til**•**la.** (Latin–sin•*till*•uh) Spark or trace. A very insignificant or trifling amount. Legal writers or commentators sometimes say, "There was not a *scintilla* of evidence."

sci•**re fas**•**ci**•**as.** (Latin–*sie*•ree *fae*•shi•uhs) *In practice.* A judicial writ based on some matter or record, and requiring the party summoned into court to show cause why the record should not be enforced, annulled, or vacated, as the case may be.

seal. The identification mark pressed in hot wax that was anciently required on many legal documents. Frequently, the impression was made from a heavy signet ring that was worn constantly, so an unauthorized person could not steal the ring and use it to duplicate the seal. The *seal* was used at a time when many people could not sign their own names. Eventually, the letters *L.S.* on a document replaced the wax impression. These letters are an abbreviation for the old Latin phrase, *locus sigilli,* meaning *the place of the seal,* which occasionally still appears on some legal documents.

sealed and de·*liv*·ered. The old English phrase still commonly used for the attestation of deeds and some other instruments, written above the witnesses' names. It is a holdover from the time when deeds were sealed as authentication, without a signature affixed by the grantor or person executing the instrument.

sealed *ver*·dict. The finding of guilty or not guilty, placed in a sealed envelope by a JURY reaching a VERDICT when the court is not actually in session at the time. In most instances the jury is allowed to separate after reaching a verdict and leaving it in a sealed envelope for the judge. Where this procedure is allowed, a jury verdict returned in this manner has the same effect as if returned in open court before any separation of the jury had taken place.

search of *ti*·tle. The examination of official records and registers made in connection with a contract for the sale of real estate. This is done to determine the existence of MORTGAGES, LIENS, unpaid taxes, or any other cloud on the TITLE of the property.

search *war*·rant. A written order from a magistrate or justice ordering a peace officer to search a specified address (house, apartment, etc.) for unlawful goods (contraband, etc.), or for property alleged to have been stolen, and to bring the same when found before the magistrate. Some *search warrants* also specify that the peace officer shall bring the person occupying the premises before the magistrate, to be dealt with according to law.

***sec*·ond·a·ry *ev*·i·dence.** That kind of evidence which becomes admissible, as being the next best, when the original has been lost or is unavailable. A copy of a document may be admitted, for example, but only after making a genuine effort to obtain the original, and explaining to the court why the original cannot be had. When the adverse party in a lawsuit holds the original, it may be obtained by a NOTICE TO PRODUCE, or a copy (*secondary evidence*) will be used in the event of default.

***sec*·tion.** In real estate law a *section of land* is 640 acres.

se·cun·dum. (Latin–si·*cun*·dum) According to.

se·*cured* cred·i·tor. A CREDITOR who holds some special monetary assurance of payment for a debt. A LIEN or MORTGAGE is the type of interest that gives a *secured creditor* protection beyond that of an ordinary creditor.

se·cu·ri·ties. Certificates that evidence the ownership of property or of a debt owed. They are evidence of obligations to pay money or of right to participate in the earnings and distribution of corporate or other earnings.

se·di·tion. A revolutionary movement towards TREASON, yet lacking an overt act. It is an attempt to overthrow the government by meetings, speeches, or publications designed to incite treasonous acts. Usually, the Supreme Court of the United States has said that mere criticism of the government is not enough to constitute the crime of *sedition;* the words must be uttered in a setting that constitutes a CLEAR AND PRESENT DANGER.

*sei·***sin (pron.** *see·***zin).** An old English legal term still sometimes used to mean full ownership and possession of real property.

*sei·***zure.** The attachment by the sheriff, or officer of the court, of property of an individual against whom a judgment has been filed. The purpose of the *seizure* is to satisfy the judgment by forced sale of the property.

self-de·*fense.* The right to defend one's person or property against some injury attempted by another. *Self-defense* is also a lawful excuse for the killing of an assailant who is attempting to do serious harm against any member of the immediate family. A peace officer attempting to make an arrest must clearly identify his or her purpose, since the criminal may kill the officer and sometimes convince a jury that the officer was never identified; in most circumstances this would justify a claim of *self-defense.*

self-help. The taking of action to help one's self, rather than wait for a court to act, which action may have legal consequences.

*sem·***per.** (Latin) Always.

*sem·***per pa·***ra·***tus.** (Latin–puh·*rawt·*us) Always prepared. Used to mean *we stand ready to perform.*

*sen·***tence.** The judgment formally pronounced on one convicted in a criminal prosecution. The punishment imposed on a lawbreaker.

*sep·a·***rate but** *e·***qual.** The doctrine formerly used to justify separation of schools along racial lines, on the claim that accommodations and facilities were equal in quality.

*sep·a·***rate** *main·te·***nance.** The money allowance granted to a spouse

193

and children for support and maintenance. In *separate maintenance* the spouses are still married, as distinguished from alimony payments as a result of a divorce action.

sep·a·*ra*·tion. A discontinuance of COHABITATION of husband and wife, either by mutual agreement or under the decree of a court.

sep·a·*ra*·tion of *pow*·ers. The division of governmental authority and power through which the EXECUTIVE, LEGISLATIVE, and JUDICIAL branches of the United States government have differing responsibilities that serve as checks and balances on the other two branches. This serves to keep any one branch from totally taking over power or placing the government in the hands of a dictator.

se·*ques*·ter. (1) To renounce or give up some claim. An heir could voluntarily sequester all right to an inheritance. (2) To place disputed property into the hands of a third person to be held pending settlement. (3) As used in international law, it is the confiscation of private property and appropriation to public use. In past years it has been common for belligerents in time of war to *sequester* debts due from its own subjects to the enemy.

se·ri·*a*·tim. (Latin–sir·ee·*ate*·im) One by one. Individually, separately.

ser·vant. An individual employed by another and subject to the employer's control as to what work shall be done, as well as the means by which it shall be accomplished. In the language of the law, the *master-servant* relationship is actually an *employer-employee* relationship. One of the basic rules of law arising from this relationship is that the master is liable for the acts of the servant. Translated into everyday terms, this means that the employer is legally responsible for the wrongdoing (TORTS or NEGLIGENCE) of the employee, so long as the employee is acting within the scope of the employment.

***serv*·ice.** (1) The delivery of a WRIT, SUMMONS, or PROCESS to the person named. If a person is being sued, for example, it is only fair that this individual be notified and given a chance to present a defense. This notification is performed by *service* of legal papers on the defendant. Personal *service* is required by law in some matters. In certain other matters publication in a newspaper is sufficient; in some matters mailing a notice to the last known address is all that is required. (2) In contract law, employment in the service of another requires the employed person to submit to the direction and control of the employer. (3) In domestic relations law, one partner to a marriage is usually entitled to damages for loss of *service* of the other partner to the marriage. A husband may recover, for example, in a lawsuit against someone who injures or kills the wife. The husband here is entitled to claim loss of comfort, aid, assistance, and society that the wife could be expected to provide. **(4)** In public utility law, the electric company renders *service* to customers.

serv•**ice by pub**•**li**•*ca*•**tion.** See SERVICE, part 1.

ser•**vi**•**ent.** That which is subject to a charge, or burden.

ser•**vi**•**ent es**•*tate.* Servitude, definition **(2)**.

ser•**vi**•**tude. (1)** Bondage or slavery. **(2)** A burden or charge on one tract of land in favor of another. A right of way to pass over the land of another is one type of *servitude.* A deed restriction on tract "A," providing that water must be allowed to flow through tract "A" and into tract "B," without diminution or disturbance of any kind, is a *servitude* placed on tract "A" (the servient estate) in favor of tract "B" (the dominant estate). **(3)** Penal *servitude* is confinement of a convicted offender at forced labor.

ses•**sion.** The sitting of a legislature, court, city council, commission, or any other official body. It is that period of time during which the organization is assembled or engaged in the transaction of official business.

set-back *or*•**di**•**nance.** An ordinance prohibiting the building of any kind of structure between the curb and the set-back line, which is a specified number of feet inside the curb. The purpose is to prevent building too close to the street.

set-off. A counterclaim which the defendant alleges, independent of and unconnected with the plaintiff's cause of action. The terms *counterclaim,* off-set, *set-off,* and CROSS-CLAIM are apparently frequently misused. A counterclaim, off-set, and set-off all involve an independent claim, while a cross-claim arises from the same transaction.

set•**tle**•**ment. (1)** An agreement to dispose of a dispute, without going through a trial; a meeting of the minds to a transaction or controversy. **(2)** To amicably close out a lawsuit by coming to an agreement or liquidation between the parties. **(3)** A right acquired by statute to claim aid or relief as a pauper, under the laws of some states.

set•**tlor. (1)** The individual who sets up a TRUST. This person is sometimes called the *grantor.* **(2)** The individual who gives the money or property or set up a trust.

sev·**er.** (1) To divide or separate. (2) To enter a plea to obtain a trial separate from other co-defendants. (3) To divide property at the request of co-owners.

sev·**er**·**able.** Capable of being separated, or divided.

sev·**er**·**al**·**ty.** A person who is the sole owner of a parcel of real property is said to be the owner thereof *in severalty.*

Shel·**ly's case.** (Sometimes called the rule in Shelly's case). The old rule declared by English courts in the 16th century, that long affected property law in England and the United States. By this rule, when an estate of freehold is acquired by gift or purchase by an ancestor, with remainder to his heirs or the heirs of his body, the word "heirs" is a word of limitation of the estate and not a word of purchase; that is, the ancestor takes the estate in fee or in tail, according to circumstances, and the heirs take nothing. The rule has been abolished in England and in most states in the United States, generally by statute.

sher·**iff.** The chief administrative and executive officer of a county. The *sheriff* gives aid to the criminal courts and judges, as well as to the civil courts of records. The *sheriff* is also the protector of the peace and tranquillity of the county, and enforcer of the criminal laws. Duties include serving PROCESSES, summoning JURIES, executing JUDGMENTS, and holding judicial sales. There are variances in responsibility and powers of *sheriffs* in England, Scotland, and the United States.

sher·**iff's deed.** A deed transferring ownership of property to the purchaser at a sheriff's sale to satisfy a judgment against the owner. While it is called a *sheriff's deed*, the deed is prepared by order of the court.

shop-book rule. An exception to the so-called HEARSAY EVIDENCE RULE, allowing the introduction in evidence of original bookkeeping records made in the usual course of business, after production from proper custody and authentication. For example, the bookkeeper of a business could bring the business journals and ledgers into court to show that a customer owed a debt to the business. The bookkeeper would be first required to testify that he or she is the custodian of the records, and that they were prepared in the regular course of business. The specific business employee who actually made the bookkeeping entry would not be required to testify.

short cause. A lawsuit, or a necessary portion thereof, that can be heard by a judge in a brief period. Some courts maintain a *short cause* *list* of matters of this kind that can be disposed of in a few minutes. For economy of time, these matters may be heard out of order between longer scheduled cases. This practice is not followed in all courts.

show cause. A judicial order to appear and explain to the court why an order the judge has under consideration should not be confirmed, executed, or put into effect. In the event of non-appearance by the individual served with the *show cause order,* the court will go ahead with the proposed action.

sic. (Latin–sick) Thus. In such manner.

sight. Demand. Upon presentation of a note or draft to the maker or draftee.

sil•**ver** *plat*•**ter** (*doc*•**trine).** The legal principle by which Federal prosecutors were allowed to use evidence that had been illegally obtained by state officers. This has been permitted only if the state officers were not acting in collusion with Federal officers or with the knowledge of Federal officials. A line of Federal decisions has held that the *silver platter doctrine* may no longer be used.

si ne. (Latin–*seen*•nay) Without.

si•**ne** *an*•**i**•**mo** **rev**•**er**•*ten*•**di.** (Latin–*seen*•nay *on*•ee•mo ree•ver•*ten*•die) *Without intent to return.* Without any intention of returning to the first position, or going back to the first issue.

si•**ne** *di*•**e.** (Latin–*see*•nay *dee*•ee) Without a day. Without a definite date specified. Thus, court adjournment *sine die* means a final adjournment, with no date set for reassembly.

si•**ne** *nu*•**me**•**ro.** (Latin–*see*•nay *noo*•me•ro) *Without number.* Without limit, or without stint.

si•**ne** **qua** *non.* (Latin) *That without which.* That without which the proposition or position would be impossible. A condition or thing that cannot be dispensed with.

sin•**gle name** *pa*•**per.** A slang term, describing a NEGOTIABLE INSTRUMENT signed by only one maker, and with no accomodation signer or co-signature by a SURETY. This means that only the maker can be held responsible for payment of the note or other instrument in question.

sink•**ing fund.** A fund set up and accumulated, usually by regular deposits, to pay off the principal of a debt when it comes due.

sit. **(1)** To hold a session of court or of a legislative body. **(2)** To perform the functions of a judge while holding court.

site. (1) A parcel of land. (2) Legally, the term is sometimes used to mean a location set apart for some specific use, and not a tract fixed by definite boundaries.

*si•***tus.** Place; location: the place where a crime or accident occurred.

*slan•***der.** Oral defamation of character; the speaking of false and malicious words concerning another, whereby injury results to reputation. LIBEL and *slander* are both forms of defamation, with libel being expressed by print, writing, pictures, or signs, where *slander* is by oral (spoken) expressions. The false words must be spoken in the presence of someone other than the person being slandered, and the speaking must be in a language understood by the third party (witness).

slip de•*ci•***sion.** A printed pamphlet of a decision of the United States Supreme Court or some other high-ranking court, issued almost immediately after the opinion was delivered, so it will be available to lower courts and attorneys as soon as possible. Later the decision is reported with others in bound volumes such as U.S. Reporter, Supreme Court Reporter, etc.

smart *mo•***ney** *dam•***ag•es.** See EXEMPLARY DAMAGES.

*smug•***gling.** The crime of carrying into this country items that are prohibited by law (such as opium), or that are prohibited without payment of tax or import duty (such as diamonds). The offense also consists of carrying out goods the exportation of which is prohibited.

*sod•***om•y.** A crime defined by statute and court decisions, that varies in meaning from state to state. Generally, it includes sexual relations between members of the same sex or with an animal, as well as noncoital, oral, and anal relations. Under the definitions in some states, BUGGERY, BESTIALITY, PEDERASTY, and the so-called *crime against nature* (oral copulation by a male on a male, also called *the unspeakable crime*) are all variations of *sodomy*. The name derives from the ancient town of Sodom in Palestine, destroyed because of the continued wickednesses and excesses of its inhabitants (Genesis 18:20, 21; 19:24–28). One of the fundamental principles of criminal law has always been the requirement that prohibited acts must be made clear for all to understand, as a prerequisite for the imposition of punishment. But for hundreds of years English and American courts and criminal statutes have almost uniformly avoided stating exactly what was meant by *the crime against nature* or *the unspeakable crime*.

sole. (1) Having no sharer; single; separate and apart. The opposite of joint. (2) Sometimes used to designate an unmarried woman.

sol•em•nize. (1) To observe some occasion with dignity, ritual, or solemnity. (2) A marriage is sometimes said to be *solemnized* when celebrated with religious rites, as distinguished from a civil ceremony.

so•lic•i•*ta*•tion. (1) The requesting, soliciting, or asking for something, usually in a vigorous manner. (2) The criminal offense of requesting or inciting another to commit any FELONY, even though the felony requested may not actually have been committed. The criminal violation is in the requesting or urging, and not in the completion of the desired criminal act.

so•*lic*•i•tor. An attorney in England who advises clients, represents them in the lower courts, and prepares cases for BARRISTERS to try in superior courts. Since a barrister can try cases in both upper and lower courts, the barrister is regarded as a step higher in professional rank.

so•*lic*•i•tor *gen*•er•al. The second ranking legal officer of the United States Government, next in authority to the attorney general. The chief duty of the solicitor general is to represent the government in all cases before the U.S. Supreme Court and the U.S. Court of Claims. The *solicitor general* is interim attorney general in the absence of the latter.

sol•ven•cy. Ability to pay one's debts as they mature; capability of meeting obligations in the usual and ordinary course of business. See BANKRUPTCY, which has a different meaning from insolvency.

sov•er•eign im•*mu*•ni•ty. The principle that the sovereign (the government) cannot be sued in its own courts, except with its consent. Some courts say, however, that this immunity exists only when the government is engaged in a governmental function. Exactly what this means is not clear.

spe•cial *ju*•ry. In some jurisdictions, a jury ordered by the judge on motion of either party, where the case may be of unusual intricacy.

spe•cie. (1) Legal coin of the realm. (2) When used in a contract, the term *performance in specie* means that that performance must be in exact accordance with the terms specified.

spe•*cif*•ic per•*form*•ance. The right of one party to a CONTRACT to require the other party to specifically do that to which they agreed. Courts will usually uphold the right to *specific performance,* especially in situations where money damages would not be adequate compensation. Sometimes, of course, *specific performance* is impossible. An example of the doctrine follows: *A* made a contract with *B* to sell a famous race horse for $5,000,000. *B* paid the money, but *A* asked to substitute other race horses of equal total value. The courts would require delivery of the horse named in the contract—*B* is seeking to obtain a quality horse to build up the reputation of a racing stable, or to obtain the horse for stud. If the contract called for the delivery of the carcases of crippled or diseased animals for use of a glue factory, it would not matter if horses of equal value were substituted.

spec·i·fi·*ca*·tion. (1) In patent law, the working papers and description of the invention, drawings, and written statement that must be placed on file with the Patent Office. (2) In military law, a statement of the charges being brought against one accused of a military offense. (3) In property law, the acquisition of TITLE to a substance or thing by CONVERTING it, or working it into a new substance from the original raw material—the conversion of lumber into plywood sheets, grapes into raisins, etc.

spend·thrift trust. A TRUST created to provide a fund for the maintenance of an improvident person. The TRUSTEE of such a fund is given the power to distribute only the income to the beneficiary; thus, the PRINCIPAL is kept free from the reach of creditors.

spin-off. (1) A process by which an existing CORPORATION sets up a new corporation, distributing shares to the old corporation's stockholders in proportion to their stock. (2) The name sometimes given to the new corporation.

spu·ri·ous. (1) False. (2) Of illegitimate birth.

squat·ter. One who settles on public lands or land of another without any claim of title. A squatter is not regarded as being in *adverse possession,* under a claim or right, and therefore cannot gain title regardless of the number of years of occupancy. See ADVERSE POSSESSION.

stale check. A check that has been held an abnormally long time before there is an attempt to cash it. Statutes in some states specify that a check must be presented for payment within a set period of time.

stale de·*mand (or stale claim).* A claim or demand that has been asserted only after an unreasonable lapse of time. Laws are not always specific as to what is a reasonable time.

stand mute. Describes an individual who fails to answer when instructed by a judge or committing magistrate to enter a plea to a criminal charge. In practically all modern courts a plea of *not guilty* is entered by the clerk of the court when the accused *stands mute.* In old English courts the failure to answer was treated as a plea of *guilty,* but this was long ago changed.

sta·re de·ci·sis. (Latin–*staw*·ree di·*sigh*·sis) *Let the decision stand.* The judicial doctrine that a court decision on a set of facts should be binding in the same court, in equal courts, or in courts of lesser rank, in future cases where the same point is in controversy. This is on the legal policy that rights should remain settled, so long as injustice was not done, so individuals may have a predictable basis on which future decisions and rights may be acquired.

state. (1) A politically organized body of people occupying a fixed territory, sometimes used synonymously with *nation.* (2) One of the component units of the United States. (3) A term sometimes used in a criminal prosecution, as the people in their collective capacity as a state, the party wronged by a criminal deed. *State* v. *Montecorvo* would be a prosecution of one Montecorvo by the state prosecutor.

state's ev·i·dence. (1) Evidence presented by the prosecution in a ciminal case. (2) Testimony by one of the defendants in a criminal prosecution against other defendants alleged to have been involved in the same crime or series of crimes.

sta·tus quo. (Latin–*stay*·tus kwoe, *stat*·us kwoe) The state of things at a given time. The existing state of affairs.

stat·ute. A law passed or enacted by a legislature or by the Congress of the United States. It is a written law, not based on judicial decision or a statement in a constitution. A law enacted by a city or municipal government is generally called an *ordinance.*

Stat·ute of Frauds. A statute providing that certain contracts will not be honored by the courts unless there is something in writing to prove that the parties have a verbal contract. FRAUD and PERJURY became so common in early-day English court trials to prove oral contracts that the British Parliament passed the first version of the *Statute of Frauds* in 1673. This British law served as the basis for statutes that have been passed in all states in the United States. Described by legal scholars as the most important single piece of litigation ever passed, the original *Statute of Frauds* has also created a stubborn popular misconception that an oral contract is not good. The basic idea of the statute is that certain contracts will not be enforced by the courts unless the contract agreement itself is in writing, or there is a substantial memorandum of it in writing, and is signed by the person against whom the contract is sought to be enforced, or is signed by his or her authorized representative. The writing need not be a formal contract signed by both parties. A written note or memorandum of the transaction is usually held legally sufficient when signed. There are some variances between state statutes throughout the United States, but the following are usually required to be in writing: **(a)** a promise to be responsible for the debts of another (a surety relationship); **(b)** an agreement by an executor to become liable out of his or her own property for debts of the estate; **(c)** a contract of marriage; **(d)** contracts for the sale of real estate or any interest in real property; **(e)** contracts which cannot be fully performed within one year; **(f)** contracts for the sale of personal property in excess of a specified value (varying from state to state). A number of states also require the following types of contracts to be in writing: **(a)** an agreement to provide for someone in a will. **(b)** the creation of a TRUST. **(c)** an agreement made when an adult to pay a prior debt contracted during infancy, or a debt outlawed by the STATUTE OF LIMITATIONS. **(d)** a MORTGAGE of personal property.

stat•**ute of lim•i•*ta*•tions.** A statute or ordinance that limits the time within which legal action may be brought, either in a civil or criminal trial. The purpose is to keep from cluttering the courts with cases that involve stale claims. If a matter goes for many years without reaching the courts, witnesses may have died or lost their recollection, and evidence may have been scattered. In civil cases, the limitation is on lawsuits arising out of a breach of contract or out of a TORT. Some criminal violations, such as murder, are considered so serious that prosecution is never prohibited by the statute of limitations. It is possible to "toll the running" of the statute (to suspend the statute) in some instances in both civil and criminal matters. For example, a written promise to pay a debt barred by the *statute of limitations* will usually revive liability for the debt. If a civil judgment is obtained, based on a debt, the judgment will be good until satisfied, even though the debtor may not have any money until after the original debt would have been barred by the *statute of limitations*. In a criminal case, if a fugitive flees the state or jurisdiction where the criminal charge is outstanding, the flight "tolls the running" (suspends) the statute. For example, in a state where there is a three-year *statute of limitations* for burglary, a burglar who fled from the state after one year, remained in hiding in another state for ten years, could still be prosecuted if apprehended. (The statute would still have two years to run.)

stat·**ute of wills.** Individual state statutes, varying somewhat from jurisdiction to jurisdiction, but generally providing that a valid will must be in writing, must be signed by the maker, and must be witnessed by a specified number of individuals and in a proper manner. Most states permit a HOLOGRAPHIC WILL, without witnesses, provided it meets strict requirements in preparation. The earliest enactment of a *statute of wills* was in the time of Henry VIII of England. See HOLOGRAPHIC WILL.

stat·**u**·**to**·**ry deed.** A printed form of DEED used in some states. By statute in those states, there are certain warranties and covenants that are legally regarded as being a part of all *statutory deeds,* although these warranties and covenants are left out of the printed form. In effect, a statutory deed is a WARRANTY DEED in a shortened form for ease in recording. The warrants and covenants listed in the statute are just as binding as if actually included in the printed form. Obviously, this form of deed is valid only in the state where the statute applies. See WARRANTY DEED; DEED.

stay. The halting of a judicial proceeding by order of a court. An example would be a *stay of execution,* by which the execution of a judgment would be held up for a limited period by a judge's order. In this sense, a *stay* is a form of INJUNCTION.

stay of pro·*ceed*·**ings.** A temporary suspension of regular judicial processes by order of the court, often to allow one of the parties to correct an omitted step, or to perform some act required by the judge as incidental to the lawsuit. A *stay of proceedings* might be allowed, for example, to give a non-resident plaintiff an opportunity to give security for costs.

steal. To perpetrate a theft or LARCENY.All three of these terms mean the same thing.

stip·**u**·*la*·**tion.** (1) A formal agreement between the opposing lawyers in a trial, admitting to certain facts or to waive certain procedures, usually to save time in presenting matters that are obvious or that would be pointless to dispute. (2) Something agreed to in a legal instrument.

stir·**pes.** See PER STIRPES.

stock. (1) A certificate representing the proportional part of a CORPORATION owned by an individual investor (stockholder). (2) The capital raised by a corporation through the sale of shares or through contribution of subscribers. (3) The goods and merchandise that is owned by a commercial firm, or that the firm has on hand.

stock *div*·**i**·**dend.** The distribution or payment by a CORPORATION of profits or earnings in the form of the company's own stock, rather than in money. This is new stock, issued without a change in PAR VALUE. There are occasions when the issue of stock could consist of shares in a *spin-off corporation* owned by the parent company. A *stock dividend* is distinguished from a STOCK SPLIT, which is a division of corporate stock by the issuance to existing owners of new shares, with a corresponding lowering of par value for each outstanding share.

stock split. See STOCK DIVIDEND, from which it is distinguished.

stock·**hol**·**der's** **de**·*riv*·**a**·**tive suit.** Either of two types of lawsuits that may be carried on by a stockholder of a CORPORATION: **(a)** One is a suit in which the corporation has some cause of action against an outsider and has neglected or refused to take action to protect stockholder or corporate rights. (2) One is a suit on behalf of some of the stockholders who have been caused damage or loss by the corporation itself in discriminating in favor of some stockholders or outside interests. This suit generally occurs when stockholders with majority control try to benefit themselves or their friends at the general expense of the corporation.

stop *or*·**der.** (1) An order to a bank by a customer, instructing the bank not to cash a specific check that is outstanding. (2) An order to a stockbroker either to buy or sell at the market price when the price of a SECURITY declines or advances to a specified price.

stop·**page in** *trans*·**it.** The right of a seller to stop goods in transit, upon discovering that the buyer does not have the funds to pay for the goods. This right of the seller is generally recognized by the courts, even though the goods may have already been given to a common carrier, such as a railroad or freight line.

straw bond. A worthless or insufficient bail bond.

straw man. (1) An individual set up as a cover or front for any questionable transaction. (2) A weak adversary or opponent. (3) A witness hired to give false testimony or put up worthless BAIL for the release of an accused criminal.

strict fore·clo·sure. A procedure for the FORECLOSURE of a MORTGAGE that vests TITLE to the property in the mortgage holder (mortgagee) on default of payment without any sale of the property or any right of redemption. This type of mortgage has been generally done away with in most states.

strict li·a·*bil*·i·ty. Liability for damage or injury, whether or not there was fault or negligence by the party held responsible. In some situations in TORT law, the courts impose what amounts to automatic responsibility. For example, a food manufacturer is the only party that can exercise control over what goes into a canned food product. The courts will usually hold the manufacturer to *strict liability* if a poisonous substance or broken glass finds its way into the product, even though the manufacturer may have been unusually careful in inspecting and supervising the canning process. This is because the consumer is in no way able to find out what caused the injury or damage.

struck *ju*·ry. Synonymous with SPECIAL JURY.

sua spon·te. (Latin–*soo*·uh *spahn*·tee) *Of his or her own will.* Without suggestion or prompting. When the judge takes some action *sua sponte,* it is on his own initiative and without a motion or urging from one of the parties in a lawsuit.

sub. (Latin) *Under.* For example: *sub curia* means under law.

***sub*·ject to.** Subservient to, governed by, or subordinate to other rights or interests.

sub *ju*·di·ce. Under legal determination; a matter still before a court or judge.

***sub*·lease.** *An underlease;* a LEASE by a tenant (lessee) of all or part of a leased premises to another individual for a shorter term than held by the tenant, and under which the tenant retains some right or interest under the original lease.

sub·*mis*·sion. (1) The act of yielding to authority. (2) A type of contract by which parties agree to refer a dispute to an arbitrator, and to be bound by the decision of the arbitrator.

sub mo•do. (Latin–sub *moe•*doe) *Under conditions.* Subject to restrictions, qualifications, or conditions.

sub•*or•*di•nate. (1) Placed in a lower class or rank. (2) To make subject to some condition.

sub•or•*na•*tion of *per•*ju•ry. The crime of bribing or requesting someone to give false testimony in a criminal prosecution.

sub•*or•*ner. One who solicits or procures another to commit a crime, especially the crime of SUBORNATION OF PERJURY.

sub•*poe•*na. A WRIT, or written command, issued by a judge or court, directing the individual to whom addressed to appear at a specified time and place, usually to give testimony in court, under a penalty for disobedience.

sub•*poe•*na *du•*ces *te•*cum. A SUBPOENA issued by the court at the request of the government or one of the parties to a lawsuit, commanding a witness who controls or possesses a document pertinent to the controversy, to bring the document to the trial.

sub•ro•*ga•*tion. The substitution of one individual in place of another, with respect to a lawful claim, demand, or right. For example, a pedestrian with an accident insurance policy was injured by the negligence of an automobile driver. The insurance company paid the pedestrian for all injuries, under the *subrogation* principle. In a matter of this kind, the party substituted succeeds to the rights of the other in relation to the debt or claim, as well as to the legal remedies or securities that were available to the wronged pedestrian. The right of *subrogation* is never accorded to a mere outsider or volunteer who has paid the debt of another without any assignment or legal obligation. In the example above, the insurance company had a legal obligation to pay the pedestrian.

sub•ro•*gee.* One who succeeds to the legal rights of another under the legal principle of subrogation. See SUBROGATION.

sub•*scrib•*ing *wit•*ness. An individual who observes the signing of a will by the maker, and who signs as a witness. See ATTESTATION.

sub•*sid•*i•ar•y. A CORPORATION controlled by another corporation that owns the greater part of its shares. Also called SUBSIDIARY CORPORATION.

***sub•*si•dy.** A grant of money by the government, usually for a project deemed advantageous to the general public.

sub si•len•tio. (Latin–sub sill•*en•*toe) *Under silence.* Without taking notice or registering objection to something. Having knowledge of a thing *sub silentio* may be taken as evidence of consent.

sub·stance. The ultimate reality, as distinguished from that which merely seems to be. The essential part of a thing.

sub·*stan*·tial *er*·ror. See ERROR.

sub·stan·tive law. That area of the law which sets forth, defines, and creates rights, as distinguished from so-called ADJECTIVE LAW, or PROCEDURAL LAW, which provides the legal rules and method for enforcing or obtaining those rights. For example, the *substantive law* states that RAPE is an unlawful and forcible sexual assault on a female. Adjective law, for example, may provide that a female victim in a rape prosecution may not be cross-examined as to whether she was previously chaste, unless some other witness testifies in open court that the victim was of questionable morals. See ADJECTIVE LAW.

sub·sti·tut·ed *serv*·ice. Process SERVICE by any means other than by personal service. An example would be service by publication in a newspaper covering the area.

suc·ces·sion. The passage of title to property by the laws of descent and distribution. The right by which individuals inherit property.

sue. To file a lawsuit.

suf·fer·ance. Toleration; passive consent, as in not hindering or forbidding.

suf·frage. The right to cast a vote in public elections.

su·i·cide. The act of deliberately and intentionally taking one's own life by a person of sound mind. Some courts have held that the term *suicide,* as used in insurance policies, means death by one's own hand, irrespective of sanity. Some life insurance policies make a distinction in this regard. An unsuccessful attempt to commit suicide was a criminal offense in early English law, but this idea has been generally done away with in modern law.

su·i gen·e·ris. (Latin–*sue*·ey *gen*·e·ris) Of one's own kind. Individual; unique.

su·i ju·ris. (Latin–*syoo*·eye *jew*·ris–having full legal capacity or right) One who has legal capability to handle legal affairs, who is mentally capable.

suit. A CIVIL action, or lawsuit. A *suit* is distinguished from a CRIMINAL action, which is termed a prosecution.

sum•**ma**•**ry** *judg*•**ment.** A lawsuit settled in favor of one party before the conclusion of the full trial. A *summary judgment* might be awarded to the defendant, for example, where it becomes obvious during the course of the trial that the plaintiff cannot make out a case.

sum•**ma**•**ry** **pro**•*ceed*•**ing.** Any proceeding by which the case can be disposed of, or the dispute settled, or the trial conducted in a simple, prompt manner, in comparison with regular proceedings. The term may apply to a criminal prosecution as well as to a civil matter. For example, some states follow a quick dispossess action for non-payment of rent, rather than the more usual lengthy eviction process.

sum•**ming up.** A procedure near the close of a trial in which the attorney calls attention of the jury or the judge to the most noticeable parts of the attorney's case.

sum•**mons.** A written notice, sometimes called a WRIT, instructing the sheriff or a process server to notify a person that a legal action has been commenced against him or her in the court where the writ issues. The summons gives the date and place of appearance where the answer must be made, or a default judgment will be taken against the defendant and in favor of the plaintiff. See: DEFAULT JUDGMENT.

sump•**tu**•**a**•**ry** **laws.** Laws designed to regulate morals, religion, or personal habits.

su•**per**•**se**•**de**•**as.** (Latin–soop•er•*see*•dee•us) *Placing in abeyance.* An order staying proceedings of an inferior court. A legal process used to supersede enforcement of the judgment of a trial court, while the matter is under review by an APPELLATE COURT.

sup•**ple**•*men*•**tal** **bill** **(or com**•*plaint***).** A bill filed in addition to that originally filed in a lawsuit. The purpose may be to correct some defect or to bring into controversy some additional matter that has occurred after the original filing.

sup•**ple**•*men*•**ta**•**ry** **pro**•*ceed*•**ings.** Statutory proceedings supplemental to an EXECUTION, usually permitting a creditor an in-court examination (questioning) of a debtor to ascertain whether the debtor has assets to pay off the debt.

supra. (Latin–*soo*•pruh) *Above, or upon.* Used in a book or writing, this term refers to a previous page, section, or reference.

su•*preme* **court.** Usually the court of supreme authority or last resort in a judicial system; the court of superior JURISDICTION or highest rank as in the Federal judicial system, and most states. In some other states, such as New York and Texas, there are variations. For example, in New York the *supreme court* is the highest trial court of general jurisdiction, having some APPELLATE jurisdiction, but is not the court of last resort. In Texas, the final appeal in a criminal case is handled by the Court of Criminal Appeals, with the state supreme court handling final appeals in civil matters.

The *Supreme Court of the United States* has ORIGINAL JURISDICTION in all matters involving foreign ambassadors and diplomatic officials, and disputes in which a state is a party. The Supreme Court of the United States has appellate jurisdiction in all cases within the judicial authority of the United States, over all the other federal courts, and over federal matters appealed from the state court systems. Under the court's present structure, it has a chief justice and eight associate justices.

sur•**charge.** (1) To charge an extra fee, over and above that already charged. (2) An excessive load or burden. (3) An additional tax, cost, or assessment.

sur•**e**•**ty.** An individual or firm that legally agrees to stand good for another person's debt, in the event it is not paid; one who undertakes to pay money or perform some other specified act in the event of failure by the surety's PRINCIPAL. In a contract of *suretyship,* one party agrees to be answerable for the debt of another, in an agreement reduced to a formal contract. The terms GUARANTOR and *surety* are sometimes used interchangeably, but there are differences. See GUARANTY.

sur•**plus.** (1) That money left over from a fund set up for a particular purpose. (2) Excess of receipts over disbursements. (3) A corporation's net worth, over and above the stated value of capital stock.

sur•*plus*•**age.** Excess wordiness in legal pleadings or a legal document.

sur•*prise.* The principle that when a party or his or her counsel is taken by surprise in a material point or circumstance which could not have been anticipated, and when there was no lack of attention, care, or skill, a new trial may be granted if it appears injustice may be done.

sur•*ren*•**der.** (1) To yield back, or hand over; to give back on demand. (2) To give up a claim or right to another.

sur•**ro**•**gate.** The name given to a judicial officer or judge who handles PROBATE matters or GUARDIANSHIPS in some states. A judge over this kind of court is also called a probate judge or judge of probate court or judge of ORPHAN'S COURT.

sur•**tax.** (1) An extra tax or charge in addition to that already assessed. (2) A graduated tax on income, in addition to a basic tax, when income reaches a certain figure.

sur•**vey.** The act by which a parcel of land is measured, determining the extent, position, and content. The courses and distances, metes and bounds are usually included in the field notes or survey papers.

sur•*vi*•**vor.** An individual who lives on after the death of another.

sur•*vi*•**vor**•**ship.** (1) The legal right of a surviving individual originally having a JOINT INTEREST with others in an estate to receive the whole estate, as the sole survivor. (2) The condition of being the one individual out of two or more who lives longest.

sus•*pend*•**ed** *sen*•**tence.** The postponement or SUSPENSION of a sentence by a judge following a criminal conviction, on condition that the convicted person remain on good behavior for a specified period of time.

sus•*pen*•**sion.** A temporary delay or interruption. A temporary stoppage of the operation of a law or right.

sus•*tain*. (1) To uphold or support a MOTION or OBJECTION by COUNSEL during a trial, thus giving it authority and support. (2) To bear up, or support, as for example the judge may say that the plaintiff's evidence *sustained* the findings of the jury.

syl•**la**•**bus.** A headnote or abstract of the points of law prefixed to the reported decision of an APPELLATE COURT.

sym•*bol*•**ic** **de**•*liv*•**er**•**y.** The constructive rather than actual delivery of subject matter of a gift or sale by giving a symbol of ownership when actual delivery might be difficult or impossible. A father's act in handing over registration papers to his son for a thoroughbred race horse would be a *symbolic delivery*. A statement by the father that he was making a gift of the animal to his son, plus the symbolic delivery, would be strong evidence that ownership had passed to the son.

syn•**di**•**cate.** (1) In business law, a combination of firms or individuals joining together in an enterprise too large for single firms or individuals to undertake. It is a JOINT ADVENTURE for profit that is neither a partnership nor a stock corporation. (2) Any kind of a union or organization for a temporary purpose.

T

tail. The limitation on the inheritance of an ESTATE to a particular person or class of persons. Instead of descending to heirs generally, property is inherited by the heirs of the DONEE'S body (to his children, and through him to his grandchildren. So long as there continue to be issue, the estate continues.) This is an old English legal idea for keeping large estates in the hands of children, grandchildren, etc. It is seldom used in American law.

tak•**ing the Fifth A•***mend***•ment.** The practice of witnesses or suspects in refusing to answer a question because of the Fifth Amendment right in the U.S. Constitution to refuse to furnish information implicating one's self in a crime. In the language of the Amendment: "... nor shall be compelled in any criminal case to be a witness against himself, ..."

tales. See TALESMAN.

tales•**man.** A person pressed into service to fill out the panel on a JURY. If a sufficient number of those jurors called to duty should fail to appear, some courts have authority to require someone off the street or a spectator in the courtroom to accept jury duty. Such an individual is called a *tales,* or a *talesman.*

tan•**gi**•**ble.** Property or items that are discernible to the touch. *Tangible* property may be either real or personal.

tar•**iff.** A list or schedule of goods or articles on which a duty, or tax, is imposed. See DUTY.

tax. A monetary contribution laid upon individuals or property for the support of the government. The most common types of taxes include: property (real estate) tax, income tax, inheritance tax, franchise tax, and license tax.

tax deed. A DEED given by the government to the new owner following a FORCED SALE of property for nonpayment of taxes.

tax lien. A claim against real property (real estate) that accrues in favor of the taxing agency (county, municipality, or state government) from taxes that are assessed against the property. If the lien is not paid when due, the taxing agency may sell the property to satisfy the lien. See LIEN.

tax·a·ble. That which is subject to taxation.

tem·po·rar·y re·*strain*·ing or·der. A temporary *injunction;* a provisional injunction, as opposed to a final restraining order or perpetual injunction; a court order forbidding an individual from taking certain actions until a hearing can be held on the merits of a legal dispute. See INJUNCTION.

tem·pus fu·git. (Latin–*tem*·pus *fyoo*·jit) *Time flies.*

ten·an·cy by the en·*tire*·ty. A type of joint ownership by a husband and wife, that is utilized in a limited number of states. TITLE is acquired by the marriage partners jointly after marriage. Upon the death of either spouse, his or her interest automatically passes to the survivor. Ownership of this kind cannot be terminated without the consent of both parties, and the property cannot be mortgaged or transferred without the approval of both. This kind of ownership is sometimes called "tenancy by the entireties."

ten·an·cy in *com*·mon. A form of co-ownership of real property. Co-tenants own undivided interests, but these interests need not be equal in quantity or duration and may arise from different conveyances and at different times. There is no right of SURVIVORSHIP. The interest of each tenant can be devised by a will, or can be passed on to the tenant's heirs. See JOINT TENANCY, from which *tenancy in common is distinguished.*

ten·ant at *suf*·fer·ance. An occupier of property who began possession in a legal manner but who has continued to occupy after the termination of a rent or LEASE agreement. Technically, a *tenant at sufferance* is not a tenant of anyone. The landlord may elect to treat such an occupier as a TRESPASSER and demand possession of the property, which demand will be enforced by the court. The only duty owed by the landlord is not to wantonly or wilfully injure the occupier of the latter's property. In some states the landlord may eject and sue to obtain double or treble rent. If the owner elects to treat the occupier as a tenant, as by accepting rent at the rate previously paid, the *tenancy at sufferance* comes to an end, and the occupant becomes a TENANT AT WILL or a periodic tenant.

ten·ant at will. One who holds possession of property by permission of the owner but without any fixed term. The arrangement may be terminated at will by either party. By statute in most states the land-lord must give thirty days' notice in order to terminate. This is the old month-to-month rent arrangement that is very common through-out the United States, but is being replaced by LEASE arrangements in many areas.

ten•der. (1) An offer of a bid for a contract. (2) An offer to buy stock for the purpose of gaining control of a corporation. (3) An offer of money or services in satisfaction of something owed or in avoiding a penalty or forfeiture for nonperformance or nonpayment.

ten•e•ment. Any kind of property that may be held by a tenant. The legal meaning is different from the commonly accepted usage of this term. In the legal sense, a *tenement* may be an elegant mansion, a slum apartment house, or a franchise that is let to a tenant.

ten•ure. (1) The act of holding or occupying, especially land. (2) The duration of length of term of an office or position, such as *tenure for life,* etc. (3) Historically, *tenure* was the system of holding lands or interests in land in subordination to some superior, such as a feudal lord or king. All concepts of property rights in old English law devel-oped from this background. (4) The status of holding one's position on a permanent basis, granted to teachers, civil service personnel, etc., on fulfillment of specific requirements.

term. (1) A fixed period of time. (2) A session of court. (3) The amount of time to be served under a prison sentence.

term of court. The designated period of time prescribed by law during which a court may sit to transact business. That period of time during which the court actually sits (is convened) is called a session. For example, a court may convene and begin business in October, in which event the occasion would be called the "October Term." If cases are to be tried during a term of court, it may be called a "gen-eral term" or a "trial term."

ter•ri•to•ri•al courts. Courts in the territorial possessions of the United States, such as Guam or the Virgin Islands. Until a territory reaches the time for statehood, the Federal courts in the territory perform the functions of both state and Federal courts.

tes•ta•ment. (1) Commonly used to mean a will. (2) In some instances the term is used in a limited sense to mean the disposition of personal property only, rather than a devise or disposition of REAL property.

tes•ta•men•ta•ry. Any INSTRUMENT or paper written so as not to take effect until after the death of the person making the document. The purpose may be to make a gift, will, or appointment. A *testamentary instrument* is revocable up to the death of the maker, who retains ownership and control of property mentioned in the document.

tes•**tate (or** *tes*•**ta**•**cy).** The state of dying with a valid will. The opposite of INTESTATE.

tes•**ta**•**tor, tes**•*ta*•**tor.** A male individual who makes or has a will made. See TESTATRIX.

tes•*ta*•**trix.** A female individual who makes a will, or has a will made. See TESTATOR.

tes•**ti**•**fy.** To give evidence as a witness before a court, or in some judicial procedure, for the purpose of establishing or proving some fact.

tes•**ti**•*mo*•**ni**•**um clause.** The clause in a legal paper or document that identifies the person signing (and/or sealing) the document.

tes•**ti**•**mo**•**ny.** Oral evidence of a witness given in court or before some tribunal or official board.

theft. The act of stealing; another name for LARCENY. Unless changed by state statute, theft is the taking and carrying away of money or personal belongings of another, with the intent to use it or deprive the owner of it. EMBEZZLEMENT is distinguished from theft in that the embezzler has been entrusted with possession of the property that is wrongfully taken; the thief has no right to possession at the time the property is taken.

tide lands. Land along the ocean lying between the low water mark and the high water mark left by the tide. Ownership of *tide lands* generally falls within the public domain. As a general principle of law, navigation may not be impeded by private interest in any tidal waterways. Oil and mineral rights in these lands have been owned by the states since 1953.

time *char*•**ter.** See CHARTER PARTY.

time draft. A BILL OF EXCHANGE, or draft, that is payable at a specified time. It is a written order from one person to another to pay a definite sum of money.

time is of the *es*•**sence.** In CONTRACT law, a statement that *time is of the essence* means that the contract will be invalid unless performance is made within the time specified in the agreement. This phrase is used when substantial compliance within the agreed time will simply not do, but total compliance is required.

time-price *doc*·trine. The practice followed by some retail stores in charging a higher price for items bought on time payments than for items bought for cash. This is usually upheld by the courts on the theory that the seller runs a greater risk of loss in credit sales and may consequently charge more. Some contend that this legal doctrine is merely a way to evade usury laws.

***ti*·tle.** (1) The union of all the elements constituting legal ownership; the means whereby the owner of lands has just possession of the property. *Title* is sometimes defined as the outward evidence of ownership, as well as the right of full possession, use, and enjoyment. (2) Something that justifies or substantiates a legal claim. (3) Legal statutes may be broken down into *titles* and chapters, by subject matter. For example, Title III of the United States Code.

toll. (1) A monetary payment for the use of a road or facility. (2) A charge for transportation or service, as for a long distance telephone call. (3) An exorbitant or ruinous price, as *scurvy took a heavy toll among Columbus' crews.*

to·*pog*·ra·phy. In real property law, the description of a particular place, such as a city, town, parish, or tract of land, in scientific description and delineation.

***Tor*·rens *sys*·tem.** A system for the compulsory registration of TITLES to REAL property, named after Sir Robert Torrens who devised the system. As used, records for the ownership of land are set up in state or county registries. Transfer of ownership takes place when a buyer obtains a DEED or other legal proof of purchase and has a certificate of registration issued by the state or county REGISTRY. This system is set up to maintain an accurate registry of ownership, MORTGAGES, and LIENS against property. A new purchaser does not need to go back beyond the registry; the title registry is legally absolute. Some states have adopted variations of the *Torrens system,* but only a few regard registry records as absolute.

tort. A private or civil injury other than one arising from a breach of contract. For a *tort,* the courts usually say there must be **(a)** a wrongful act or omission, or a failure to obey the law, and **(b)** a resulting injury to some person. The injured victim has the right to sue for the damage that results, and corporations are responsible for the *torts* of their employees committed within the scope of their employment. Commonplace *torts* often arise out of negligent operation of

an automobile, assault and battery, false imprisonment, injuries arising from negligent maintenance of store premises available to the
public, from selling adulterated products that cause injury, etc.

tort·*fea*·sor. One who is responsible for the commission of a TORT,
civil wrong.

tor·**tious.** A wrongful act; in the nature of a TORT or personal injury.

Tot·**ten trust.** (Sometimes called a savings bank trust.) A TRUST which
arises from the deposit by one individual of that individual's money,
in his or her own name as trustee for another; the transaction is revocable at will until the depositor dies or gives evidence that TITLE has
unequivocally passed to the beneficiary, by gift.

tow·**age.** In admiralty law, the service involved in towing a ship.

to wit. Specifically; namely; that is to say.

town·**ship.** A territorial subdivision six miles long and six miles wide. It
contains 36 sections of land, each one mile square.

trade·**mark.** A distinctive mark of authenticity, by which the product
of a particular maker may be distinguished from the products of
others. A *trademark* is registered with the United States Patent Office in Washington, D.C., and use of the mark is reserved exclusively
for the holder. Unauthorized use of the *trademark* is actionable in a
lawsuit for damages, and an injunction may also be issued to forbid
unauthorized use.

trans·*ac*·tion. (1) A completed piece of business; a business deal. (2) The
published records of the activities of a society or organization.

tran·**script.** An official copy of a court record. For example, a certified
copy of a court judgment. Transcripts of the testimony of witnesses
in a trial can usually be purchased by paying the court stenographer
for transcribing the testimony.

trans·*fer*·a·ble. That which may pass from hand to hand, carrying all
the rights of the original holder; capable of being transferred or assigned.

tran·**sient.** (1) That which is temporary or of short duration. (2) Someone who has no permanent address.

tran·**si·to·ry.** That which is unstable and fleeting; that which may
change from place to place.

tran·**si·to·ry** *ac*·**tion.** A lawsuit in which the plaintiff has the option
to initiate action in any one of several locations.

trav·*erse*, *trav*·erse. A term used in old forms of legal pleading to signify a denial of the facts alleged in the declaration of the opposing party.

trea·son. An overt attempt to overthrow the government to which one owes allegiance.

treas·ur·er. An officer of a private CORPORATION, society, etc. or a public official charged with the receipt, custody, and disbursement of money.

trea·ty. (1) In international law, a compact or agreement between two or more independent nations intended to be of benefit to all the nations involved. (2) In the law of sales or CONTRACTS, that discussion of terms which immediately precedes the completion of the understanding.

tres·pass. (1) An old legal designation for a great variety of civil wrongs or TORTS. Any injury of another's person or property. (2) Any unlawful entry onto the REAL PROPERTY of another.

tri·al. The formal examination before a competent court to determine the verdict of those matters in issue in a civil or criminal case.

tri·al **at bar.** A trial had before a full court composed of several judges, rather than one had before a single court, or NISI PRIUS.

tri·al **term.** See TERM OF COURT.

tri·*bu*·nal. (1) Generally used to mean a court. (2) The place where a judge holds court; where justice is administered. In early Roman times it was an elevated seat occupied by the judge (praetor) while dispensing justice. (3) The whole body of judges who are members of an appellate court.

tro·ver. One of the old forms of COMMON LAW action brought to recover the value of goods wrongfully converted by another to his or her own use. Seldom of any practical use today, the old form of action is of interest in the development of property law.

true bill. An INDICTMENT returned (voted and approved) by a GRAND JURY as warranting a criminal prosecution of the accused.

trust. A FIDUCIARY relationship in which property or money is held by one party for the benefit of another. The property is retained or controlled by the trustee for the benefit or use of a beneficiary, sometimes called the *cestui que trust*. A trust can be created for any purpose that is not illegal. It is set up by the giving of money or property by a grantor or trustor, so long as the fund is sufficiently identified for title to pass to the TRUSTEE. An express trust may be set up by explicit words or action, as by a devise in a will, while others may be set up by operation of the law. The trustee, of course, may be liable personally for mishandling trust assets.

trust deed. See DEED OF TRUST.

trus·*tee*. An individual or trust company representative in whom an estate or power is vested under an agreement to manage it for the benefit of others or another. One appointed or required to carry out a TRUST.

***trus·*tor.** (sometimes called the grantor of a trust) The individual who creates a TRUST, either by will or by some other legal instrument.

trust re·*ceipt*. A surety transaction is represented by a document called a *trust receipt,* by which one individual lends money to another for the purchase of goods or merchandise, and the borrower promises to hold the goods or merchandise for the benefit of the lender until the debt is paid.

try. To try a case means to represent one side in court as a lawyer, or to hand down a decision as a judge presiding over the trial.

***tur·*pi·tude.** Shameful wickedness; moral depravity, or lack of character.

***tu·*te·lage.** The state of being under a legal guardian.

U

***ul·*tra *vi·*res.** (Latin) *Beyond the scope.* Not in accordance with the powers. Sometimes a CORPORATION is granted a charter by the state to do one type of business. If the corporation engages in some completely different kind of business, it is said that this latter activity is *ultra vires.* Or the directors of a corporation may vote to give themselves each a salary of $100,000 a year, although the corporate charter stated they were to serve for $10,000 a year. Here again, the director's vote would be *ultra vires.*

u·na·*nim·*i·ty. Agreement of all parties concerned.

***u·*na *vo·*ce.** (Latin) With one voice. Without dissent; unanimously.

un·*clean* hands. The legal principle that a party seeking relief in a court of EQUITY must come in without fault in the transaction complained of. The doctrine has no application unless the party's wrongdoing is reasonably related to the subject matter in dispute.

un·*con*·scion·a·ble. Beyond the limits of good conscience; unduly harsh and shocking.

un·con·sti·*tu*·tion·al. In conflict with the Constitution of the United States.

un·der-ten·ant. One who holds property by a SUBLEASE, or under one who is already a tenant.

un·der·write. The assumption of risk by an insurance company in providing life insurance or various forms of property insurance. For example, the insurance company providing coverage is frequently said to be the *underwriter.*

un·der·writ·er. (1) A company or individual who insures another. (2) A firm or individual that undertakes to purchase an entire issue of bonds, stocks, or other securities, or subscribes to underwrite a whole block of securities.

un·due *in*·flu·ence. Pressure, constraint, or improper persuasion of such nature as to interfere with the exercise of free will, choice, or judgment.

un·fair com·pe·*ti*·tion. A general term applied to all forms of dishonest or fraudulent rivalry in commerce or trade. Those methods by a competitor that deprive the operator or owner of the rightul profits of a business. Under the legal doctrine of *unfair competition,* a buyer may be induced to purchase goods because they are packaged in a similar way, or are simulated by name, symbols, logo, color scheme, or other imitation. The equity principle of *unfair competition* applies to all cases in which one party seeks to sell goods as those of another. Generally, fraudulent intent is a necessary ingredient.

u·ni·*form*·i·ty. Conformity to the same patterns; conformity to one type. Legal requirements for *uniformity* are generally said to be met when the law applies uniformly to all persons or groups within the relations and circumstances provided in the law. *Uniformity* in taxation, for example, does not require that all inhabitants or firms be taxed, nor taxed alike. But the tax must be levied alike on all that fall within the same class or kind.

u·ni·*lat*·er·al. Pertaining to one side only.

un·i·**trust.** A type of TRUST set up for the beneficiary to receive a fixed percentage of the trust property on a yearly basis.

un·*just* **en**·*rich*·**ment.** The legal doctrine that one obtaining or retaining money unfairly shall not be allowed to enrich himself or herself at the expense of others. For example, A could say to B, "Hold this one thousand dollars for me, as it is dark and I might be robbed while going home." B kept the one thousand dollars, and A was killed in a car wreck enroute home. B refused to turn the money over to A's heirs, saying, "I kept the money for A, and no one else should get it." The courts would say that B is not entitled to enrich himself at the expense of A or A's heirs, and must give up the money to those legally entitled to A's property.

un·*law*·**ful.** That which is illegal or in violation of law.

un·*law*·**ful de**·*tain*·**er.** The unlawful retention or possession of REAL PROPERTY by a person whose right to such possession has terminated and who refuses to quit the property.

un·*liq*·**ui**·**da**·**ted** *dam*·**a**·**ges.** Damages that are to be awarded, but where the amount owing has not yet been determined. See DAMAGES.

un·*sound* **mind.** Characteristics of an individual incapable of handling himself or herself: the lack of capacity to understand and act with discretion in the ordinary matters of life, includes all who are insane or those classed as idiots or imbeciles. Courts have said that mere uncleanliness, neglect of person, clothing, or eating habits, or mere eccentricity do not constitute unsoundness of mind. However, any or all of these factors may be taken into consideration as to the mental state.

un·*writ*·**ten law.** (1) That part of the law observed administered by the courts which is not based on a constitution, statute, or ordinance. In general, the *unwritten law* is identical with the COMMON LAW, deriving authority solely from usages and customs accepted by the courts from time immemorial. Even though state statutes may specify that there are no crimes in the laws of that jurisdiction except those acts forbidden by specific statute, the courts may turn to the common law in their decisions. For example, the state statute may specify that rape consist of forcibly having sexual relations by a man with a non-consenting female. In a case of this kind the accused male could claim that the act was not completed and he was therefore not guilty. In the past, the courts have looked to the old common law of

England in upholding a conviction, even though the state statute was not specific as to whether the act had to be completed. The old common law of rape considered any penetration, however slight, to constitute the crime. **(2)** The traditionally assumed rule that an outraged man may kill the seducer of his wife, when the couple is caught in the act. This *unwritten law* is allowed as a defense to a charge of murder of the paramour in some states (but not to killing the wife). It is not allowed as a defense to a murder charge in many jurisdictions, however.

up•**set price.** A specified price below which any land or goods put up for sale in an auction is not to be sold.

us•**age.** Those customary and accepted practices that are followed in a particular locality or business. It is a custom or practice that is so well known that the parties must be presumed to act with reference thereto. In the meat business the local *usage* may be to put the meat back into the seller's meat locker until the buyer calls for it. Placing the meat out on a table, where there was no refrigeration and it would deteriorate, would not be in conformity with accepted *usage,* and would subject the seller to legal responsibility for loss.

use. The right of one person (called the beneficiary) to the enjoyment of the rents and profits of lands and buildings, the legal TITLE to and the posession of which are vested in another in trust for the beneficiary.

u•**su•fruct.** The right to reap the benefits from property, so long as the corpus or substance of the property is not harmed. Crops could be taken from a farm so long as the lands are not seriously depleted. Building stone could not be taken from a quarry on the property, however, as this would be depleting the resources.

u•sur•*pa*•tion. **(1)** Marking unlawful use of property which belongs to another. An interruption or disturbance of the right to the use and posession of property. **(2)** The seizure of supreme or governmental power by force or illegality from the regularly constituted government or ruler.

u•**su•ry.** Charging a rate of interest in excess of the maximum rate allowed by law.

ut•**ter.** **(1)** To attempt to negotiate a fraudulent check or document, whether or not it is accepted; an attempted or an actual circulation of a counterfeit coin. **(2)** To give public expression to.

ux•or. (Latin–*ucks*•or) Wife. A married woman.

V

v. Abbreviation for VERSUS.

***va*·cate.** To set aside; to annul. When a court vacates an entry or judgment, it is competely set aside. To vacate is not to suspend judgment, but to completely set aside the judgment for all time.

***va*·grant.** A person with no visible means of support, who wanders from place to place, and while apparently able to work lives on charity or handouts.

***val*·id.** That which is sound; LEGITIMATE; sufficient and efficatious; legally sustainable.

***val*·u·a·ble con·sid·er·a·tion.** Something of value given up in good faith in exchange for something received or the promise of something of value from the other party. It is the kind of CONSIDERATION that courts will enforce against another party that does not live up to the other side of the bargain. In short, it is the kind of consideration needed to make a CONTRACT.

val·u·*a*·tion. The process for determining the worth of a thing. An appraisal. The setting of a price.

***var*·i·ance.** (1) Permission or license to do some act that is contrary to rules or laws. For example a *zoning variance* may be granted by the zoning commission to permit construction of a cement block wall eight feet in height, although city ordinances specify seven feet as the accepted height for such a wall. (2) A discrepancy in a civil lawsuit between the pleadings as to what one party says will be proved (alleged), and what the evidence actually shows at the time of trial. If the *variance* is so great that the defendant was seriously crippled in preparation of the defense, courts usually hold that the plaintiff cannot recover. In a criminal prosecution, the prosecutor must prove the crime actually charged, and proof of another crime will not be sufficient to convict of either.

***ve*·hi·cle.** (1) A conveyance used in the transportation of passengers or merchandise. (2) A medium through which information is expres-

sed. **(3)** An agent such as a solvent, carrier, or binder, holding chem-
icals in solution or holding substances as chemical agents.

ve•**nal.** Open to corruption or bribery. That which can be had for a
price.

vend•*ee.* One who is a buyer.

ven•**dor.** A seller.

ve•**ni**•**re fa**•**ci**•**as** (Latin–vuh•*nye*•ree *fay*•she•us) An order, or a writ,
from a judge ordering the sheriff or coroner to call a specified num-
ber of persons from which a jury could be selected (a jury panel).
Sometimes shortened to *venire*.

ve•*ni*•**re**•**man.** An individual called to serve on a jury by a writ of *venire facias* ordered by a judge; a member of a panel of jurors.

ven•**ue.** **(1)** The county or other geographical or political division from
which the jury must be summoned and in which the trial must be
held. **(2)** The place where a crime is committed or a cause of action
arises.

ver•**dict.** The JURY'S finding on a question of fact in a civil or criminal
proceeding. If a jury is waived, a verdict may be the judge's findings
while sitting as a jury. It is usually said that the jury's findings are
not a verdict until accepted by the judge. It is distinguished from a
JUDGMENT.

ver•**i**•**fi**•*ca*•**tion.** A sworn statement in a lawsuit confirming the truth,
correctness, or accuracy of PLEADINGS by DEPOSITION or AFFIDAVIT.

ver•**i**•**ty.** The state or condition of truthfulness; conformity to fact.

ver•**sus.** (abbreviated as *v.* or *vs.*) (Latin) *Against.* The term used in the
title of a lawsuit to distinguish between the opposing parties, as
Smith versus Jones, or Smith vs. Jones, or Smith v. Jones.

vest. To take immediate effect. See VESTED RIGHTS.

vest•**ed.** Fixed; established; not susceptible to change; not subject to
any conditions that could change the established relationship.

vest•**ed** *in*•**ter**•**est.** A present fixed right of future enjoyment of property, not contingent on anything; an established property right. For
example, if an individual sells you a lot and delivers you a DEED, you
have a vested interest in the land, even though the sale contract permits the seller to grow vegetables on the land for the next year.

vest•**ed rights.** Rights that are absolute and not subject to any conditions. It is the certainty or uncertainty of enjoyment that distin-

guishes a *vested right* from a contingent interest in an estate (property). The *vested right* or *vested interest* is immediate, with no contingencies.

ve•to. (Latin) I forbid. **(1)** The power vested in the chief executive of the United States or a state (President or governor) to prevent temporarily or permanently the enactment of a statute passed by the legislature. The holdup by the chief executive is sometimes temporary. Under Federal law, the legislature (Congress) can overturn the *veto* by voting a second time with a two-thirds majority of the legislature. Most state governments have simlar provisions for overturning the veto of the governor. **(2)** The power of any of the five permanent members of the Security Council of the United Nations to cast a negative vote; one such vote prevents action.

vi•*car*•i•ous li•a•*bil*•i•ty. Liability of an employer for the wrongful acts of an employee during the scope of job activities. This is also the indirect liability of a master for the TORTS or NEGLIGENCE of a SERVANT, or of a PRINCIPAL for the wrongful acts of the principal's AGENT during the scope of that agency relationship.

vice. **(1)** Moral corruption or depravity, frequently of the type that is forbidden by law. Usually, this kind of *vice* includes gambling, PROSTITUTION, PANDERING, and sale or use of drugs or alcohol under conditions forbidden by law. **(2)** Any moral fault, defect, imperfection, or character blemish.

vide. (Latin–*vye*•dee, *vee*•day) *See. Vide ante* is a reference to a previous passage in a written work, while *vide infra* or *vide post* refers to a subsequent passage in the same writing.

vide ante. See VIDE.

vide infra. See VIDE.

vide post. See VIDE.

vin•*dic*•tive. See EXEMPLARY DAMAGES.

vi•o•*la*•tion. A breach of duty or right; an infringement; a transgression; a RAPE.

vis *ma*•jor. (Latin–veece *may*•jur) *A greater or superior force.* Any act of God or natural disaster beyond the control of human agencies, and which happens independently of human neglect or action. Earthquakes, tornados, tidal waves, disastrous fires caused by lightning are all examples of a *vis major*. There is no TORT liability for a disaster of this kind.

vi•sa. (1) Any official endorsement on a document to verify that it has been inspected and found to be in due form or correct. (2) The approval to visit a country stamped into the passport of one desiring to make the travel. This approval is given by the consul or other official representative of the country to be visited.

vi•ti•ate. To cause to fail or to impair. To make faulty or defective. In contract law, there is a legal maxim that *fraud vitiates a contract.*

vi•va vo•ce. (Latin-*vee•*vuh *voe•*see) With the living voice. By voice vote. The word *ballot* usually signifies a secret vote, while *viva voce* means a voice vote by public outcry. The term is also used to mean oral testimony, as distinguished from giving evidence by written affidavit or deposition.

void. Of no legal effect; without force; without the legal authority it was intended to produce. *Void* is to be distinguished from VOIDABLE, in that a *void* document or agreement is regarded as never having had any effect, and that nothing can be done to cure this inadequacy.

void *con•***tract.** A contract which is regarded as never having had any legal effect. It involves a situation in which the parties went through the form of making a contract, but in the eyes of the law none was ever made, since some essential element of the contract was left out. Such an agreement is *void* from the outset, creating no legal rights. Either party may ignore such an agreement at their wish. A typical *void contract* would be one in which no valuable consideration was ever offered. See VALUABLE CONSIDERATION.

void•a•ble. That which is capable of being adjudged VOID. It is not void in itself, but may be considered so, at the will of one or more of the parties involved. For example, a contract made by a minor to buy a car may be *voidable* when the minor comes of legal age. The minor can back out of the contract and return the car, but cannot keep a car that has not been paid for. The minor can choose to go ahead with the contract on becoming of age. In that event the buyer will thereafter be bound by the *voidable* contract.

voir dire. Preliminary examination of a juror by the opposing lawyers and/or the judge, to determine if the individual has an interest in the case, is incompetent, biased, related to the disputants, attorneys, prosecutor, judge, or in any way is unfit to serve as a juror.

vol•un•tar•y **lien.** A LIEN placed on property with the consent of the owner, or as a result of a voluntary act of the owner. Some *voluntary* *liens* arise by operation of the law, and others by stipulation of the parties.

vot·ing trust. A TRUST created by agreement of a number of shareholders to deposit their stock in the hands of a trustee or trustees. Under such an agreement the shareholders retain ownership of the stock but delegate their power of voting it to the trustee or trustees.

vouch·er. A document or receipt which evidences a transaction, especially a document that will show the discharge of a debt. An account book showing the disbursement of money may also be known as a *voucher.*

voy·age char·ter. See CHARTER PARTY.

vs. Abbreviation for VERSUS.

W

wage as·*sign*·ment. An agreement of a voluntary nature by which an employee or worker permits earnings to be paid directly by the employer to a creditor of the employee or worker. An arrangement of this kind is now illegal in many jurisdictions.

waive. To intentionally and voluntarily abandon or give up a right, claim, or privilege.

waiv·er. The voluntary giving up of known right. A *waiver* may be either express or implied, involving either CIVIL or CRIMINAL matters. An accused individual may have the right to a trial by JURY, but may *waive* this right in open court, permitting the judge to act as both judge and jury, to save time. *Waiver* of most rights in a criminal prosecution must be done in the presence of the accused's attorney and in open court in such a manner that the judge is satisfied the accused understands the implications involved.

wan·ton. Completely undisciplined, foolhardy, and in reckless disregard of the rights of others.

ward. **(1)** An individual placed by a court under the care of a guardian. Usually the *ward* is a child, or is incompetent due to mental or physical disabilities. See GUARDIAN. **(2)** An area or section of a city, usually set up for elections or administrative purposes.

*ware•**house** re•*ceipt.* A receipt showing storage of goods or property in a warehouse. It is sometimes used as a NEGOTIABLE INSTRUMENT, and is evidence of TITLE to the property in storage.

*warf•**age.** A slang usage for WHARFAGE.

*war•**rant.** (1) A WRIT or order for the arrest, search and seizure, or other legal act directed to an officer, who will be relieved of liability in carrying out the writ. **(2)** A promise in a CONTRACT or DEED OF CONVEYANCE to defend the TITLE and possession of the property to the purchaser and heirs against all claims. **(3)** An order by which the drawer authorizes one individual to pay a sum of money. **(4)** An order by a municipal council, board, or other official body to the treasurer of the organization to pay money to those whose claims have been approved.

*war•**ran•ty.** (1) In REAL PROPERTY law, a convenant (legal promise) in a deed whereby the GRANTOR binds himself or herself and heirs to secure to the GRANTEE the estate conveyed. In this covenant the grantor promises to guarantee the conveyance with other land of equal value if the TITLE should fail. **(2)** A promise or undertaking, either express or implied, by the seller of property, that the property is as represented to the buyer. For example, merchandise sold in a store must be as claimed by the salesperson. **(3)** In insurance law, a pledge or legal stipulation on the part of the insured that the facts claimed in relation to the person or property insured are as stated. The enforceability of an insurance contract depends on the literal truth of the insured's representations. For example, in applying for health insurance the applicant may be required to *warrant* that the applicant has never had a heart attack or a stroke. If the insurance is issued and the insured has in fact had such a heart attack or stroke, the insurance will not be paid by the insurance company. This is because of the insured's false *warranty.*

*war•**ran•ty deed.** A legal document by which ownership of land is transferred from one owner to a new owner. In giving a *warranty deed,* the grantor (seller) does two things: **(a)** transfers the seller's ownership or title to the property, and **(b)** legally agrees to defend the validity of that title forever for the benefit of the purchaser. A *warranty deed* gives the buyer the right to collect from the seller if anyone subsequently establishes a claim or incumbrance against the property. A QUITCLAIM DEED does not give this right to go back against the seller. A *warranty deed* is sometimes called a *general warranty deed.*

waste. The dissipation, destruction or abuse of property by one in rightful possession; a material alteration or spoilage of real estate by an individual entitled to use it. For example, a grandfather left a LIFE ESTATE in a walnut grove to his son, with the FREEHOLD INTEREST in the property passing to his only grandson. The father, of course, can harvest the crop and spend the proceeds, as well as live on the property. Resentful that he did not get outright TITLE to the property (a freehold interest, rather than a life estate), the father tore out the irrigation system, and many of the walnut trees died. The grandson could go into court and obtain money damages against the son (his father) for the destruction done to the property for *waste,* and could get an injunction ordering the life tenant (son) from committing further *waste.*

wa·tered stock. Stock issued by a corporation for which the PAR VALUE has not been paid in. Stock not backed up by additional assets.

wa·ters. Waters are either public or private rivers, streams, lakes, or arms of the sea. The sea, its branches, and navigable streams are publicly owned. Water itself is neither land nor tenement nor susceptible to absolute ownership. If it escapes, the right to ownership of it is gone forever. The right to use of water on private lands is a complicated legal subject, varying in legal implications from state to state.

wharf·age. Sometimes called *warfage.* The fee paid for transferring goods onto a boat or barge, or for unloading the goods at a wharf.

wil·fully. Same as WILLFULLY.

will. (1) Wish, choice, or desire. (2) In CRIMINAL law, that INTENT of the mind which directs the action of the individual. (3) A revocable legal document by which an individual disposes of property, which takes effect after the maker's death. The person making this disposition of property is called the *testator* if a male, or the *testatrix* if a female. Under the law in most states, a will must be signed in the presence of two or more witnesses, who sign in the presence of each other and the *testator* or *testatrix.* It is usually advisable for a will to be drawn up by an attorney, especially if there is an extensive amount of property. There are a number of different kinds of wills. See HOLOGRAPHIC WILL, NUNCUPATIVE WILL.

will con·test. A lawsuit to determine whether a purported document or instrument should be admitted to PROBATE. The *will contest* is not concerned per se with the legality or validity of the contents, but only with whether this particular document was intended to be a will of the deceased and was the last will written.

will·**ful.** (1) In criminal law, describes an act done intentionally, knowingly, and purposely, without justifiable excuse. It denotes an evil disregard for what is right. It distinguishes from an act done carelessly or thoughtlessly. (2) Perversely and obstinately self-willed.

will·**ful·ly,** *wil*·**ful·ly.** (1) Deliberately, in a premeditated or headstrong manner, intentionally. (2) With criminal intent.

with·*out* **day.** An old expression still used to mean that an adjournment is final, with no time fixed for another meeting or session. It is usually used to mean that court has closed down until the next session.

with·*out* **prej·u·dice.** A phrase used to mean current action cannot be regarded as an admission of liability or as a final adjudication of a matter. For example, dismissal of a lawsuit *without prejudice* means that the judge has dismissed the action because some technical requirement was left out; the lawsuit may be reinstated without harming the rights of any of the parties involved. The judge's dismissal was not intended to be final on the merits.

with·*out* **re·course.** Without liability. The phrase endorsed on the back of a check, promissory note, or other NEGOTIABLE to relieve the ENDORSER (other than the original maker) of liability. In short, the intermediate holder is passing the instrument on, and will not be responsible if the maker does not honor the obligation.

wit·**ness.** (1) To give evidence. (2) A person who can testify concerning what happened in a particular incident, since this person observed, heard, smelled, etc., what transpired first hand.

words of *pur*·**chase.** The language in a will or deed that relates who is to receive the estate in question.

work *prod*·**uct.** Work performed by a lawyer in his professional capacity for a client.

work *prod*·**uct rule.** The legal principle that an attorney need never disclose any of the work done or facts assembled for the party he or she represents, unless the opposing attorney can persuade the judge that it would be basically unfair not to disclose those matters that affect the other party.

wreck. (1) In admiralty law, a ship rendered unnavigable or unable to pursue the voyage without repairs for at least half of the ship's value. (2) Goods cast ashore by the sea. (3) To ruin, damage, or imperil. (4) A person or animal of broken spirit.

writ. A written order issued by a court or judge. *Writs* may take many forms, and may be used to handle many aspects of legal proceedings.

writ of *er·ror*. (1) A writ issued by an APPELLATE COURT in a CRIMINAL case, directing a lower (inferior) court to send the record and proceedings in a case for review. (2) In some states a *writ of error* is the procedural method by which appeals from civil court decisions in lower courts are brought to APPELLATE COURTS, including the court of last resort, which is usually called the State Supreme Court.

writ of ex·e·*cu*·tion. An order from a court to a sheriff, marshal, constable, or other officer directing the officer to execute and enforce a JUDGMENT of the court.

***wrong*·ful death *stat*·utes.** Statutes that allow the dependents of one wrongfully or negligently killed to sue for civil damages. The theory here is that the cause of action died with the victim, but that the dependents have a different cause of action.

Y

yield. (1) To surrender or relinquish control. (2) The return on an investment, based on the percentage of the sum invested.

Z-mark. A mark used in the preparation of legal documents to show that writing in the document concluded at the point where the Z begins, and that writing or entries in this space have been added without authority after the completion of the document. The first line of the Z begins at the end of type immediately preceding the blank space; the bottom line of the Z extends across the bottom of the blank space; a diagonal line joins the upper and lower lines to form a "Z."

zon•**ing.** The division of a municipality into areas or zones by ordinance specifying the uses that may be made of property in that area. For example, some areas may be zoned for industry, others for commercial, residential, or other uses.

REFERENCE

DATE DUE

USE IN LIBRARY ONLY

1-25-89